GROWING UP
in
DUBLIN

Reflections from the 1950s

John E. Mullee

Copyright © 2015 John E. Mullee
All rights reserved.
ISBN-13: 9780990362418
ISBN-10: 0990362418

Cover Design: Bernard Agard, with the author.

Front cover: Dublin City, time-stitch montage from several different periods. Background: St. Stephen's Green, ca. mid-2000s (photo by Tom Mullee). Inset, front row holding hands: my brother Louis, sister Marie, my dad, brother Tom, 1945; back row: two unknown men, 1945, unknown woman, probably 1930s (photos by street photographers).

Back cover: Boys digging bait on Sandymount Strand in the 1950s.

Book Layout: CreateSpace (www.createspace.com)

Published by

Chac Mool Books, Houston

For my children: Tara, Amanda, and Mark.

CONTENTS

Introduction..1

1. Setting Lines......................................5
2. Turf Smoke..19
3. The Lamplighter...................................38
4. The Hay Rakers....................................46
5. The Coalmen.......................................51
6. My First Catapult.................................61
7. The Foghorns Fall Silent..........................68
8. Backyard Beekeeping...............................77
9. Salley Branches..................................103
10. The Messenger Boy...............................109
11. The Crystal Spring..............................119
12. All the Faces of Snow...........................132
13. The Blackberry Pickers..........................163
14. Ballsbridge Library.............................168
15. The Carbide Lamp................................199
16. The Windmaker...................................202
17. Going to The Row................................206
18. Ethics in Marbles...............................246
19. The Sixties—All Change Here!....................252
20. My First Bike...................................267
21. How I gave Up Smoking...........................283
22. Born in World War II............................293
23. Learning School.................................310
24. Climbing Trees..................................320
25. Chestnut Brown..................................323
26. Dún Laoghaire Pier..............................328

Acknowledgements....................................349
About the Author....................................351

Some shattered dishes underneath a pine,
The playthings in the playhouse of the children.
Weep for what little things could make them glad.

—Robert Frost

INTRODUCTION

Dublin is the city that mothered me. It is a city of rich and diverse character kept lively by a robust human core. It can be refined, gritty, earthy, even crass. Its people are naturally inclined to be open and friendly, but may lapse into frivolity or bestow kernels of native wisdom at little or no prompting. This can make it quick to loosen up the restrained or weary visitor. One thing you can rely on: Dublin will always arouse strong emotions—of some sort. It is a city that never completely weans you of its earthy nourishment, never openly binds you to it, yet never actually lets you leave.

When my three children were growing up, I used to tell them stories about my own childhood in Ireland, a country largely unknown to them. In 2002 my oldest daughter gave me a blank notebook with the request (or the challenge) that I write down all the stories I had been telling them, without the puns. Ten years later the pages were still blank. It was not until I retired from my day job that I started to write the stories down, and this book is the result.

So I have at least three guaranteed readers.

I was born in Dublin. It was 1942—in the middle of World War II. Much of Continental Europe had already fallen to Hitler's Germany, and Great Britain was under fierce assault. At that stage in the war, the outcome was by no means clear. But the air-raid sirens did not whine over Dublin as they did in Britain, because the Irish Republic was neutral in the war. In spite of this neutrality, however, some bombs did fall on Dublin, and with very deadly effect. The Luftwaffe apologized, claiming the pilots had erred. Or was it a crude warning to stay out of the war?

The Irish Republic was still very much affected by the breakdowns in industry and commerce, of course, but I was too small, and the violence was too far removed, for me to feel any direct pain from the war. In fact, some of the very earliest memories I can retrieve from childhood are of grownups counting wartime rationing cards and talking about "ten shilling notes" in tones that let me know it was no concern of mine. And I can remember very clearly that our family cat had kittens on the back seat of our Austin Eight, which was laid up on blocks because petrol was rationed.

Before the war had ended, my mother died in childbirth. I was two years of age, the youngest of four surviving children. My father remained a single dad for the rest of his life, and brought all four of us up until we passed through the rapids of adolescence and sobered to the deep wide waters of adulthood. We did not have much, but we had enough, so in the well-accepted sense we were actually rich.

In 1964, at the age of twenty-two, I left Dublin on the Mail Boat—a passenger ferry that sailed across the Irish Sea to Great Britain, and one that had become an icon of Irish emigration. I had a year's savings, a backpack, and a warm sleeping bag to crawl into as soon as I found a decent spot between the lifeboats on the open deck of the boat. I also had a compelling urge to steep myself in a totally different culture for one whole year.

It was two years before I returned to Dublin. But that was only for a brief visit, and I would spend another two full years working on the Continent before moving back to Dublin for any length of time. By then I had become weary of low-end landlords, I was hungry for higher education, and I just wanted to live in my home town again. And: I had saved enough money for the first of four years in University College Dublin.

After that I left Ireland again—for good, as it turned out. I left by boat, again, but this time I had a regular suitcase—rather

INTRODUCTION

than a backpack—and a secondhand Morris Minor parked in the car bay. Folded up inside my suitcase was a degree in civil engineering. I rolled off the boat in Liverpool, took another ferry from England to Holland, and started a new career in Schiedam, a satellite town of Rotterdam.

I was thirty years of age, and broke.

In Holland I met Yvonne. We got married in Singapore, and for over thirty-five years we lived in various countries, following my work, or following our fancy whenever we could make these two coincide. We have three children—now adults—and together the five of us have been rearing one another through all that life has had to give, and to take away. We are still doing this, now with the willing and energetic help of two little grandsons. Through all this we kept a home in the welcoming and diverse city of Houston, Texas, and this is where we now live.

In 2006 I became an American citizen, and in 2011 I retired from my career in civil engineering.

The stories in this book are stand-alone episodes in no particular order and with no coherent thread. They are intended for anybody who might identify with the places and the events described—and how I reflect upon them—either directly or from other experiences that may have invoked similar thoughts. The core material is taken from the twenty-odd years between 1945 and 1965, when I was growing up in Ireland, from age three to twenty-three. To put that period into perspective, it would take another full generation for the "Celtic Tiger" to spring—the economic surge that would utterly transform Ireland's social and urban landscapes, obliterate some of the culture I write about here, and make the country almost unrecognizable to me when I returned on short visits.

The events of youth are often taken at face value, and we do not see at the time—or need to see—that they are merely fragments of a far larger pattern—pieces that we will put together later from those "Aha!" moments that come from the joys and troubles of life. That is why I have grafted some later experiences onto "stems" grown in that core twenty-year period growing up in Dublin. I couldn't resist, either, the odd attempt at drawing some philosophical conclusions from all this.

So I invite you to come back to Dublin with me and relive some of the experiences I had growing up there. Along the way, we might stray into other countries, other topics, and other times.

1
SETTING LINES

We were so excited that we got out of bed and had our clothes on before most of the city was even awake. We walked out over the sand flats in Dublin Bay, with the salt breeze in our faces, and watched the engorged sun burst out of the Irish Sea. We had never seen the sun so big and yellow, and as we walked towards it in silent wonderment we thought: It really *is* a huge ball of fire. The terse cries of hungry seagulls followed us all the way out as they circled and circled overhead. We learned the signatures of the sea at a time when our senses were exposed and raw.

Setting lines was a simple way for my boyhood pals and I to fish the open sea, because we didn't need a boat, or even a fishing rod. We simply went down to Sandymount Strand at low tide, walked out to the edge of the tide, set down our fishing line, and went home. When the tide came in, our line would be deep under water, and the fish would find our baited hooks. When the tide went out again, we would walk back out and pick up our catch.

Occasionally, we would bring home a fish that usually could only be caught from a boat—a fish that was "big" compared with the height of a twelve-year-old.

The squealing seagulls, the sound of our own footsteps splashing rhythmically through the water, the vague sensation of sand ripples giving way under the soles of our bare feet: all this helped to put us into a sort of private reverie.

Setting lines was a pastime that took up most of a summer's day, because we had to wait for the tides to come and go as they pleased. But even when the tides were unfavorable and we could not go fishing, we would be busy mending our lines.

The further north you live in Europe, the longer your summer days are. As Dublin Bay is more than halfway from the equator to the pole—it lies about fifty-three degrees north—we had nice long evenings to enjoy our summer holidays. And those of us who did not stay too long in bed had early sunrises, too. Around midsummer's day, if there were no clouds, the last glow of sunlight would linger in the western sky long after eleven pm.

Not only did the drawn-out days give us generous time to spend on the sand flats, but the geology of Dublin Bay was kind to us as well. It sheltered us from the Irish Sea with mighty Howth Head on the north and rugged Dalkey Island on the south. Into this sand trap flows the staid River Liffey and her two little sisters, the Dodder and the Tolka. Today, when the moon lines up with the sun to pull a good spring tide, the sand flats stretch about two miles from Sandymount Strand. So much sand is exposed at low tide that it takes about forty-five minutes to walk out to the point where the first timid little waves come arcing in from the sea. By that time your perspective of the bay has changed because of the sheer distance traveled—you have left the suburbs of Merrion Gates and Booterstown behind and are now abreast of Blackrock.

But tidal flats are not permanent features of the bay: their shapes change continually as they are washed by tides and churned up by storm waves. Twice a day the tides move a huge amount of water into and out of the bay. If you stand at the advancing line of tidewater, well after the tide has turned, you can see the water pooling in around your feet at an alarming rate. This can even be a bit disquieting; you feel powerless against the overwhelming might of the sea.

In fact, the water has found a way to speed up this filling and emptying of the sea by gouging itself some deep channels through the tidal zone. Once a channel is formed, it tends to monopolize the flow of tidal water, getting deeper and deeper until some natural limit is reached. And so it was that one undisputed channel dominated the sand flats of Dublin Bay: the "Cockle Lake." We held the Cockle Lake in some awe because, though we accepted it as the true soul of the sand flats, we knew it could show its treacherous side if we did not respect its moods. Between tides—when the flow was strongest—it would come alive with a fierce current. But what made it treacherous was that this current snuck in *behind* you. So, for example, if you mused too long over the beauty of the incoming tide snaking its way through the sand ripples, you might not notice that the Cockle Lake had filled up behind you and cut you off from the shore. You would then have to swim across the channel against a very brisk current, or wait in the hope of being rescued before there was no more sand left to stand on.

I never knew anybody who actually had to be rescued from the wrong side of the Cockle Lake, but the fear was always there. It was said among the boys that there was always a man who kept watch near the Poolbeg lighthouse, with binoculars and a boat, ready to rescue any unwary beach walker who got trapped by the incoming tide. I remember very well the shock I got one evening when I came in from the outer banks a bit too late after the tide had turned; when I reached the Cockle Lake I was alarmed to find that it had become greatly swollen since we had paddled across it through a listless current that barely came up to our knees. The surface was roiled by a nasty current, driven by a tide impatient to fill up the bay. My buddy and I waded in with our fishing gear but quickly found ourselves up to our chests in a strong current trying to drag us out to sea. Luckily we were not in over our depth, and we still had enough positive weight to dig our toes into the sand and win this scary fight for equilibrium. That, more than any rumors of rescue boats, was what gave me high respect for the Cockle Lake in Dublin Bay.

Towards the end of the 1800s cockles were fished in this area—as food for humans—and that is where the name of the "lake" comes from. Records show that up to about ten tons were being landed every year at Ringsend, an inner suburb of Dublin. In the early 1900s though, it was reported that the cockle beds had become grossly polluted, probably by sewage, and that the high incidence of typhoid in the city was due to the eating of contaminated cockles.[1]

When we walked out over the sand flats in the 1950s, the only shells we noticed much were the razor shells. These stood out because they were long and narrow, like the steel blade of a straight razor. (My dad still used a straight razor for shaving, then.) When the mollusks died, they left their hard shell-backs in the little tunnels where they had lived. Now and then—particularly in the Cockle Lake—a broken razor shell would be sticking out of the stiff sand to surprise the barefoot walker.

We could only set lines when the first low tide of the day occurred early in the morning, and the second one late in the afternoon, since otherwise one or the other would occur during darkness. By eagerly studying the tide tables in the *Irish Independent,* we soon learned how spring tides and neap tides varied with the cycles of the moon, and that the best time for us was when a spring-low tide occurred just after dawn. Each day the low tide would come about fifty minutes later—following the moon's rotation around the earth—until it became too late to fish because the evening tide got too close to nightfall. Then we would have to wait until the tides favored us again.

But long before you got to savor the salty fresh air of the sea, there was a lot of preparation to do. No problem, because that had its own rewards, and, besides, we enjoyed the expectations it raised. First, we had to visit the little shop filled with fishing tackle, a task that probably gave me as much excitement as shopping for a stereo or a car later in life. That is, if one allows for the inflation of expectations as one matures into adulthood.

A profound finding, though not surprising.

The tackle shop was down in the dockland, near George's Quay. I could get to it easily on my own by taking a train to Tara Street Station. My fishing buddies and I would gaze in amazement at all the gear stacked in nooks and on shelves—slender, varnished fishing rods with big winders and fantastic mechanisms for reeling in quickly, without the horrors of knotted balls of tangled line. From this we would select about fifty hooks, around an inch in length, made of brassy-looking metal, and about 100 yards of strong cotton fishing line. We were impressed by the shiny look of the new hooks and the pleasing smell of new cotton line.

At home we would rig up the line in the back garden, looping it around the trunks of the apple trees and anything else that would make a suitable return point, such as a drainpipe or a gooseberry bush. Then, at intervals of a yard, we would attach snag lines with hooks dangling down on the ends. A stiff wooden stake at each end would finish the job.

Sometimes we made up two or more strings. Then we would bundle the line into a compact roll so we could carry it on our bikes. This required care, since the hooks were sharp. Anybody who has ever had the barb of a one-inch fishing hook embedded in their finger, and has tried to get it out without ripping out too much flesh, will understand this. We coiled the cotton line around the wooden stake, holding the dangerous barbs against the soft cotton pile with one finger while winding the next loop tightly and safely over it. If done properly the rolled-up line and its snag hooks could be transported and unwound successfully without any stubborn tangles or flailing fish hooks.

We dug our own bait on the sand banks at low tide. The best place for this was the seaward bank of the Cockle Lake. The bait-rich sections were easy to find, as there would always be others quietly digging away there. Also, you could see the wormholes on the surface of the sand, and the gulls circling overhead. There was no question of our *buying* bait—our pocket money was already stretched very thin, and anyway the bait was abundant and plentiful on the sand banks.

We would dig bait in the afternoons, on our way out to recover the catch from the morning's tide. For this we used my dad's spade, that most reliable and versatile of garden tools. The sand bank was high enough to dry out and harden a bit when uncovered by the outgoing tide. We only had to dig down one spade-length, as the worms lived close to the surface. Nearly every upturned clump of sand would yield several worms. Some would be hanging from the open ends of what had been their private underground tunnels—where they thought they were safe—while others would be delivered intact inside the upturned clump of sand. Often we would cleave through a worm, leaving half on one side and half on the other. We ought to have found this at least a bit distressful, but we were not sensitive to the welfare of worms then.

In the mornings we would get up very early and cycle to Sandymount Strand. We left our bikes propped up against an old granite wall—near the Martello Tower—and stuffed our shoes into a bush behind the wall where they would be out of sight. (At that time there was no need to lock our bikes.) Then we walked out barefoot to the sand flats of Dublin Bay.

Our most prized catch was the magnificent salmon bass. This was a well-contoured, sleek fish with nice silver scales. In the 1950s it was common to catch a salmon bass over two feet long in Dublin Bay (no, *honestly*). The salmon bass was not really a salmon, but it looked so much like a salmon that nobody really knew (or cared) about the false label. It even had pink flesh. Besides, "salmon" sounded so much better, especially if you were telling somebody how well your fishing day had gone.

Next, and possibly the most valuable to the consumer, was the plaice. This is an attractive flatfish with pretty orange spots. The coloring no doubt gives it the advantage of having a good camouflage underwater, but unfortunately it is well recognized and highly prized in restaurants for its fine taste. Like most flatfish, both of its eyes are on one side of its head—the side that looks up: it is a bottom-dweller. Some of the plaice we caught would be the size of a full dinner plate (no kidding).

Less exciting to us were the dabs—light-brown flatfish with dark spots. We probably valued these less because they were usually small, and tasted bland, at best. Occasionally we would catch a flounder—another bottom-dweller, mottled brown, with both eyes "flattened" on one side. At that time I thought flatfish were flat because they were squeezed by water pressure as they floundered on the bottom of the deep.

As we approached the furthest point of the beach, where we had staked our baited lines on the sand, we would strain to see what the night's tide might have brought us. This was the most exciting part, of course, but it was also tinged with some anxiety. Would we find a big silver-backed salmon bass? Some nice big spotted plaice? We knew it was just between us and the sea; there was nobody to guarantee anything for us.

And it seems that whenever you work to produce something of value, you may expect some form of theft. In our case we had to watch out for seagulls and humans. The seagulls were much more difficult to deal with than the humans, since they had evolved with features well suited for hunting fish, such as big sharp beaks. And, after all, they could fly.

As the tide went out, the sand flats would gradually drain, leaving our fishing lines exposed among the sand ripples and shallow pools of water. Fish unfortunate enough to have got hooked by our bait would then become sitting ducks for seagulls. Flatfish were a bit more fortunate than the round-bodied ones. More fortunate until *we* arrived, that is. They could ripple the fins on their flanks, burying themselves out of sight while the hungry seagulls circled overhead. It also helped that their sandy-colored backs looked just like the sandy bottom. Fish that normally swam well above the seabed, however, had little to protect them. As the water in their huge fish bowl slowly drained away, their flapping only dug them into a big, open crater very visible from the air. Enter ravenous seagulls.

But, at that time, we were not sensitive to the plight of fish, either.

It would be obvious to us when our catch was being stolen. As we got near our line, we would see a flock of squealing seabirds circling over it. We would run, paddle into the water as far as we could, wave our hands, and shout.

The best, of course, was to get there before the seagulls.

It was more difficult to catch human thieves in the act, because of course they would not hang around at the scene. If you were tardy, other boys might reach your line before you did, and nip some choicy specimen. The only evidence you would have when you finally arrived at your line would be a big crater in the sand. By that time the boys who lifted your big fish would be half way back to the seawall on Sandymount Strand.

One morning my buddy and I were late as we walked out hurriedly to our lines. That was never a good feeling, perhaps the only unpleasant one in the whole fishing season. Just beyond the Cockle Lake we met two boys coming back. We stopped to chat and to admire the huge salmon bass they were carrying. I thought I detected signs in their behavior that betrayed their having taken booty from our line, or somebody else's. But with nothing more than speculation, and our self-reproach for not having got up on time, all we could do was hurry out to our lines. Sure enough, when we arrived we found a huge, empty depression in the sand about the size of that big salmon bass.

The sand flats became wide and featureless when you walked far out to the low-tide mark and looked back. Finding the spot where we had set our lines provided us with some early training in orientation. As Dublin Bay had plenty of prominent landmarks, we could navigate by eye fairly well, with some practice. The south wall of the shipping channel was dominated by two tall, striped chimney stacks known as the "candy sticks." These undisputed icons of Dublin Bay stood out very clearly—from a long way off—and they still do today. At that time the chimneys discharged smoke and steam from the Pigeon House Power Station, which burned coal. Today the old power station is obsolete and the chimneys are redundant, but they still have plenty of "fire" in them: Are they eyesores that should be demolished (and the real estate freed up)? Or are they so dear to Dubliners that they should be preserved at all cost? As dear, perhaps, as the memory of cockle sellers pushing their wheelbarrows through old Dublin's streets? Would Dubliners just stand and watch the dynamiter light his fuse?

In the 1950s, though, we just took them for granted and were happy to have such good landmarks.

To the south, there was a tall church spire in the suburb of Blackrock that usually stood out well against a lightening skyline. As we walked out from Sandymount Strand, we kept our eyes keen to discern how our lines of sight were changing relative to these two landmarks, and in this simple way we could triangulate ourselves to our fishing line.

It worked well as long as there was enough daylight.

On good days we could sell off the best fish in our catch to recoup some of the cost of our lines. Far more important, however, was the satisfaction of having produced, on our own, something of real value—something that the adults would actually *pay* us for.

There were two catches each day, since we would bait the lines in the late afternoon, let the night tide cover them, and return in the early morning to bait them again for the day tide. On the way home after taking our morning catch—thus still very early by others' standards—we would simply go cold-knocking on doors near St. John's Road. Usually, a rather surprised woman in house clothes would open the door to two boys with ruffled hair and sand wedged between their toes, holding up beautiful, plate-sized, orange-spotted plaice. We would open with our carefully chosen sales pitch:

"Would you like to buy some fish? We just caught them ourselves."

We were surprisingly successful. After all, plaice was a highly valued fish, and we had some great specimens to offer. Or maybe we cut a lonely, pitiable figure standing on the doorstep so early in the morning, when most kids were still in bed. But of course that aspect would never have occurred to us then, since we were enjoying that unquestioning confidence that comes with youthful achievement without adult help.

One morning we sold some of our catch at a house not far from the seawall. We knew that a famous person lived there—Ronnie Delaney—and we assumed that the lady who opened the door was his mother. A few years earlier, in 1956, this very amiable athlete had given Ireland an electrifying boost by winning an Olympic gold medal in the men's 1,500 meters (and immediately kneeling down on the running track to offer a prayer of thanksgiving). We got a little boost that morning, too.

Now, getting out of bed early in the morning never came naturally to us boys. But enthusiasm is a great motivator, and our enthusiasm for setting lines spurred us to achieve some firsts in the area of self-discipline, for our age. Nevertheless, strong will can only go so far, and since we had to get up around four o'clock to catch the tide, a reliable alarm clock was just as important. Neither one on its own was enough. Since I had a fairly good alarm clock—with stainless steel bells and a good hard hammer—I agreed to act as a human alarm for my fishing buddy: as soon as I got up, I would go to his house and rouse him. He lived close by.

I cannot recall doing anything as normal as having breakfast before I left the house, but there are two things I do remember vividly. The first is that eerie sound of the early morning. This should perhaps be called that eerie *non-sound*. It seems that during the day there are so many sounds—cars on the street, birds singing or screeching, kids playing, people talking, and so on, that they mask the ever-present background noise. The Pigeon House—that power station with the tall chimneys—produced a low, whining drone twenty-four hours a day, but you would only notice it early in the morning. At that time, the only person you would expect to see would be the milkman. The droning seemed to rise and fall as if were being carried on the morning breeze. It diffused through the senses, adding to that somewhat mystical feeling one gets from being out under the stars when the first hint of daylight appears. To this day my mind flashes back to that arresting sensation whenever I hear the sound.

The second lasting memory is not mystical at all: it is the sound of throwing small pebbles at my buddy's upstairs window to wake him up. This usually required two or three throws, and they had to be well aimed. Throw too hard, and you could wake up his siblings, or worse still his dad; throw too timidly, and you might have another few minutes to wait, and then another pebble-throw. Each time the pebbles bounced off the glass, they would make a hollow "pang–g–g" that seemed sure to rouse all the sleeping dogs in the area.

Finally, a lost, expressionless face would appear behind the window pane, barely visible against the reflection of the brightening sky. A weak hand signal would finally relieve the tension: your buddy was awake. He would get dressed and come down as nimbly as a fireman sliding down the pole in a fire station.

There was plenty to do.

I was the youngest of the three boys in our family. When I wanted to learn how to set lines, my two older brothers took me along one morning to fetch the catch. It was cold and windy. The sun had barely risen, and visibility was poor. As we were a bit ahead of the tide, the water had not yet uncovered the wooden stakes that marked the fishing line we had left on the seabed the day before. A stiff morning wind was beating away at the coast and whipping up sharp ripples in the pools of water left on the sand flats. The thin layers of water at the edge of the receding tide were churning and sloshing as if trying to find a way out of the trap they were in.

It was difficult to get any bearing for direction, or to judge how near we might have been to our lines. With our flimsy clothing flapping at our arms and legs, and no immediate prospect of finding our lines, we decided to wait until the tide went out further, and the sun rose a bit higher. Perhaps it would be a bit warmer, too.

We began to shiver.

As we waited, peering into the dimness where we thought our lines might be, we instinctively shifted positions on the sand to protect our bare legs and scantily covered bodies from the cold wind. After a while I noticed that my oldest brother had "naturally" fallen into the upwind position. My next-oldest brother had fallen in just downwind, while I stood well shielded behind both of them. We remained there for a while in silence, miles from shore, my eldest brother protecting his two younger siblings from the cold.

SAND SWIRLS IN DUBLIN BAY

Restless tides have scoured these channels into the sand flats of Dublin Bay. The big one is known as the Cockle Lake. Dotted white lines mark roughly where we walked out over the sand to set our fishing lines at the furthest reaches of the tide. It was about two miles. If you waited too long out there after the tide had turned, you risked being cut off: the Cockle Lake would circle in behind you.

THE BAIT PICKERS

We dug our bait on a low sand bank created by the Cockle Lake. It was the only place where the sand drained enough at low tide to become a bit firm. The rag worms and lug worms loved the spot, at least until our rude spade cut them in half, or left them wriggling helplessly on an upturned clump of sand. If we missed any worms (or half-worms), the seagulls would soon take care of them.

The candy-stick chimneys of the Pigeon House would guide us to our fishing lines when we walked further out to the edge of the tide.

---

[1] A.B. West, J.K. Partridge and A. Lovitt. 1978. "The cockle *Cerastoderma edule* (L.) on the South Bull, Dublin Bay: population parameters and fishery potential," Department of Zoology, Trinity College, Dublin.

2
TURF SMOKE

It's hard to forget the atmosphere created by a turf fire in a country kitchen. Whether on a late summer afternoon, when the kitchen has become a busy hub, the fire has been stoked high, and a blackened kettle nestled among some burning sods starts singing—or on a Saturday night, when all the hay has been saved, all the chairs have been set out for the visitors, the accordion and the tin whistle have been taken out, and little glasses of spirits are passed around discreetly.

Turf smoke is a bit pungent to the nose, but it's actually quite pleasant to sense inside a cozy kitchen, or when walking past a farmhouse on a country road. It's as if the smell of turf smoke actually *creates* an atmosphere, from association, and its distinctive smell can trigger pleasant memories decades later.

Often on Saturday nights, on my uncle's farm in County Mayo, the local farmers would linger in the kitchen. As daylight faded, the glow from the turf fire and the yellow flame from the paraffin lamp took over. My cousin Tom would go into the back room and take his melodeon out of its protective case. If we were lucky, somebody would pull a tin whistle out of a breast pocket and the obligatory coaxing ritual would start:

"Ah sure I can't play at all" was the prescribed response—at first.

The coaxing was designed to protect the performer from being accused of being too eager to play. One night I remember somebody playing a fiddle. Then some Guinness bottles were opened and black porter was poured into kitchen mugs until the tan-colored froth overflowed onto the ground. Tiny glasses were filled with Paddy's Irish Whiskey and passed around to selected guests. That must have been strong stuff: I have seen farmers well past eighty dance jigs to the warmth of the music, the company, and the turf fire.

My relatives harvested their own turf on the farm, and I helped eagerly when I spent my summer holidays there. We needed no more than a spade, a donkey, and a cart. If a dry spell seemed likely to last another day or so, my uncle would disturb the donkey's grazing, harness him to the cart, and off we would go. I sat beside my uncle on the little bench up front. We soon settled into the steady rhythm set by the donkey's docile clop–clop–clop and the grating of iron-rimmed wheels on the road. We quickly got used to the cart jerking from side to side in response to the ungraceful gait of our little farm animal, who would pull us obediently in whatever direction we turned his blinkers.

Soon the hardtop road turned to gravel, then to twin parallel tracks of crushed white limestone with a center path beaten out by many donkey hooves. The sound of the cart's wheels would have turned to grinding–crunching by now, as the iron hoops on the wheels cut into the loose stones. Perhaps the white gravel on this little bog road had come from limestone basins that nature had kindly prepared for trapping vegetation and turning it into peat.

My Uncle Tom was a taciturn man. It would be nothing for him to remain completely silent during this hour-long trip to the bog. I used to wonder what he was thinking about as we sat side-by-side on the little cart, moving slowly but steadily down the country road. On other occasions, when he was working alone in the fields, my cousin Mae would send me out to him with lunch: strong tea in a candy can recycled from her little country store, and soda bread dabbed with salty homemade butter. The can had a tight-fitting lid to keep the tea warm on the journey, and to stop me from spilling it as I sought to keep balance while scrambling over earthen ditches. When my uncle saw me coming across the fields, he would abandon whatever tool he had, lean up against a grassy ditch, and lay his tired legs out in front of him. Then we would sit together in silence.

So here we were again, sitting side-by-side—this time on a little donkey-and-cart— together but far apart. Perhaps my uncle was studying the clouds as they moved across the sky, hoping the weather would hold long enough for us to cut and stack a decent load of turf. They would need that turf to keep the cold and dampness out of their thatched cottage when winter closed in with its long dark nights. By that time I would have returned to my home in the cozy, well-lit streets of suburban Dublin.

The bogland seemed to stretch away forever on all sides. Soon, you noticed that the usual background sounds were missing: birds, mooing cows, hens, chickens. The ground was covered with mosses, grasses, and scraggly heather. Every few hundred feet or so there was a sheer drop where a bank had been cut away to harvest the turf, a bank that would move back slowly with each passing year's cut. The turf exposed on the newly cut face was like Christmas plum pudding: a dense, wet "pie" with a black or very dark-brown color. Its surface texture was fairly smooth, except for slight seams or ridges left between successive strikes of the turf spade. A stringy matrix of root fibers ran through the turf, and some of them stuck out like an untidy person's scraggly hair. If the ground had not been permanently saturated with water, and did not have all those plant fibers, it probably would have turned into hard-packed soil.

Water would pool at the bottom of the bank where the deepest sods of turf had been dug out. If you stood close enough to this, and pranced around a bit, little waves of moving moss-carpet would radiate out from your feet over the soggy ground. Sometimes I thought it would not be strong enough to support me, and that at any moment it would open up and swallow me. It evoked scenes from the jungle movies we used to watch then, where at least one person had to be sucked into quicksand to satisfy the director. If it was the "chap," or the "girl," they would be saved, otherwise they would slowly disappear, struggling in agony as if they had been loosely tied with rope and thrown into a pool of water. Would my uncle save me if I started to sink into this quicksand?

The natural infusion of plant fiber into the water had discolored it to dark reddish brown. In clear sunlight, though, you could still see about a foot down into the water, and it was easy to understand why the Irish used this sun-glinted brown to describe very strong tea: "bogwater." Tea that is best thrown out. If you had put too much tea into the pot—or left it stewing on the gas while you were at something else—you would be mercilessly accused of serving up bogwater. That was a heavy charge: the Irish take their tea drinking most seriously. But you had to see and even taste actual bogwater—in the bog—to fully understand the force of this accusation.

I'm sure the botanists would have found the spongy mosses very interesting—and would have been able to name each one of them—but we who worked the bogs had less scientific interests. My uncle never bothered to explore this netherworld of bog like I did: there was work to be done up on the bank.

Cutting sods of turf out of the ground was hard work, and quite tricky. Too hard and too tricky for a boy visiting from the city. This was my uncle's task. The turf spade was shaped like a half-box open at the bottom so you could cut out an oblong sod of manageable size. I'm told that strictly speaking it is "peat" until you take it out of the ground, whereupon it becomes "turf." On our farm, however, I never heard the word "peat." Regardless of what you called it, some effort was required to drive the spade into it, craft a sod, and throw this up over your shoulder onto the high ground. My uncle let me try it, once, just to show me, but I had to struggle with the spade just to overcome the suction put up by the bog trying to hold on to its turf. This was one of the few times my uncle showed his feelings: the lines on his normally serious face reshaped completely into a broad-writ smile that included his eyes and all their surrounding wrinkles. Of course, he was beaming at having shown this city boy how hard farming really was.

That lesson was not lost on me.

Soon my uncle would settle into a good rhythm, cutting sods from their long-time home and spading them sprightly over his shoulder. By then I had worked a lot with him on the farm and had figured out that this was his secret for accomplishing *any* repetitive task: find a good rhythm and stick to it.

Another good lesson.

My job was to gather the wet sods and stack them up to dry. Stacking was relatively easy, though it certainly required—and promoted—good back muscles. Good for a city boy, my uncle probably thought, behind all that silence. When first taken from their watery pudding, the sods were so soft that you could not lift them without their breaking apart. First, you had to upend them in what Boy Scouts call the "tepee shape" used for stacking logs when starting a campfire. With time and a bit of good weather (something you can never take for granted in the west of Ireland), the breeze blowing through the little tepees would dry out the sods and firm them up a bit. This would be enough to prevent them from sagging or breaking in two when you lifted them up. Then you could stack them "log cabin" style, several layers high, to get the best air circulation.

After about a week—a week of good weather, that is—the sods would dry out as much as they were ever going to, at least in the open air. You could judge their dryness by their reduced weight, too. Time to bring them home before they got drenched again by rain. Working together, my uncle and I would gather up the sods and throw them into the cart. You could stack the turf quite high by putting sideboards in place to keep it from spilling out. Then we would climb on top of the pile and resume our jerking cart ride, each left to his own private thoughts. Including the donkey.

Here in the US a scene very like this is often used to attract tourists looking for a total change of scene: A farm donkey with shaggy hair hauling a bockety cart loaded to the rims with turf. A farmer dressed in rumpled clothes. A girl-and-boy or two with big brown freckles spattered all over their faces—and at least one mop of wild red hair. A farm dog circling. And, preferably, a background of low mountains disappearing into a blue haze. The farmer and the kids should have expressions of indeterminate meaning as they look at the photographer.

Back at the farmhouse we offloaded the turf from the cart and built it into a big stack called a rick. We slanted the sides and top of the rick so that they would shed the rain and keep the sods dry underneath. If we had a sheet of plastic or tarpaulin we draped it over the top. This was not absolutely necessary, though, if you placed the sods correctly.

Throughout the year the rick was slowly eaten away as sods of turf were brought in to keep the kitchen fire going.

Turning soggy slices of peat into dry sods of turf and bringing them home was an oddly satisfying experience for a city boy like me. It required a certain resolve to leave the fun of riding the cart, or to stop plodding carefree over the spongy bog, and get down to work stacking sods. But once you got into that repetitive work rhythm, the rewards were great: the rawness of uncultivated bogland, the abiding quiet made palpable by a lone bird flying past, the healthy breeze, the cadences of buzzing all around you as bees sought out nectar from tiny blossoms. Perfect for daydreaming. I could not have known what my uncle's adult daydreams were—and he surely had them—but mine were usually about evening time when my cousin Tom would come home from his day job on the railway and take me with him to hunt rabbits with the greyhounds.

And a big country meal made on the turf fire in the kitchen.

Turf Smoke

For many people in Ireland, turf was the only abundant fuel they had for cooking and for getting through the cold damp winters when pneumonia was never far from anybody's mind. In school we were always told that the country was shaped like a saucer: low-lying plains ringed with mountains. The mountains make for some terrific hiking and sightseeing, while the low-lying areas are spotted with lakes and small waterways, ideal for boating and fishing. The midlands also host the Bog of Allen, an enormous raised bog stretching over an area equivalent to about twenty miles by twenty. (Only Seamus Heaney could have come up with the proper words to describe the deeper meanings of this bogland in culture: in a poem[1] loaded with metaphor, he says of it: "The wet centre is bottomless.")

In a decidedly more literal sense, Bord na Móna, the Irish Turf Board, has harvested this dormant energy for years. They scrape the peat off the surface with huge milling machines and compact it into "peat briquettes"—highly compact, fine-textured sods of turf. In the 1950s the briquettes were sold in clean bales—ideal for young singles living in small flats where fuel (like beer) was bought in hand-carried packages and lugged up several flights of stairs. Or for seniors who could only manage one brick of peat at a time (and carried their spirits in a body flask).

With so much turf, and so many people depending on it, the bogs have turned out to be an equally rich source of fuel for natural history, anthropology, folklore, and snide jokes. "You can take the man from the bog, but you can't take the bog from the man" is the most polite one I know.

One can only guess what jokes were being told two thousand years ago—and there surely were some because there seems to have been a lively culture in the boglands. When I last visited The Natural Museum of Ireland in Kildare Street, Dublin, the mysterious Iron Age "bog bodies" were so well preserved that you could clearly see folds and creases in the skin.

(The acidic soil and lack of oxygen prevent the corpses from decaying.) You could also see how the bodies were mutilated for reasons and by persons unknown. These finds, and others such as "bog butter" preserved as well as if the bogmen had General Electric refrigerators, help the museum deliver on its promise to build a picture of what daily life was like in Ireland two thousand years ago.

But before you go to the museum, be sure to read Seamus Heaney's description of the half-faces and half-bodies recovered from bogs (including other European bogs), and the emotions evoked by speculations on what human relationships and beliefs might have motivated such violence.[2] (No doubt if the Iron Age bogmen could read today's newspaper[3]—23rd May 2013—they would be curious to know why a man hacked a total stranger to death on a London street.)

Indeed, the bogs of Ireland are full of lore. Some of the lore definitely has to be told to the young—to warn them about the fairies that may take them away if they are bold; other parts have to be told in hushed conversations—the fearful sound of banshees keening the dead, or calling out to those who are soon to join the dead and scaring the bejazus out of everybody else.

Other stories could only be told in the confessional. It was said that occasionally one would find an old handgun in a bog, thrown there, probably, to hide the evidence of a secret landlord assassination.

My dad lived through the Irish Civil War of the 1920s. Although he never spoke to me of his personal experiences in that war, it is well known from open history sources[4] that brother was set against brother, neighbor against neighbor. And for some who were caught on the "wrong" side of this argument, their last sensations of life may have come to them down some boreen that dead-ended into an open bog.

The bog hides many things.

But for every scary aspect of the bog, there were plenty of pleasant ones, too. Even in summer, life centered on the turf burning in the hob, where all our meals were cooked. There would still be a pile of glowing ashes in the hob when I went to bed, and by the time I got up in the morning somebody would have brought new life to them: red embers cradled in spent ash, lively new flames licking new sods and giving off fresh grey smoke. As soon as I appeared in the kitchen my cousin Mae would take the black tongs and pull a few sods aside to boil our battered black kettle. What in the world would we have done without turf?

As noon approached, a big fat-bellied pot was filled with potatoes and swung in over the flames. A heavy lid kept the swirling smoke and the ashes out, and kept the heat in. A hefty swing-arm let you move the pot in and out of the fire easily to see if the spuds were done.

The big black pot with its round belly and short stocky legs looked exactly like the one in a stock image. This icon is still used today by the Gods of Advertising to make us salivate over good things promised at the end of the rainbow. But for us the pot just meant dinner; that was our gold. And when we had eaten our fill of fluffy potatoes with salt and homemade butter, scallions, or curly cabbage, the remaining spuds were fed to the farm animals and the fowl.

No wonder the big black pot is revered so much.

We also baked our own bread on the turf fire. My cousin would knead a cake of dough on the deal-wood table in the middle of the kitchen and put it in a cast iron pan, like the "Dutch oven" so useful to campers cooking on an open fire. Then she would nestle the pan among the glowing sods, placing some on the lid so the bread would bake evenly on all sides. After a while she would take the long black tongs and lift off the lid to see if the dough had swelled to that nice crusty brown.

In the early evening, after a day of raking hay or stacking turf, I often sat on the little wooden stool by the fire in the kitchen. Gazing idly at the kettle squatting on the fire, I would fall into a mild trance as I waited for it to start simmering. And who better than Yeats could have described the profundity of this simple experience? Who more deeply understood its loss?

> He'll hear no more the lowing
> Of the calves on the warm hillside
> Or the kettle on the hob
> Sing peace into his breast,
> —Yeats[5]

"Sing peace into his breast": the sound of a kettle singing on a turf fire should be bottled and sold as a tonic to soothe the mind.

When daylight was nearly gone, my uncle would come into the kitchen and take his accustomed spot by the window. Reading glasses on, newspaper in hand, he would quietly adjust his sitting position to catch the last glow of light coming through the little squares of glass. When it got altogether too dim inside, somebody would stand on a stool and put a match to the big oil lamp that hung from bare rafters of the roof. Rafters made from tree branches. That yellow light, and whatever light came from the turf fire, was all we would get in the kitchen for the rest of the evening. Time to pull up a stool and sip tea by the fire. Tall stories would sometimes come out then, and I would have to judge for myself which ones were true. I was a young boy from the city eager to hear new and strange things, and my cousins could tell all their stories in the same tone of voice, giving no clues to help me decide which ones were real and which ones had been invented for the naïve. Nor did their expressions give anything away. There was no use telling a country story unless you had full mastery over your face muscles as well as your vocal cords.

Turf Smoke

When it was time to go to bed my cousin would light a candle from the turf fire and put it into a holder shaped like a saucer with a small handle. I would take this into the bedroom, lighting my own way as I went, put it down on a small table, and blow it out just before hopping into bed.

In a minute I would be fast asleep.

Even in the daytime the kitchen could become a meeting place, at least on Sunday afternoons after everybody had been to Mass and had finished with their Sunday dinner. If there was an important football match being played in Dublin's Croke Park, the men would gather in our kitchen to listen to it live on the radio. Since there was no electricity, the radios ran on enormous dry batteries. The battery that powered our radio was the largest I have ever seen: it took up the entire bottom part of the old tube set.

Our farmhouse in Murneen was the mecca for people working the small farms nearby. Since we had a post office and a little country store, it seemed natural that the local farmers should meet there to listen to the football match. This was Gaelic football—somewhat like soccer but requiring the skill of hand play as well as foot play. All available seats were placed in the kitchen to accommodate the listening spectators. Some sat on simple stools; others sat backwards on chairs—legs out behind, hands resting on the back of the chair (and sometimes chin resting on wrists). One hand might move occasionally to bring a cigarette or a pipe to the mouth for another puff. Most listeners would keep their eyes fixed on the floor, as if they had been asked to keep track of a tiny spider that was not allowed to get away.

But in their minds' eyes they could clearly see the football players dashing across the field over a hundred miles away in the big city. The gripping commentary and the vivid imagery that came through that little loudspeaker were the work of the incomparable sports announcer Michael O'Hehir. The cadences and tonal inflections of his voice seemed to stay as close to the game as the ball itself, captivating anyone who came within earshot of the loudspeaker. Whenever a goal was scored for County Mayo—or not scored—the room would erupt with the release of pent-up emotions. Instant, gratuitous, and of course expert analyses would be provided by the listeners (usually all together). Pipes and cigarettes would be forgotten temporarily as arms were waved and feet stamped to affirm that justice had been done by some outcome, to malign an unfortunate player for missing an easy shot, or to hurl a bland insult at a referee for making a stupid call.

By the time the game had entered its final quarter-hour—and tensions had risen—the sun would have dropped towards the western horizon and reduced the light in the kitchen to a kind of pleasant gloom. With only indirect daylight entering now above the half-door, the listeners would become silhouettes against the glow of the fire. To complete this scene, turf smoke would blend with cigarette smoke rising in thin stems from poised fingers.

That memory too, I owe to turf.

Unknown to me the first few summers I went to Murneen, that scent of turf smoke was engraving itself into my memory. I first discovered this at home in Dublin one cold, autumn night. It was the custom then to post a night watchman at ongoing road repair sites to guard materials and tools. He would have a tiny watchman's hut to shelter him from wind and rain. A big coke fire would burn all night in an iron brazier right in front of his cozy hutch. It radiated so much heat that you could feel your face getting a welcome warm-up as you passed it on your way home. We boys would sometimes linger near these beacons of fire and chat with the night watchman, partly because of the heat radiated from his fire, but also because of the guy's idiom, which was often full of wisecracks and colorful city jargon. In a typical ten-year-old's fantasy, I envied him for his cozy little refuge, and how he got to stay in it all night.

One evening I was passing by a glowing brazier like this, at Sandymount Railway Station, when the scent of turf smoke hanging in the air sent me back instantly to that country kitchen in County Mayo. The night watchman was burning *peat briquettes* (probably from the Bog of Allen).

Nor am I the only person for whom the smell of turf smoke can invoke lingering, emotional memories. Long after I left Ireland my sister sent me a small piece of turf—a souvenir of Ireland skillfully targeted at the emigrant and foreign visitor alike. Now I could take an instant trip from my home in Houston back to my childhood days in County Mayo simply by letting that little piece of turf smolder away on my windowsill. This was my little pot of gold.

One night I was returning home with some buddies to my uncle's farmhouse in County Mayo, around midsummer's night. There was no moon, and we would have been in total, utter darkness had it not been for some low clouds that still reflected the last vestiges of sunlight. The lone farmhouses in off the road did not have electricity, and all you could see of them were a few tiny squares of feeble yellow light from their windows. They say it is best not to use a flashlight at all in these conditions (even if somebody has one), because your eyes automatically lower their thresholds of sensitivity to pick out the slightest trace of light. In fact, we thought it was fun to walk in near-total darkness, something that is almost impossible to do in the city.

There were a few pasture fields on our left, beyond which the land dropped off into a vast bogfield. My cousin Tom had told me that it went all the way to Claremorris, five miles away, because if the hunting dogs rose a hare in that area, the chase would be so long you would not see either the hare or the dogs for the rest of the night. We were stepping along the narrow blacktop road, carefully guiding ourselves by the barest outline of some furze bushes along the edge, when all of a sudden a sheet of white light flashed across the bog. Its whiteness was like the cleanest bed sheet you have ever seen, illuminated by the brightest light you have ever seen. It seemed to flit along the ground and spread or jump to an adjacent patch of ground in one, instantaneous flash. Then it was gone. Those who had been looking to the other side of the road did not see it at all. It lasted no longer than one second, maybe less.

My dad had explained to us several times what this was, in a knowing, matter-of-fact way. It was called *ignis fatuus*, he said, Latin for foolish fire, and was caused by the spontaneous combustion of marsh gas. This simple hydrocarbon gas is produced by dead plants rotting in water. If the temperature and pressure in the bog are "right," the gas can "light itself" when it rises and mixes with air, without anybody—or anything—giving it a spark. The right conditions for this spontaneous combustion can be found fairly easily in a bog on a warm summer's night.

And strange things are known to happen on warm midsummer nights.

It is not difficult to imagine country people coming up with other explanations for sheets of light dancing over the marshes and bogs. This is true for the present as well as the past, before discoveries in organic chemistry took some of the fizz out of the more imaginative interpretations. White lights darting across bogs without any *living* human lighting them or carrying them is simply too much for the legend-makers to leave alone. Especially those who can keep a straight face while explaining them to children.

In the reference books you will find many other names for marsh gas, such as: "will-o'-the-wisp," "jack-o'-lantern," "friar's lantern," and so on. Most of these seem to build on the fleeting nature of the gas—how it appears very suddenly but never stays in the same place—and of course they often link it to the paranormal and the supernatural. But nevertheless, even some august and erudite sources cannot resist the temptation to include the beliefs of popular culture. My American encyclopedia, for example, provides these colorful insights from folklore:[6]

> Ignis fatuus. In meteorology, a mysterious light seen at night flickering over marshes; when approached, it advances, always out of reach. [...] In popular legend it is considered ominous and is often purported to be the soul of one who has been rejected by hell carrying its own hell coal on its wanderings. [...].

My American Heritage dictionary[7] adds this interesting second meaning after the scientific one:

> Something that misleads or deludes; an illusion.

Literature is in fact very rich in accounts of lights that spring to life without anybody having to put a match to them, and that don't need organic chemistry to explain themselves. Most of these accounts are rather disquieting, making them out to be the spirits of human dead or of non-human beings living in a parallel world of their own. The spirits are at best quite mischievous, but some have a downright mean streak and love to lure unwary travelers into danger with their "lanterns."

The will-o'-the-wisps come to life vividly in German folklore, too, where none other than Faust's hoped-for prize, Mephistopheles, asks one of them to light his way up a hill on a dark midsummer's night:[8] Will-o'-the-Wisp hesitates because it (or he, or she) knows it cannot stay put for one second and fears it may not be able to control its flighty zigzagging. But it does, anyway.

On top of Brocken the human guests dance and sing until they lose their gusto, complaining that they have worn their shoes down to the bare soles of their feet. But along come the Will-o'-the-Wisps, reveling at being able to stay so lively and so bright even though they are only made of rotten vegetation:

> We came here from the marshy waste,
> That's where we were created;
> Yet we're already in our place—
> Glittering, gallant, and elated.
> —Goethe[9]

In Ireland the will-o'-the-wisp has a special place, since it is well known that the fairies like to romp in the open bogland. My own aunt Mary Ellen warned me several times in Murneen that I would be taken away by the fairies if I did not behave well. Yet the fairies, or whatever else they might have been who were dancing with Faust and Mephistopheles that night, appeared to delight in being so much more carefree and sprightly than the humans. So it is not really clear to me whether children might not be better off if they *were* taken by the fairies. Granted, we had a lot of fun as human children, but you never know...

Indeed, Yeats entices the human child by telling how the faery-children play all night on a flat, moonlit beach in nearby County Sligo:

> Where the wave of moonlight glosses
> The dim gray sands with light,
> Far off by furthest Rosses
> We foot it all the night,
> Weaving olden dances,
> Mingling hands and mingling glances
> Till the moon has taken flight;

Who has not thrown themselves into the carefree momentum of a ring-a-round, letting one hand go just in time to grab the next one, half-wishing to understand the secrets in those shared glances? In the end Yeats convinces the child to join the faery-children for an apparently never-ending life of pure play:

For he comes, the human child,
To the waters and the wild
With a faery, hand in hand,
From a world more full of weeping than he can understand.
—Yeats[10]

Nevertheless, we are left with the feeling that the human child may miss the lowing of the calves and the singing of the kettle. I know *I* should.

Seeing bog lights in Ireland is not always dismissed as an inconsequential event of no significance: many terrifying stories have been told in hushed conversations late at night around a turf fire, to folks with somber faces and bowed heads. Nor do these tales only deal with the "old days," for as recently as 2011 I was told that seeing the bog lights meant you will be leaving the human world soon, like hearing the wailing of a banshee prompting you from the wings of life's stage to go out and do your closing act.

My dad had only given me the dry explanation of bog lights: simple, natural gas obeying school book physics. So on that warm summer night, on the road in County Mayo, I was just happy to see for myself those milk-white sheets of light fleeting over the bog.

Or should I say… *ghost*-white?

We never did find any old guns in the bog. Nor any rusty artifacts to fuel speculation about dark deeds carried out furtively, and then suppressed by fearful minds. Nor any trace of the people who worked the sidecuts in the bogs long before us: no half-mummies telling stories of violence; no enigmatic half-faces. One can only wonder what these people would tell us if we could gather them around a turf fire today.

* * *

Whenever I smell that turf smoke, fifty years collapse in a split second—adolescence, college, years of travel, career; all vanish as if I had never left that country kitchen. And the vivid imagery comes complete with all the emotional trappings. Our childhood sense of smell appears to be unique in that it is hardwired directly to the brain's "emotion room"; it bypasses the analytical antechambers where, in later years, rational analysis will be applied.

My own experiences with these vivid flashbacks led me to the French writer Marcel Proust, who dwelled on the theme to a truly amazing extent.[11] For Proust, one could not recapture certain past experiences with the conscious intellect alone, yet they could be re-awakened unexpectedly, and with great fidelity, by pure chance.

The writer had come home to his childhood village, Combray, where he and his mother shared a little treat of butter cake, *petite madeleine,* soaked in hot tea. The sight of the madeleine, alone, did nothing for him, but as soon as it hit his palate, he suddenly got an extraordinary thrill. The exquisite feeling rescued him from his mundane thoughts about life's ups-and-downs, minor mishaps, and illusions. He even compared having this powerful feeling of joy with the way one is affected by love (he was French, after all). Searching for the cause, he figured out that that the taste of the tea-soaked madeleine had triggered the memory of a very pleasant, but long-lost, childhood experience: he would visit his Aunt Léonie on Sundays and they would have some petite madeleine together, before going out to Mass. As Proust put it, even though nothing material may survive the passing years, the tiniest droplet of taste or smell can recreate a whole scene from the immense edifice of our memory. So it was that years later, sitting with his mother, his childhood village sprang back to life—out of a cup of tea—complete with gardens, flowers, the parish church, and all the colorful town folk.

Waiting for a blackened kettle to start simmering; stacking wet turf on tufts of scraggly heather; lost in thought on a bockety cart clop–clopping down a blacktop road, or crunching through loose gravel on a bog road.

Or listening to whispered stories about small people rarely seen by day, some better not seen at all.

Not bad, turf smoke.

---

[1] Seamus Heaney, "Bogland."
[2] Seamus Heaney, "The Tollund Man" and "Bogland" (from his *Bog Poems*).
[3] "Terror fears heighten after slashing attack," *Houston Chronicle*, 23rd May 2013.
[4] Ernie O'Malley, *The Singing Flame* (Cork: Mercier Press, 2012).
[5] Yeats, "The Stolen Child."
[6] *Encyclopædia Britannica Ultimate Reference Suite* (Chicago: Encyclopædia Britannica, 2011), under "jack-o'-lantern (phenomenon)."
[7] *The American Heritage Dictionary of the English Language,* Fifth Edition, under "Ignis fatuus."
[8] Goethe's *Faust,* "Walpurgis Night," starting up Brocken Mountain.
[9] Ibid., "Walpurgis Night's Dream," or "The Golden Wedding of Oberon and Titania Intermezzo" (author's translation).
[10] Yeats, "The Stolen Child."
[11] Marcel Proust, *À la recherche du temps perdu / Du côté de chez Swann (1913), Première partie, Combray I, pp 52-56,* often translated as *In search of lost time / Swann's way,* ISBN 9781500499396, author's interpretation.

3

THE LAMPLIGHTER

The lamplighter came down the street on his bicycle, weaving from side to side, from lamppost to lamppost. Up till then you had been enjoying the summer's day and hadn't really thought about when it would end. The lamplighter stopped his bicycle close to where you were playing with your pals, placed one foot on the ground, and, keeping the other on the pedal, reached down to a little hatch in the base of the lamppost beside you. Supervised now by a small group of boys, he inserted a key into a matching hole in the hatch and flipped it open. Then, after an easy flick of his wrist and a click from inside a little switchbox, the bulb at the top of the lamppost sprang to life and began to shine brighter than the fading background of the sky.

That clinched it: daytime was officially over.

The lamplighter closed the door of the hatch with a decisive clap, wobbled to a start on his bicycle, and pedaled off towards the lamppost on the opposite side of the street. His pace was leisurely but steady.

I was probably born into the last generation that would see the lamplighter do his job on the suburban streets of Dublin. By the time I came on the scene in the 1940s the streetlights in our area were run on electricity, not gas, but they still had to be turned on and off by hand. For this you needed the lamplighter.

Granted, it might have been more romantic if the street lamps had to be turned on by putting a flame to a gas jet rather than flipping an electric switch. Nevertheless, I did not miss that custom completely, for there were gas lights in the trains that I rode to school. At least until steam gave way to diesel in 1954. Nightfall came early in winter—sometimes even as early as school quitting time. If I boarded the train early—while it was parked on a side platform—the man would come through the gloomy carriages and light the gas lamps one by one. Occasionally, the trainman-lamplighter would replace the little shroud on the gas jet that made it burn so fierce and white. One day I asked him what he was doing and he taught me the word "mantle."

But it was in our suburban neighborhood that I got to know the traditional street lamplighter. Our lampposts were placed on alternate sides of the road, so that the pools of light would overlap. The base was fairly low, and a bit stocky. A tapered, fluted post rose up to a crossbar with decorative balls on either end. Above that, a hook decorated with a few iron curls curved over like a bishop's crosier. A single shamrock was cradled within the last decorative swirl of iron, and at the end of all this was the lampshade with its lightbulb nested in the center.

The shamrock indicated that the lampposts had been manufactured after 1922, when this part of Ireland effectively became free of British colonization. Otherwise—as with many postboxes—you would be likely to find a British royal insignia embossed on the casting such as "VR," for "Victoria Regina." But the Irish postboxes did not display the Queen's favorite postbox red, however, because that would have been smothered by several coats of Ireland's then favorite paint: patriotic green.

Cast into the base of our lampposts stood the Dublin coat of arms and its motto *Obediencia Civium Urbis Felicitas*. Loosely translated, if we live by the rules of our city we will make it a happy one. Fair enough.

In my day the lampposts were of course painted green, but when I visited them many years later, in 2013, they were teal blue (even the little shamrock on top). The teal-colored paint was flaking off in some places, showing my old green paint underneath. (There was a curious *bright red* layer under the teal, but on top of the green, meaning that either the British had reconquered the city and painted all the lampposts red again while I was in exile, or the painters had applied a redlead anti-rust coat on top of the original green.)

Besides providing back-to-back pools of light to reassure you that no (imaginary) creature was creeping up behind you in the dark, lampposts had other important uses for boys. For example, the base made a nice wicket for cricket games. In the course of these and other games on the street, many balls were "canted"—lost to high-walled back gardens, high-hedged front gardens, or delicate flower beds. The flower beds in particular caused a lot of friction between us and certain inconsiderate grownups. We were in fact convinced that one particular neighbor stayed on duty behind the curtains whenever we appeared on the street, because she would dart out and confiscate any ball that landed among her dainty flowers. In another case, after a particularly insensitive neighbor moved out (probably because of us) the new owner of the house found a big box full of assorted balls in the garage. They all had signs of heavy usage—threadbare tennis balls, faded plastic footballs, cheap, punctured rubber balls—all confiscated from our street leagues. The new owner gave them all back to us, marking him instantly as a friendly neighbor and therefore one to be protected.

The sight of a twenty-foot-tall lamppost could instantaneously unleash the instinct to climb. One of us would suddenly break into a run as we approached the post, and jump onto the base. This was an implicit challenge to the others. To continue climbing you had to ratchet yourself up the pole by gripping it tightly between your legs, pushing your body up by straightening your knees, embracing the pole tightly with your arms, and bringing up your legs to start the cycle all over again. Supporting your weight with your lower legs and feet was the most difficult, because whereas hands and fingers are made for grasping and holding on with, we humans are no good at grasping things with our feet (any more). Nevertheless a practiced lamppost climber could get up and grab the crossbar without slithering back down too much (or too noticeably). A really advanced climber could even do this with some grace.

As a final flourish—if you trusted your remaining strength—you could use the crossbar as a trapeze and swing out over the footpath, letting your legs flail in the air. Then you would slide back down the post like a fireman and jump back onto the footpath, landing with a look of accomplishment.

Your pals had to match that.

Compared with Texas, at least, Ireland is much further north, so the sun sets much later on summer evenings. It is not unusual to still have some light in the sky after eleven pm on a cloudless night, especially around the summer solstice. On the other hand the winter nights are l—o—n—g. You learned to make the most of both seasons: stay out late into the summer evenings, enjoy the cozy atmosphere in your warm home on dark winter nights. Also, our clocks were set to the local time of the central meridian in Greenwich, England, so when the sun set on Greenwich it still had another twenty-five minutes to go before it set on Dublin. True, there was no net gain, since we had to give the twenty-five minutes back the following morning, but we were rarely awake then.

On nights when the sky was clear, daylight "switched off" very abruptly because the sun nipped all too suddenly behind the Dublin Mountains, or the roof of the house next door. On overcast days, however, it would take much longer for day to fade into night, because the cloud shell would scatter the sun's rays like a giant frosted lightbulb.

But whatever the conditions and whatever the season, somebody somewhere had to decide when the streetlights were to be switched on. To anybody who loved being outdoors, the lamplighter's arrival was a cue that it was time to start changing from day things to night things. If you went home right then there was a good chance the table would be set for tea. It was time to disband and switch to things better suited to the dark.

We were never around when the lights were turned off in the mornings. Nor did we ever even think that the lamplighter might have been out there, weaving his way across the street from lamppost to lamppost just after dawn, while we were fast asleep in our beds. In winter, too, he must have been out— even when the roads were iced over, or covered in slush and snow, because the lights were always on at night and always off in daytime.

Streetlights will always have their romantic side, of course. Regardless of who or what turns them on, they will always create their own unique aura—a comforting oasis of safety—when you walk under them. The aura gets even more enjoyable when there is wind and rain. (It rains and blows a lot in Ireland.) As you walk home in the dark, a wavy curtain of rain descends unseen until it reaches the shining bulb below the iron shamrock on top of the lamppost; then, suddenly, the droplets light up and spread out like a meteor shower. Sometimes this process is reversed: a blustery wind drives the little droplets *upwards* and they suddenly *dis*appear above the lampshade.

And, finally, what would the suburban carol singers have done without streetlights? This tradition was very much alive in suburban Dublin during the 1950s. Television was either waiting in the wings or had already arrived but had not yet infected all homes. On your way home from the bus stop you would come across the little group of singers huddled together beneath the tungsten star of the lamppost. Bright, cheerful faces; colorful scarves, song books held up to the light; lips moving in sync with lyrics of adulation or light-hearted tales. It made a nice contrast to the vague sensation of emptiness or even uneasiness one can get hurrying through the shadows between pools of light. Just what you needed to put you in the right mood before you reached the front door of your cozy home.

Or, if you were already at home, you would hear the slightly subdued singing outside. When you answered the doorbell the singing would turn itself up to full volume and a cheerful, hopeful face would look up at you, holding out a little money box.

* * *

The lamplighter's job fell to higher technology at some time after I stopped paying attention. Now, the aptly named "electric eye" does the work of the lamplighter's human eye, and the electromagnet does what the lamplighter did with a deft flick of the wrist. There is no need any more for a human lamplighter to wobble across the road on a bicycle. When the cool eye no longer sees any sunlight, it sends its unseen message to a hidden magnet and the bulb springs into life. The lamplighter's ceremony is over.

Nothing there to interest an eight-year-old boy.

THE LAMPLIGHTER'S CEREMONY

The lamplighter doing his rounds, in the 1950s. We watched him with a passive curiosity as he opened a little door in the base of the lamppost and flicked a switch to turn on the light. That was a signal to us that the day was soon to turn into night: time to be going home for tea.

The lampposts were also used for climbing contests, for playing cricket, for hiding behind, and for casting light on carol singers. The decorative ironwork was topped with a little green shamrock, indicating that our suburb had been built after Independence in 1922.

In 2013 the shamrock was still there, but it was painted teal blue, like the rest of the lamppost.

4
THE HAY RAKERS

I had expected the afternoon to be uneventful at best, yet it taught me a lesson that lasted a lifetime.

The field at the top of the farm straddled a small hill. There was a ditch running diagonally across it. This ditch was only a foot and a half wide, but it was about three feet deep, cut with sides perfectly straight and vertical. Uncle Tom must have dug the ditch because the water had been collecting at the top of the field and was not draining away. There was usually a little stream flowing in the bottom of the ditch.

When the grass was tall, it was difficult to see the ditch, and you might not have known it was there unless you had seen it before the grass grew, or after the hay was saved. I used to love to get down into the ditch and walk from one end to the other, looking for frogs, butterflies, ladybirds, strange bugs, or anything else that I could find living in the watery, stony bottom.

One day Uncle Tom and I were out in this field making hay. The grass had been cut already some time, and the weather had been good. The hay had been spread out loosely on the ground, so that the wind could blow nicely through it. The wind and the sun would dry it out. You could not bundle the hay up together immediately after cutting, because it would stay wet inside and this would almost certainly cause it to rot. We had already turned it several times and it appeared to have dried out nicely now; it could safely be raked up into larger heaps.

Uncle Tom and I went to work in the field, raking the hay up into large square or rectangular areas, each just the right size to make one cock of hay. The sun was out in full strength, and it was hot. The ground was dried out and hard. The strong, thick stalks of the grass were left sticking out of the ground when the hay was cut and this made sharp stubble that could prick your feet if you were not careful. There was only a small trickle of water flowing in the bottom of the ditch now. I imagined there would not be many frogs or other interesting creatures down in the ditch that day anyway, so I was probably not missing very much by making hay instead of exploring the ditch.

We had worked for several hours, and I was getting tired. I began to think about what I would be doing that evening when my cousin came home from work. The hay rakes we were using were very common tools, found on every farm. At the bottom of a long pole there was a long, flat board with pegs sticking down from it, spaced every two inches or so. When you drew the rake through the hay, the pegs would fall between the sharp stubble and scrape along the hard ground, taking the hay with it. You usually had to make at least two passes with the rake to be sure not to leave any hay behind: it would remain embedded in the spiky stubble, or would simply be pushed out of the way of the rake. You held the pole of the rake firmly with one hand and let it slide through the other as you drew it along the ground. I was not used to this work (since I was a city boy). Small red marks were beginning to form on the palms of my hands and on my fingers—red marks that I knew might become blisters if I did not keep changing the parts of my skin that came into contact with the pole. (I knew that after I had worked a few days on the farm calluses would form on these parts and this would protect the skin from blistering.)

Uncle Tom knew perfectly well that I was not able to rake as fast as he was. He would give me a small area to rake, and then go off to another part of the field himself where he would work away continuously for long periods, leaving me to rake away at my own pace. I imagine Uncle Tom was thinking of different things than I was; perhaps he was worrying whether the weather would stay fine one more day so we could get all the hay into cocks. It would not matter then because the rain would just roll off, keeping the hay inside completely dry.

My uncle was gradually working his way towards me. Finally, after a long while, he was in the square next to me. When he finished raking this he slowly walked over to the square I had been working in. We were both somewhat lost in our private thoughts, slightly subdued by the rhythm of the raking and the sunny warmth of the afternoon. Without saying anything, he began raking the parts that I had already been raking for the last hour. He raked closer and closer to me, still not saying anything. By now I began to feel a little uneasy. For a minute, I put to one side the thoughts that were running through my mind regarding what I was going to do that night when we were finished working in the fields. Why was Uncle Tom raking where I had already raked? Then I looked around and suddenly realized that I had left big, long streaks of hay behind: I had tried to rake too much at one go. More hay was left trampled into the stubble, passed over by the pegs of the rake. Now, Uncle Tom was standing right beside me. He was more weary than annoyed.

"I don't mind if you only rake a little bit," he said, "but leave the ground clean behind you. If you don't, I still have to come back and rake your part for you."

From that day onwards, I never forgot what Uncle Tom had taught me: If you're going to do something, do it right.

Author's note: By exception this and one other story were written in 1989, over twenty years before the other stories in this book. My children were young then and I wanted to pass on Uncle Tom's lesson (because it had helped me long after I left the hayfields of county Mayo). Text essentially unchanged; old photos added 2015.

The Hay Rakers

COCKS OF HAY

This hay has been raked and gathered into cocks ready to be brought home by donkey power. The field is just over the railway from the one in my story, though the photo was taken some fifteen years after I worked there with Uncle Tom.

When a train was due I would put my ear to the track and listen anxiously. As soon as the track started to sing I would dash up the embankment and see how long it took until the train appeared suddenly from around the bend. This railway line had so many bends and level crossings that it was dubbed the Burma Road by railway men. In 1975 it was abandoned to the weeds and the thriving saplings.

Photo: Louis Mullee, 1968 (edited to remove distracting telephone poles).

1950s ITINERANTS

A typical 1950s itinerant family with their caravan, livestock, and belongings. In this un-posed shot they were passing my relatives' farmhouse in Murneen, County Mayo. At that time these people with their highly distinctive way of life were called tinkers,[1] gypsies, or (in song)[2] The Traveling People, or (in the official media) itinerants. Later they were also called The (Irish) Travelers. They would sometimes drop in to our farmhouse and ask for a little milk, or for some other commodity that was not easy to get on the open road.

Unfortunately, there was not much understanding or trust between our respective cultures then: my aunt would always keep an eye on the back door when talking to a tinker at the front door.

About twenty years later I came across several more of these caravans winding their leisurely way along the country roads: German tourists.

Photo: Ca. 1958 (partially restored), spectators from left: my Uncle Tom, brother Tom, Cousin Tom, brother Louis, my dad.

---

[1] A singer-songwriter nicknamed "The Pecker Dunne" wrote the folk song "O'Sullivan's John," and would delight us by performing it in "singing pubs" across the West of Ireland around the late '60s–early '70s. It tells of a farmer who left his country home to roam the road with a tinker's daughter. One of the ways tinkers made a living was to call in to farmhouses along the road looking for odd tin-smithing jobs. The Pecker sang: "...And it's where would you get an old pot to mend..."

[2] Ewan MacColl's folk song "Freeborn Man of the Travelling People" was very popular in the 1960s. The Irish adopted this English song in the 1960s, and surely they could be forgiven for thinking it was written about their own traveling people.

5

THE COALMEN

In the 1950s it was common to hear a primal jungle call echoing through the streets of our otherwise sedate suburb.

"Whooooo–uup. Whooooo–uup. Whooooo–uup," it would go.

The call came from a species of human that had evolved an oversized voice box: the chimney sweep. Covered in soot from head to toe, he came down our street slowly wheeling a bicycle loaded with mats, old jute sacks, and what looked like oversized bottle brushes. He turned his head to the left and right continually as he emitted his whooooo–uup call. It was just a matter of survival: the call had to reach into your home so you would know that he was in your area. If you thought your chimney was choked with soot, you invited this ball of bottle brushes into your house. Once in your living room he would start shoving various types of brushes up your chimney on long, extendible poles. And—oh yes—he would lay down some old cloths to protect your fireplace and your carpet from any stray puffs of soot.

In 1950 I turned eight years of age, the youngest of four children in a single-parent home. The decade just beginning would offer few choices to the average parent of young children in Dublin. Those who took the risk of running a business instinctively squeezed wage-earners as much as possible. In turn, those who lived from paycheck to paycheck squeezed everybody around them who might make a claim on their weekly wage. But text books on economics could never catch the ways in which this continual squeeze created its own imprint on the city's culture. In some parts of the city, a mother raising a family at home had to go to the factory on Friday afternoons to pick up her husband's wages, as otherwise the local pub or the racetrack might claim too much (or possibly even all) of it. My dad was an insurance agent living on commission. Late Friday afternoon was by far his busiest time, because if he did not knock on the door early enough to collect the cash premium due every week, all the available money might have gone to others. He had to rank his clients by their reputation for disciplined spending as well as their earning power. If the shaky ones were spread too far apart, he would deputize me to be at a certain house before the wage-earner went out for the evening. Less critical cases could be handled on Saturday, the next busiest day for dipping into people's weekly wages.

But, people adapt. Always. They look for and find ways to compensate. I, for one, have no memory of ever lacking anything that I *needed*. These basic needs having been met, I was free to relish the things that punctuate a regular day with little sparkles of delight. Treats like HB ice cream, Cadbury's chocolate, toffee bars.

All these child "needs" were met.

By far the most memorable "extra" was the box of toys I found under my bed every Christmas morning, wrapped in brown manila paper and tied with sisal string. Inside it was stuffed with small toys from Woolworths. None of these treats were very expensive, but they were more than enough for us.

This kind of upbringing served well in shielding children until they had toughened up to where they could handle things for themselves. But looking back I see that my screened experiences did mask the hard facts: times *were* very difficult, at least compared with later decades. (It remains to be seen whether the cycle will come around again.) Clothes were worn threadbare until some important seam ripped apart unexpectedly; holes in socks were sewn up with thick woolen thread until the heel became more repair than sock. Concentric rings formed on the soles of shoes as the leather thinned down to the upper, then to the sock, sometimes even to your bare skin. But if I came home with wet feet my dad would get out his cobbler's last and nail on a new leather sole. Patches were sewn onto the elbows of jackets long before designers began to emulate this style for people who never had to wear the authentic originals out of prudence or necessity.

To warm your sheets before you went to bed, you filled a glass Cidona bottle with boiling water—very carefully—and wrapped it in a big sock. There were not enough of those floppy rubber hot-water bottles for everybody in the family. This worked well as long as the stopper did not leak hot water, and as long as the bottle did not come out if its sock and touch some sensitive part of your body. There was of course one other danger—one with unspeakable consequences—and this led to another of my dad's basic rules for living a successful, and long, life:

Never put two glass bottles in one bed.

Indeed: We had nice cozy beds. But occasionally when we awoke we found red spots on our skin: the bed bugs had dropped by. Our simple and effective remedy was to sprinkle DDT between the sheets. This was around the 1950s, "Silent Spring"[1] had still not been written, and DDT was freely used in the home to kill bugs.

Those were the years when charcoal grey became very common in men's clothing. At least in winter it was common, before the soft Irish spring arrived, when the faithful little primroses pushed their heads up and banks of wild daffodils appeared under the pine trees in Wicklow.

But, in winter, motley was the color of our clothes, and motley was the tenor of our lives.

So when the long dark nights arrived, the coal fire became the center of the home. It was like the North Star—everything revolved around it. We did not have central heating (except in the sense of having one fire in the center of the house). Nor was anybody I can remember ever put out by the concept of clean air—the lack of it I mean. Coal fires burned everywhere in Dublin City and in its suburbs. Coal smoke was in your nose, in your throat, in your lungs, in your eyes, on your clothes, on your skin. If there was not enough wind to carry the smoke upwards, it would cling to the damp air close to the ground. You would soon smell and even taste this pungent, sticky blanket clinging to the ground.

My dad always made sure we had enough coal to keep the kitchen fire burning and to isolate us from the damp cold outside. When it was time to fill the coal shed, an order would be placed with a supplier and a few days later the knock on the door would come.

"The coalmen are here."

We bought coal by the quarter or half ton. It was delivered in reusable jute sacks (as opposed to clean paper bags). The coalmen were around middle age, though it was hard for me to tell just how old they were because at that age I tended to lump all adults into the general category of grownups. But I do remember that they were fairly stocky. Coal dust is very fine; it lodged in the creases of their faces and accentuated their leather-like wrinkles. I imagined some of this black-lining would have survived daily face-washing. The whites of their eyes contrasted against their coal-darkened faces, their hair, and their uniformly dark clothes. Taken together—the coal-dusted faces, the dark hair, the dark shades and shapeless forms—on recollection I could easily imagine them as somber Rembrandt etchings.

The foreman would have two or more porters with him. Each porter would take a heavy sack of coal from a lorry or a horse-drawn cart parked outside, positioning it on his beefy shoulders to distribute the load evenly. Each sack would weigh 112 pounds—a hundredweight. Twenty sacks was one ton. All this weight would be taken on those strong shoulders; one hand grasping a corner of the sack to keep it from shifting, the other held out to one side for balance. They must have had strong legs to keep their gait steady without wavering or stumbling from the momentum of the heavy sacks. And, of course, it added 112 pounds of dead weight to their feet. Still, a coalman could lift a sack onto his back, tramp through the front door, hall, and kitchen, out the back door, and tip the contents into the coal shed all without breaking rhythm.

The coal shed was a narrow brick storeroom attached to the main house. Wooden battens were spaced across the front opening to hold the coal in. At the bottom, a slightly wider opening allowed you to shovel out the coal without anything getting stuck or anything collapsing on top of you. The coalman would lean forward and tip the load over the top, raising a small cloud of black dust. There would be a brief, muted crash as the coal on the bottom absorbed the impact and shifted to make room for the new dump. Then the porter would carefully fold the empty sack and lay it neatly on the ground. He would not look at you as he did his work, preferring, I presume, to keep focused on balancing his weighty loads. It never occurred to me to speculate on what the porters were thinking about.

When all the coal had been unloaded, they brought in the slack—coal that had been broken down to dust and gravel-sized fragments. Unlike the larger, angular pieces of coal, slack could flow like gravel or sand. When dumped in a heap outside the coal shed, it would slump down and fill whatever space it had. When all the slack had been delivered, the foreman would give you the nod to count the empty sacks and verify the quantities. While you were doing this, and as you signed the delivery docket, the porters would take a little rest. There was no small talk: this was hard work. Any time not spent straining under a hundredweight sack of coal was savored in silence.

When the coalmen had left, and you had swept the coal dust from the ground in front of the shed, you could look at the coal stacked high behind the battens and feel secure that you were well covered for the cold winter nights.

In later years I often wondered how the coalmen fared when they got older, given the amount of coal dust they must have inhaled into their lungs.

I could see into their faces, but not into their lungs.

These men were the next-to-last in a very long chain of actions by nature and man to give us our cozy kitchen fires. The coal that was carried through our front door had probably come from England, or Wales, if not from one of the coalfields in Ireland itself such as Arigna. It had started as plants and trees growing in a world very far removed from the one we now live in. Far removed, that is, in terms of climate and land form, though not far removed in distance, for those green forests grew where the cities and towns of England and Wales now stand. When the trees could no longer stand firm and catch the sun with their leaves, they fell to the soggy bed of the forest. With time—and nature had lots of that before the Corporate Age—the dead vegetation built up into thick layers like a giant Black Forest cake. In thousands of years these layers of cake can turn into peat, and in millions of years they can turn into lustrous black coal.

If the vegetation had remained exposed to the wind and rain after it fell—and not become waterlogged in the ground—it would have decayed and given its energy back to the age it had taken it from. But without the oxygen in the air it remained half dead—black treasure buried in a tomb. Until fathers and sons went into that tomb to dig it out and deliver it to my home.

It was the Coal Age.

The Coalmen

In the early mornings my dad would get up before anybody else and get the coal fire going in the kitchen. Later, my eldest brother took over this vital chore. You started with a few loosely compacted balls made out of yesterday's newspaper, a few sticks of soft kindling wood, and some hand-picked pieces of coal in different sizes. A well-set coal fire needed one match and no nursing. You did not want it to fizzle out behind your back—and have to resuscitate it by puffing into it with your eyes closed and your face a few inches away from yesterday's ashes. The trick was to leave enough spacing in the stack of wood, paper, and coal so the fire could breathe well. In proper proportions the kindling flame would lick the coal long enough to set it alight before the tinder burned up. As long as you could see that the coals had started to burn on their own—no matter how feeble the flame—you had the needed edge over the cold and could get on with making breakfast.

As the fire took hold, tar oozed out to form little bubbles that boiled away on the surface. Micro-eruptions of trapped gas released plumes of flame and thick brown smoke—after millions of years of sleep. There would be pops, snaps, and puffs. Now and then the fire would play a plaintive song in one long, fading note, like a cane flute with only one tuning hole.

When the chances of the fire going out were very low, you could shovel on the slack. If you put the slack on too early it would fill the voids between the coals and smother the fire. On a nicely burning fire, however, the slack would weld itself into a rigid crust, slowing the air flow and dampening the fire so it would not burn too quickly on you.

After a while the mass of burning coals would become white-hot at the bottom. For fun we would stick a poker into it and watch as it too became white-hot. Then we would pull the poker out and see how long it took the heat to drain off to red-hot, a faint glow, then black. (If it made a burn mark on a piece of wood, it was still hot.) Or we would throw a few pieces of copper wire into the burning coals and watch the curious green tongues of flame fly out.

"Now lad, don't play with the fire," my dad would warn.

But his warning was often in vain. (Much later in life, when I had to supervise campouts in Holland and Texas, I confirmed that all boys and some adults have a primal urge to mess with open fires.)

Probably nothing can match the atmosphere of an open fire. A coal fire radiated such intense heat that it could turn the room into a veritable oven that quickly lulled you into a stupor of inactivity. Sometimes you had to hold a newspaper in front of your face to shield your eyes from the heat rays. Nevertheless, on really cold days, it was considered poor manners to stand between somebody and the fire.

One day my dad showed me how you could heat up a mug of Guinness stout with a hot poker taken from the coal fire. I was told that the country people did this in the dead of winter. Before dismissing this idea, try it: you'd be surprised how much good it can do you on a really cold night (all else aside). And if the fire started to die, you could brave the cold or rain and go outside to the coal shed for a few big lumps of coal. They would keep the fire going till you finished your cheese and crackers and went to bed.

But back to the main function of the kitchen fire. By closing an internal metal flap—the damper—the air flow would divert the flames to a water heater at the back of the fire. The narrow air duct would turn your kitchen fire into a tiny blast furnace, sending scalding water up to a copper tank in the bathroom. After a few hours, there would be enough hot water to bathe four kids and still have some the following morning to wash your face and take the chill away. The fire range even had an oven for cooking, and a compartment to keep your socks warm.

I never remember suffering from cold in winter, thanks to that long chain that ended with the coalmen.

In the evenings, especially on Sundays, we would light a second coal fire in the living room. This would become the center of life for the family; we would often spend the evening there with legs and arms sprawled over the sofa, reading from my dad's small but broad-ranged library. (Family reading ended for most when the television arrived in the 1950s.)

Sometimes, on a sleepy morning after a late night around the fire, you might come down and find that there was still some life in the embers. If you were so inclined, you could reflect quietly on the pleasant hours spent with family and friends the night before.

Where there is a potential to make a mess in a home, some form of etiquette usually develops. And coal fires are essentially messy. The lazy way to start this second fire was to take a pan full of lighted coals from the fire already burning in the kitchen. This was not good etiquette, however, because even if you didn't drop any hot coals on the carpet, the traveling shovel would smoke like a factory chimney. Little hook-shaped pieces of black smut would float around in the air and come to rest on the mantelpiece, a windowsill, or your shirt collar.

To avoid criticism from one's family, one could develop proper fire-setting skills, as described above, and set the new fire from scratch.

Or tell them to make the fire themselves.

Whereas everybody loved a coal fire, nobody loved a chimney fire. It was easy to dismiss carbon soot as powdery dust, but that carbon may not have burned itself out completely before heading up your chimney. In fact it often had enough fuel left to put on that spectacular encore, the chimney fire.

Walking home, on occasion you would smell very acrid smoke and then look up for dark red flames streaking from a chimney that you hoped would be a neighbor's. When our own chimney went on fire we would climb into the attic to check how hot the bricks on the chimney stack had become. It was usually best to let it burn out, because if you called the fire brigade they would pump water down your chimney and make a terrible mess in your living room.

By the 1970s the chimney sweep had evolved into a completely different species: the man in white overalls. They came into your house and sucked out your chimney with powerful vacuum pumps, leaving your living room (and their white overalls) spotless.

* * *

Coal fires were phased out in Dublin households sometime during the late nineties or the early 2000s. After that, natural gas and electricity kept the homes cozy. This was truly a righteous and even noble move.

But apparently that ordinance only covered the big city. In early winter 2011 we happened to be in the town of Boyle, County Roscommon. Even though it was cold, wet, and blustery, we lingered on the old stone bridge in the center of town to watch the inky waters of the River Boyle slip beneath us. The narrow streets and tall gables channeled the wind into gusts that blew parallel with the crown of the bridge, that is, straight into our faces. Suddenly I was transported back to the streets of 1950s Dublin: a down-draft from the chimney of a riverside pub had sent a cloud of acrid coal smoke into my lungs.

---

[1] Rachel Carson, *Silent Spring* (1962). This book stimulated widespread public concern over the dangers of improper pesticide use and the need for better controls. Nevertheless, in September 2006, the World Health Organization (WHO) declared its support for the indoor use of DDT in African countries where malaria remained a major health problem, citing that the benefits of DDT as a pesticide outweighed its health and environmental risks. ("DDT - A Brief History and Status," US Environmental Protection Agency (EPA), http://www.epa.gov/pesticides/factsheets/chemicals/ddt-brief-history-status.htm, last updated 9th May 2012.

6

MY FIRST CATAPULT

The age of ten is an exciting time for any child, but especially for a city boy suddenly let loose on a farm. It is also an age when some boys get into mischief without really meaning to.

I was about ten when I got my first catapult.

Farmer Mark lived alone on his small acreage in Murneen, County Mayo. Every summer for many years I would spend my holidays on a neighboring farm owned by my uncle and aunt. It was a complete contrast: from the capital city to a forty-acre farm where almost everything was homemade. I shared a surname with Mark, though I never knew how closely we were related, if at all. I would have been glad to find a family link between us, though, because he had a big heart and could relate easily to people from a different culture and a different generation.

Mark was about eighty when I was ten.

We had met often in the small store run by my cousin Mae on my uncle's farm. The store sold the few essential things that the local farmers could not produce themselves, such as sugar, salt, and flour. It also housed the area post office, with its own trail of creosote-tarred poles carrying the wires that led to the only telephone around for miles and miles.

On a typical summer's afternoon, Farmer Mark would come to our little shop to buy some things, or to collect his "pinchin"—the state Old Age Pension. Even though it was summer, he always wore the same heavy black coat, tied at the waist with a piece of coarse sisal string. His compulsive smile revealed gaps in his bite where several teeth had been lost. This did not in any way diminish the measure of his smile, however. In fact, I don't remember Mark ever half-smiling or even *not* smiling.

He never seemed to be in a hurry, and always had plenty of time for me. With great interest, he would ask what *I* was up to, never talking about himself, or what he was doing on his little farm. The 70-year age difference between us would shrink to nothing when we started to talk, and I always felt that *my* life was the most important thing in the world to him. In fact, he was just like a ten-year-old buddy, because he always read me so well and guided the conversation to keep me excited about whatever I brought up.

One day I was playing on the road outside my uncle's house when Mark came up on his big black bicycle. It was typical summer weather for County Mayo: several clumps of fluffy white cloud were moving across the sky, but they were moving too quickly for comfort, meaning we were probably in for some more showers before the day was out. The rain from the last shower was probably still visible as little globules of water clinging to blades of grass and wildflower blossoms. (If there had been no rain, I would have been working in the fields making hay, and so would Farmer Mark.) I probably checked for wild strawberries on the roadside that day, hoping that one or two of the bitter green buds I had seen the day before would have ripened into juicy red berries. I may have focused for a while on the droning buzz of a passing bumblebee, trying to spot it from the rising and falling cadences of its pitch. Or listened to the coarse caw–w–w–w! caw–w–w–w! of the crows dotting the branches of the trees high above the old abandoned farmhouse. Certainly, in the background, there would have been the bucolic signature of the rural farmyard: hens clucking and scratching for food.

I greeted Mark very eagerly as soon as he arrived, for I was delighted to see him. He dismounted slowly from his sturdy farmer's bicycle and gently leaned it against the wall outside our thatched cottage.

"Hello-a Hugh-a-gene!" he said, in the accent common for the "hWesht" of Ireland.

"Sure a fine day that's in it, too!"

(In County Mayo, it was a "fine day" if it had not rained for a few hours.)

"Now what's that you've got there, young lad?"

"Oh, nothing," I said. "I was just trying to make a sling."

I showed him the crude sling I had made by knotting a strip of bicycle inner tube into a band. I demonstrated how it worked by flinging a few pebbles down the road. He watched with wide-eyed interest, not saying anything. Then his face lit up as if a great idea had just hit him. He flung his arms out, stooped down to my level, and looked me intently in the eyes:

"What you need is a *catapult!*" he said, and threw his arms into the air with a flourish of animation that spread through his whole body. His eighty-year-old eyes filled with wild excitement and his face turned into one huge smile. (Now what would a ten-year-old boy do with a catapult?)

He spread his index finger and his long finger apart to make the "Y" shape of a catapult. Then he put the thumb of his other hand through the base of his "Y" to show me that I had to hold the fork very tightly to stop it from bending back or twisting when I pulled hard on the rubber sling.

All I needed then were two strips of rubber to make the sling, and a doubled-over patch of leather for the "pocket" that held the missile to be catapulted. I would have to cut a branch from a fairly strong tree to make the fork; fresh new-growth would not do. A blackthorn bush would be ideal if I could get one. Mark made the fork shape with his fingers several more times to drive the idea home, all the while bubbling over with unrestrained enthusiasm.

He had convinced me: I needed to make a catapult.

Over the next few days I carved a Y-fork (probably with my jackknife) and borrowed the kitchen scissors to cut two strips from an old bicycle tube for the sling. Farmer people rarely throw anything out, so I easily found an old boot with a soft leather tongue. This would become the pocket for the projectile, after I trimmed it and cut slits on either side to thread the slings through. Next I bound the slings to the top of the Y-fork with some copper wire that was lying around. My excitement rose. I put small stone in the leather pocket, drew the slings back, and let go. With a "thwang–g–g" and a rush of air the stone shot out of the weapon and covered an impressive length before dropping to the ground and skipping to a stop. I was satisfied with the range and force. A lot of fun was ahead.

After a few more test shots I decided I needed to practice much more because I could not hit the same spot twice. That is, I could not be sure what my stone-bullet would hit. Something would have to improve before I put my catapult to use on real targets. I was not sure yet what these would be. Small birds were friendly things to me, so not these; the crows were safe because they were much too wary of ten-year-old boys, which was why their rookery was high up in the trees above an abandoned house. I knew that a catapult was not a trivial toy—that it had the potential to do damage. But I had plenty of time. At the back of the farmyard behind the henhouses there was a pile of rubble with plenty of empty glass bottles.

Glass bottles! Ideal for target practice…

They even came in varying shapes and colors.

The bottles rewarded me with a sharp "ring–g–g," for a glancing hit, or a series of tinkles for a direct hit that shattered the glass. After a day or so of diligent practice the supply of bottles began to run out. What I needed was a target that would either not shatter at all, or could be put back together easily if it did shatter, yet would still make a definite ping when I hit it. One that left you in no doubt about your marksmanship. Also, it had to be reusable, so I would not be wasting my practice time looking around the farmyard for new targets (a "sustainable resource" is today's buzzword).

But what could that be?

A bucket!

Buckets were always to be found in farmyards. They were used for almost everything—for milking cows, feeding calves, hauling fresh water from the well. And they were strong—made of metal. They would not shatter like glass bottles. I got hold of one and set it up with the bottom facing me. It made a nice round target that stood out from the weeds and stones.

The bucket-target rewarded me with a metallic "pj–ong–g–g!" when my slingshot found its mark on the galvanized iron. To improve my technique I collected some of the limestone pebbles that had been dislodged from the road surface by passing cars. They had sharp edges—having been crushed and sieved in some big noisy machine—not like the rounded ones lying in the farmyard. The harder missiles made an even sharper pj–ang–g–g on the bottom of the bucket. But most important, they were all about the same weight, too, so there was less guesswork in adjusting your aim for the fall during flight.

Things were looking good. I could hardly wait to share my success with farmer Mark.

Later that day, my Uncle Tom was walking around the farmyard busy with the daily routine of milking the cows and feeding the calves. It was then that he noticed a trail of milk tracing his steps from the cowshed to the hut where the bleating calves were waiting to be fed. The milk was coming from the bucket he had used to milk the cows. There was a hole in the bucket.

The forensics started immediately. Very quickly I was identified as the only person on the farm who could possibly have made a hole in that bucket. It was not a simple case of the bottom having rusted out with age: the metal had been torn, and the fracture face had a bright luster. Clearly, the hole had been made by the impact of some small, sharp object. But most incriminating of all: I had been sighted behind the henhouse shattering glass bottles and pinging some metallic object with a homemade catapult. I tried to be as meek and contrite as I could: I had no idea that the force behind those limestone bullets could have been enough to puncture a sheet of iron.

My uncle, never one to waste time trying to undo the past, took out his patch kit immediately and got to work fixing the hole. He put a small, cork gasket on either side of it, followed by shiny metal washers for stiffening, and bolted them all together. The quick fix was effective in restoring the bucket for its original intended function—milking cows and feeding calves—but not for honing catapult skills. My punishment was a few terse, humiliating words from Uncle Tom, and pointed avoidance for a couple of days. Nor was any further punishment needed: I had learned my lesson.

I have no memory of the matter ever having been brought up again, for example the next time my catapult mentor came to visit me. Perhaps there *was* some kind of an open confrontation, and I have suppressed that memory, but I doubt it. Most probably Cousin Mae told Farmer Mark how effective his coaching had been, how it had disrupted peace in the farmyard, and that he should not bring up the subject of catapults with me ever again. If this is so, then Cousin Mae would just have been using her highly acclaimed gift for defusing potentially divisive issues before they escalated out of hand.

"We'll leave it at that," she would declare, drawing on the respect she had won through years of selfless caring for others. That meant, unequivocally, that it was time to drop the issue, and for good.

Either way, I'm sure Farmer Mark chuckled to himself as he cycled off home, not regretting it one bit for having shown me how to make my first catapult.

* * *

Today, in 2013, I have a powerful catapult safely stored on a high shelf in my Houston home. It is the real thing: cast metal frame, strong slings, official Boy Scout issue. I bought it for my son when he was about ten years of age, intending to show him how to use it.

I never did.

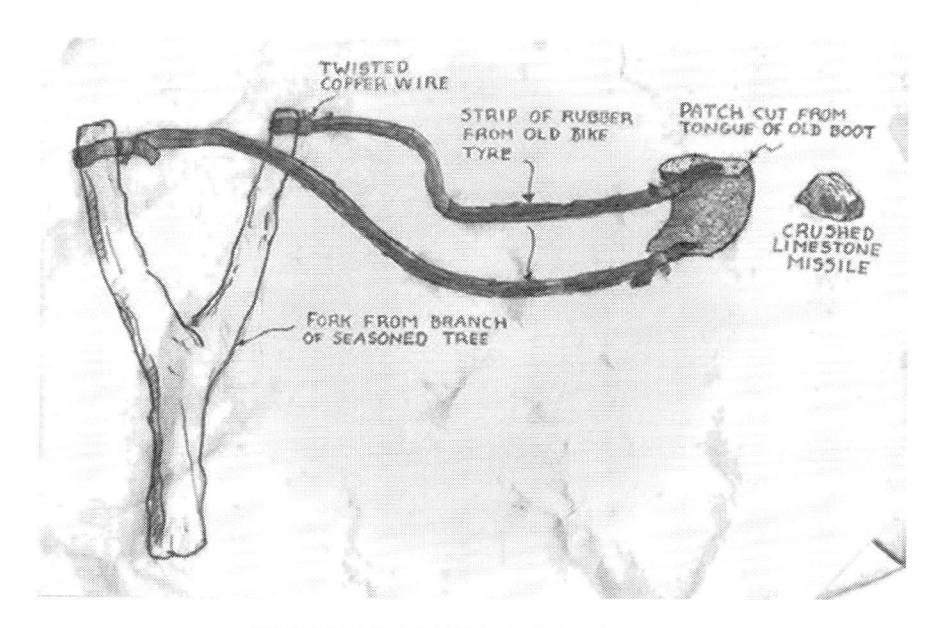

HOW TO MAKE A CATAPULT

7
THE FOGHORNS FALL SILENT

Our history books tell us many stories of ships being wrecked off Howth Head and Dalkey Island when Dublin Bay was shrouded in fog. It is easy to visualize a captain straining behind the glass in his wheelhouse, peering anxiously into a continuum of nothingness where the sky merges unnoticed with the water. They knew they were near land, but all they could see was a curtain of fog—a curtain that could lift suddenly at any moment to reveal some dreaded danger. How anxious the sailors must have been to detect the sound of a foghorn.

So imagine my surprise when I found out that the last of Ireland's foghorns had been switched off for good. On New Year's Day in 2011, a headline in the *Irish Times*[1] ran: "Signal of change: Remaining foghorns fall silent."

I got this news by chance exactly one year later while skipping through the Internet on some other business. I immediately forgot what I was looking for and went tumbling down Memory Lane, back to when I used to hear the mournful brooding of the foghorns as I lay half-awake in bed. Somehow, that plaintive sound had reached deep into my consciousness and evoked strangely different feelings—from a reassuring comfort to an eerie disquiet.

Dublin Bay is a big semicircle cut out of the eastern seaboard—a cove about eight miles wide between rocky Howth Head and the stony headland at Dalkey. Looking seaward from almost anywhere along the coast of the bay, one cannot help feeling a bit humbled—sometimes even a bit misty-eyed—at the wide sea platter rimmed with hazy landmarks. It is even more refreshing and inspiring at dawn, when Dublin Bay hosts the sun's arrival over the Irish Sea. Even in drizzle or fog, the moisture-laden air suffused with morning light will do the trick. After that you can go home to your breakfast of rashers and eggs spiritually charged for the day.

After the nostalgic trigger of the story in the *Irish Times,* I came across a string of comments on a Dublin blog lamenting the last stand of the foghorns.[2] I was not alone, then. "Strum" was tucking her youngest daughter into bed when the child heard a new sound and asked:
"Mom, listen! What's that sound?"
"That's the foghorn on the end of Dún Laoghaire pier."
The girl's mother was then whisked back to her own childhood. She began to think of how she had loved the sound of the foghorn when she herself was a child, but how she had never heard it before in her new home, with her own children. The foghorn's sudden return that Christmas week was due to unusually heavy snowfall that had smoothened the lumpy landscape and dampened out competing sounds. There's nothing like a good blanket of snow to reveal the interesting sounds normally masked by the city's constant din. That snowfall was an extra Christmas gift for the child, her mother thought, because it gave her "a last chance to fall asleep to the comforting, regular, heartbeat of the fog horn on Dún Laoghaire Pier."
Before the foghorn was silenced forever.

Around Dublin Bay, at least when I was growing up, the foghorns appeared to be of the type called a diaphone—a kind of reed trumpet driven by compressed air. Their sound was pitched intentionally low—a bass note not all that far above the threshold of human hearing. Low notes carry far, and can penetrate the fog banks far out to sea. A boat approaching from the open sea could hear the foghorn a long way off, and be alerted to something hard that was coming up—a stone wall or the base of a cliff, for example. Or one of those shallow sand banks notorious for shifting from place to place. I imagine the sailors could have judged distance from the loudness of the horn, to some extent at least, but they would not have been able to judge direction well enough to be absolutely sure where that hard object was. Very low sounds may travel well, but they cannot be focused into narrow beams so you can tell where they are coming from (like your hi-fi tweeter). Not being able to tell exactly where the danger was from the sound of the foghorn alone surely helped the Harbor Board decide to turn them off for good on the 11th of January 2012.

Some of the foghorns were at the mouth of the River Liffey, where it enters Dublin Bay. The river slows as it enters Dublin's city center, like a long-distance train easing itself between the platforms at its final stop. After flowing somewhat sluggishly under the graceful arch of the Ha'penny Bridge, it continues a short distance before gliding past Daniel O'Connell standing on his monument overlooking his bridge. Then it slips past Butt Bridge and under the oily tracks of the railway bridge. That was the last bridge on the river when I was growing up in Dublin. Big cargo boats could sail up-river all the way to this bridge and tie up to George's Quay. As boys we would marvel at the unbelievably strong mooring lines made of giant chains and massive braided ropes sloping down from the capstans on the boat decks to the bollards on the quay. To us the ropes were much bigger and thicker than any we could have imagined. There were ship's chandlers along the quay who sold ropes, chains, and fishing gear: beautiful high-tech reels with complicated winders, shining hooks, catgut lines, and slender fishing rods gleaming with new varnish.

    The rough-faced sailors, the seagulls squealing overhead, the unmistakable smell of the sea, and the odd fish rotting on the wharf completed my boyhood dockland experience.

The spot where the Liffey starts to widen at Butt Bridge is close to the city center. Standing anywhere along the bank, and looking out into Dublin Bay, the river seems to swell up to meet the open sky. Here, the rainy Irish weather conspires with some unremarkable temperatures to keep the dew point low. When the air cannot hold any more water, it makes fog banks out of it. You have to actually stand on the docks yourself and look out into Dublin Bay when the fog is hanging over the water (where the horizon should be) to fully understand its effect on the soul. As with many other memorable experiences in life, the effect seems to be purer when it hits you unexpectedly as you are in the middle of doing something else.

If you cannot catch the real experience, however, a good second is to listen to the verse below from one of Ireland's revered ballads, "The Foggy Dew." It describes how gunboats sailed this far up the Liffey to shell-blast the General Post Office where MacDonagh and MacBride and Connolly and Pearse had made their stand. It was of course Easter 1916, when a group of independence rebels, whose most dangerous weapon turned out to be their idealism, had taken on the British Empire to remove Ireland from it forever. Of the poorly armed men marching towards this part of the city with freedom on their minds, the ballad sings:

> No pipe did hum, no battle drum,
> Did sound out its loud tattoo.
> But the Angelus bell o'er the Liffey's swell,
> Rang out through the foggy dew.
> —Canon Charles O'Neill[3]

I wonder if the foghorns were working that morning.

I grew up about a mile inshore from the Martello Tower at Sandymount Strand, in Dublin Bay. There were two foghorns nearby: one on the North Wall—less than a mile-and-a-half away—the other on Poolbeg Lighthouse at the end of the South Wall—about three miles away. The one I heard when I was going to sleep was probably Poolbeg, because, though further away, its sound would have traveled over open water and sand flats rather than bluff factory walls and residential houses.

The foghorn had a downbeat by design—one very low note lasting a second or two (as far as I can remember), dropping to an even lower note at least an octave below. This two-note cadence was no doubt designed to penetrate deep into the fog, but it penetrated deep into the mind as well. The feelings it evoked were subjective, depending on your state of mind. At first, lying under the blankets but still hanging on to your day thoughts, the sound was strangely comforting and reassuring. But if you floated up from a deep sleep at around three thirty in the morning—when all else was dead quiet—it was inexplicably disquieting. The bass downbeats seemed to weave themselves into your half-dreaming: It's dark and foggy out there... *somebody's in danger...*they are having a tough time in the bay while I lie safe in bed.

Yet to people living *very* close to a horn, or to those accustomed to sleeping far away from city sounds, the foghorns seem to have been a curse. Discussing where exactly the horn was mounted, one blogger[4] said he thought it was "in [his] bleedin' bedroom." Another said his visiting country relatives asked him how he could "live with that din," whereas he himself had trouble sleeping in *their* place—a country house soothed in quiet.

Then there is the radio broadcaster[5] who likened the sound to "a bull grunting" (sure to give you unquiet dreams). In the same broadcast we learned that during a period of prolonged fog a lady had actually got the lighthouse keeper to turn off his foghorn: her dog did not like it. That was at least better than asking him to turn off the fog. But in fairness to people and dogs, that particular fog signal (heard from inside the building) was not the low, two-note downbeat I have been writing about here: it was a penetrating, attention-demanding, electronic whine that would draw secrets from the bravest spy.

As boys in the 1950s we had been very impressed by the technology that automatically turned the foghorn on when visibility got dangerously low. We were told by our older pals that it was switched on and off by an "electric eye" that could "see" how foggy it was outside. That technology was leapfrogged by still more clever devices until, now, radio beams from earth satellites give sailors their precise position, on a precise map, regardless of how foggy it is outside. The space age has relegated the foghorns and their smart switches to, at best, the maritime museums.

Also to be retired would be the old joke about the lighthouse keeper who woke up suddenly when the foghorn *stopped* blasting in the middle of the night: "What was that!" he asked, startled by the sudden quiet. It seems he had an inverted sense of silence.

All this begs the question: How close to a foghorn must one live before the romance gets lost?

Finally, I can't help thinking about a comment in that same *Irish Times* article: "However, should a blanket of cloud descend over Fastnet Rock it may be that passing craft will still hear a ghostly warning sound from the fog signals for some time yet." No doubt the writer was thinking of the many sailors who had strained behind the glass in their wheelhouses, listening for the lowly but welcome sound of the foghorn.

And perhaps, too, he was thinking of those for whom neither the sound of the foghorn nor the call of the Angelus bell would ever again come through Dublin's foggy dew.

Should you ever visit Dublin, and stay anywhere near Sandymount Strand, and wake up from a deep sleep in the bottom of the night, listen for a low, mournful sound...

Growing Up in Dublin

WISTFUL GAZES

High above Dublin City's most famous street, Daniel O'Connell shares his monument with an uninvited guest. Both appear to be wishing the warm winter sun was not about to go down. Both are far removed from the world of the impatient pedestrians massing on the crosswalks below, playing bluff with cars and busses in the late-afternoon dash for home. One level down, under O'Connell Bridge, the River Liffey glides quietly towards the open waters of Dublin Bay.

There might be fog in the bay tomorrow.

Image: Digitally modified photo, December 2011.

POOLBEG LIGHTHOUSE, DUBLIN BAY

Poolbeg Lighthouse still welcomes ships entering Dublin Bay, but the haunting downbeat of its foghorns no longer slips into the thoughts of half-sleepers in their cozy beds on shore.

Some mourn the loss, recalling the how the brooding sound used to evoke poignant feelings late at night. But others, living closer to the source, are glad that the din has finally quit, and that they no longer wake up thinking the horn is in their very bedroom.

In daytime, strollers enjoy the popular walk along the South Wall, while fishermen stand on the lighthouse's rocky foundation to raise their rods and lose themselves temporarily among the sounds of the sea.

Image: June 2012, digitally modified photo.

---

[1] "Signal of Change: Remaining foghorns fall silent," *Irish Times*, 1st January 2011.
[2] "The Foghorn's last shout," *Dún Laoghaire BlogSpot*, comment posted by Strum, 12th January 2011, http://www.dunlaoghairecounty.ie/viewtopic.php?f=24&t=1958.
[3] Canon Charles O'Neill, "The Foggy Dew," Irish ballad inspired by the tragic events of the Easter 1916 rising, set to the air of "The Moorlough Shore," http://www.bbc.co.uk/history/british/easterrising/songs/rs04.shtml, last updated April 2012. My favorite version is by Sinéad O'Connor, with The Chieftains.
[4] "The Foghorn's last shout," *Dún Laoghaire BlogSpot*, comment posted by jordo, 12th January 2011, http://www.dunlaoghairecounty.ie/viewtopic.php?f=24&t=1958.
[5] Ella McSweeny and Pat Kenny, "The Death of the Fog Horn in Ireland," RTE Radio 1 report, *Audioboom* blog entry probably December 2010, http://audioboom.com/boos/243757-the-death-of-the-fog-horn-in-ireland.

8

BACKYARD BEEKEEPING

I had just spent another long summer day in the giant playground I loved best—my uncle's small farm in Murneen, County Mayo. My cousin Tom had come home from his day job on the railroad and, as usual, I had helped him bring in the cows, milk them, and feed the calves. The hens in the roost had quietened down, and the hound dog had stopped prowling the farmyard. Daylight was getting scarce. Those with outside tasks were dribbling back to the farmhouse and lingering in the kitchen. The turf fire was getting low, and the big oil lamp hanging from the rafters had been lit. Normally, in another hour or so I would take a candle to the bedroom and reluctantly admit that the day was over.

But not that evening: suddenly, my cousin rushed into the kitchen looking for me.

"Quick–quick, lad: there's a swarm!" he said, with his trademark halfsmile that understated the exciting things he had in store for me.

"Oh boy!" I said, "This is what I have been waiting for!"

The bees were flying aimlessly along a line of trees bordering a pasture field. They had formed a cluster about ten inches wide, with a head and tail like an upside-down, flying comma. Most of them were in the head of the comma—a brownish blob barely visible against the darkening sky.

That was about fifty years ago.

About two hundred *million* years ago, the insects that would develop into today's bees were living on the supercontinent of

Pangaea, a land so huge that nearly all of today's continents could have fit into it. Eventually Pangaea broke up into separate plates that rafted away from each other to form the shapes we now recognize on our world map. It took time of course, but there was plenty of that. The insect-ancestors got separated, too, and drifted off to different parts of the world depending on which raft they took.

We know that as far back as eighty million years ago, a fully formed bee of a species closely related to the honeybee got stuck in a bead of resin, probably on a tree. The resin hardened into amber, trapping the bee inside and turning it into a fossil. But we don't have to resort to science fiction to bring the bee back to life, for its descendants live in all tropical areas of the world today, even though these parts are now separated by thousands of miles. It is theorized that this is so because the now-separated bees share common ancestors that once lived together on Pangea, before the continents drifted apart from each other.[1] (This drifting is still going on, so in fifty million years airfares to Australia should be lower, because that continent will have merged with Africa.)

Bees have indeed been around since long before we came along, and may still be around long after we are gone. It is very rewarding to look at how the surviving species live, and what worked best for their ancestors on their long journey from Pangaea.

If you really want to get close to bees, you should host a colony and care for them. You can even do this in a suburban backyard, as I did, if you have good relations with your neighbors and don't mind a little sting now and then. If you live close to touchy neighbors, or are sensitive to bee venom yourself, you can always host a nest of stingless bees.

The scientific name for the western honeybee, also called the European domestic bee, is *Apis mellifera,* a name that immediately brings up the word "mellifluous"—flowing like honey.

This species has in fact been selected and bred for a number of traits, including gentleness.[2] Folks living in Texas or any other southern US state will value this gentleness very highly, and will be very aware that hundreds of humans have been stung to death by a new, invasive subspecies of bees that is most definitely *not* domesticated and *not* gentle.

Schoolteachers rightly stress that nectar is not honey: bees gather nectar from plants, swallow it, break it down into simpler sugars, and (to use the nicer word) regurgitate it partially digested, as honey. When we humans eat honey, we can absorb the simpler sugars directly, thanks to the work done by the enzymes in the bees' stomachs. Thank you, Miss Bee.

The nectar that the domestic bees are eternally looking for is produced by the stamens of the flower blossoms they visit. The stamen's main purpose is to produce pollen—the male cells that fertilize plant seeds for procreation; it only produces nectar to reward birds and insects for dropping by. Most plants keep their generations healthy by cross-fertilization—seeding their young from a diverse gene pool. So most plants would like their pollen to be spread from one plant to another as much as possible. When the bee drops in to pick up her nectar, she also picks up some pollen and carries it to another plant. It is a good bargain: the plants spread their pollen and the bees get their nectar. The bees have a good use for pollen, too: they mix it with wax secreted from their bodies and feed it to their young.

* * *

I got drawn into the lives of bees in a very simple, practical way: watching my cousin Tom tending a few hives on that little farm in County Mayo. My practical interest held long enough for me to build two hives in the backyard of my home, in the well-populated suburbs of Dublin. This lasted several years, before adolescence diverted my thoughts and efforts in ways that adolescence does. But many people have devoted their whole lives to studying bees and working with them. Others have filled books with incredibly realistic drawings of them.

Cousin Tom's beehives were set up a safe distance behind our little thatched farmhouse. I would approach the hives very carefully and spend my leisure time passively watching the routine comings and goings of honeybees. It was immediately obvious that sun and warmth played a big role in motivating bees. On hot days one or two bees would leave the hive or return to it every second. They would stride out of the entrance briskly, with the purposeful manner of somebody who had no doubt at all where they were going, and why. They would rise gently from the hive and veer off to one side smoothly like an airplane climbing to align itself with a well-defined flight path. By the time I suddenly caught sight of an incoming bee, she would be heading dead straight for the hive like an airplane on its glide path to the runway. (Yes, a beeline.) A second later she would alight on the board at the entrance to the hive.

You could see the pollen baskets on their legs—big globs of pollen-wax mix—hanging like fat missiles from the wings of a miniature fighter plane.

Western honeybees are called "social" insects, but that does not mean that they behave like humans who are called "social," or "socialized." In a way, we have borrowed the term "social" to describe bees in our language because we don't speak any bee languages, but it is very easy to see the limitations. It would be interesting to hear a bee talk about how humans socialize, say, at cocktail parties, football matches, not to mention in a welfare state. In fact, the realities of the bee world can be harsh in the extreme. There appears to be little sentimentality and no place at all for any bee who whose job is not essential to keeping the colony alive, or producing new colonies. Individual bees are safe from layoffs—or worse—only as long as they have useful work to do.

There are three distinct classes, or casts, within the domestic bee family: workers, queens and drones. There is no King of the Bees. As in other societies, each class has a distinct job to do. The worker bee is a female that has been deliberately, that is, instinctively nurtured in a certain way to "engineer" her for defending the hive, gathering food, caring for the young, and keeping the nest clean (nothing else). She can lay *unfertilized* eggs, but these only produce drones, and she only does this when drones are really needed.

The queen is a fully developed female: she can attract males and mate with them to fertilize her eggs. She has in effect a personal "sperm bank" in her own body that can keep sperm alive for several years. (Not by freezing, of course.) She fills this up on her nuptial flight by mating with as many as twenty drones. Thus she has a nice diverse mix of genetic material in her sperm bank, a vital factor in keeping the colony healthy (like the flowers that they pollinate). She fertilizes the eggs as they are laid, or, if required, she can close the faucet of her sperm bank and lay her eggs without fertilizing them. Those eggs will produce drones. The vast majority of her eggs are "designed" to staff the hive with diligent female worker bees. She doesn't go out and gather nectar or pollen, clean the hive, or care for her young; all that is delegated to the worker bees. She does have a sting, however, but she uses it to settle royal disputes, not to defend the hive; that, too, she leaves to her loyal subjects the worker bees.

Eventually, a younger queen will replace the reigning queen. Thus, over the long term, the colony is constantly refreshed with a healthy mix of new genes.

The drone is a male; that's all. He does not cruise over flowery meadows and gather nectar or pollen; he does not risk his life in gallant battles to defend the hive, and in fact he doesn't even have a sting; he wants nothing to do with rearing the bees he has sired, nor does he care about cleaning the hive. His only function is to mate with the queen, and even for this he has plenty of willing help from other drones. But fertilizing a queen's eggs is a seasonal job. Worse still, there is only one season: the queen can fertilize a whole batch of eggs on that one nuptial flight. (It would be much different if each egg had to be fertilized separately, say at repeated intervals of about a week.) So when the drone has done with this single job, he himself is done with: the worker bees sting him to death. Ouch.

There are no retirement benefits for drones (but then, they never live long enough to need them).

Once the queen and her consort drones have finished the fertilization ceremonies, she only has one more job to do: lay those eggs. She may lay somewhere around one thousand five hundred eggs *a day*, making her in effect and egg-laying machine. Normally, worker bees place the queen's eggs into those neat hexagonal cells, where they hatch into larvae (also called grubs). Then they secrete a sort of bee milk known as "royal jelly" and feed it to the larvae for the first three days of their lives. Royal jelly is full of carbs and vitamins and even offers a rich serving of B_5, the vitamin essential to all forms of life. So the bee children are very well looked after and will never have to fly to a vitamin shop for supplements when they grow up (just as well, because they won't have the time).

After this royal treatment the grubs are switched to a diet of nectar or diluted honey and pollen. Soon, hormones start to drive the complete change of form that in three weeks will turn the grub into a fully formed worker bee, with wings and all.

Once the new hand is out of the wax, she loses no time. On her first full day as an adult she carries out waste, cleans cells, and secretes a disinfectant into them so they are ready for the queen to deposit the eggs. Then she moves on to the crèche and feeds the older larvae their honey and pollen. On the sixth day, she starts work in the critical Postpartum Department, feeding newborns with royal jelly. At about three weeks she works for a short while in Security, defending the entrance to the hive. Finally, after her apprenticeship as inside worker, nest builder, and soldier, she starts her lifelong career as breadwinner. The bread is made of honey and pollen.

Watching bees always had a calming effect for me. It was nice to listen for the low hum of an arriving bee, and to track those taking off. I would try to guess where they were headed, and to see how long I could keep them in sight before that tiny dot vanished from my radar. Most probably they were headed for the clover in the pasture fields all around us, because clover is a favorite source of nectar for bees and is famed (by humans) for the honey that the bees produce from it.

Occasionally I would see some drones hanging around the hive. They were a bit bigger than the worker bees. I was not afraid of them: drones have no stings, and I had taken good note of that. (Besides, a horse fly sting is far worse than a bee sting. You don't feel anything while the horse fly is sucking up your blood, and by the time you do feel something and swipe the insect away, you already have a disgusting smear of fresh blood on your skin, and a disgusting feeling of having been had. Give me a bee sting any day—but only one, thank you, not a mass attack.)

I soon noticed that the traffic near the hive was much lighter on cold days. The bees seemed to lack motivation. I imagined that they were inside the hive building new hexagon cells, capping the cells that were filled up with honey, or disinfecting empty cells to make them ready for the queen's eggs. I couldn't imagine that they would have been absolutely idle, or just hanging out on comb corners gabbing. (What was there to gab about anyway, besides work?)

I tried to see the world as the bees did. It was well known that a bee had to die after stinging an animal, because the barbs on her sting won't allow it to be removed without ripping out the viscera from her own abdomen. Perhaps she attacks on pure instinct, and does not care—or know—that it will be her last, heroic act. In addition to being totally dedicated to her work, she is expected to sacrifice her life without flinching if the good of the colony requires it.

In the end I decided to become a beekeeper myself, and asked my cousin how to build a hive. He told me there was a free government leaflet with detailed carpenters' drawings for the hive and instructions on how to manage bees. For the farmers, beekeeping was not a hobby, of course—it was a job that produced valuable food for the table and promoted the spread of pollen to help flowering plants flourish. For me, though, beekeeping was just going to be summer fun.

But first it would teach me a useful lesson on life, one that had only a coincidental connection with bees.

When I saw the drawings my cousin had got from the government, I decided I needed to study them thoroughly. This was serious work, so I set myself up in the barn with paper, pencil, and ruler, and started to copy as much as I could. The barn was the quietest place in the farmyard. Important stuff was stored there—cream skimmed off milk that had come straight from the cows, fresh yellow butter made from that milk, and other things that had to be kept in a cool place out of reach of geese and hens. I had made myself a comfortable little "office" there, taking a kitchen chair from the thatched dwelling house and setting up a makeshift table for my drawings. Occasionally I would sneak a spoonful of the delicious thick cream from the basin. I was a bit older now compared with the previous summers I had spent on the farm, and I fancied I had really seen all there was to see of making hay and bringing turf home from the bog. Yes indeed, I was very comfortable in what now had become the Barn Academy of Beekeeping.

Too comfortable: that was the problem.

On about the third day of study in the barn, my newfound academic serenity was jolted severely. My Uncle Tom—father of Cousin Tom and owner of the farm—was talking to my aunt within earshot of the barn door. Either by chance or by design,

I overheard what he was saying, and it was about *me*. My uncle's voice rose in a mixture of criticism and frustration:

"But he's so bleddy lazy!"

This really jerked me back to reality: I had completely overlooked the fact that it was good weather outside and I was expected to *literally* "make hay while the sun was shining." (You have to live in western Ireland, where rain can come out of clear skies, to appreciate the truth in that maxim.) I really should have been out in the fields helping my hosts with the unending chores that make a farm a farm. I had been blinded by my fascination with all things bee. I immediately got the message. How could I miss it?

So I stopped studying beehive technology in my Barn Academy and turned to haymaking. Alas, the holidays were nearly over and I was only able to undo a little bit of the harm.

After I returned to Dublin I went to the Department of Agriculture in Henry Street and picked up my free copy of the beehive drawings. I went to a store near Tara Street and had the man cut several pieces of wood to sizes small enough for me to carry home on my bicycle. That meant balancing the wood on the handlebars with one hand and steering the bike with the other, ready to brake suddenly with the same hand if necessary. That was easy then, as there was not much traffic on the road through Ringsend.

At home, I went to work in the garage sawing and nailing. The most sophisticated tool I had was a simple handsaw. My big brother Louis had very strong hands and I would ask him to make the critical wood cuts for me. I was not able to make right-angled cuts true enough to avoid ending up with ill-fitting joints with telltale gaps. (The bees would surely have complained of the drafts when winter came.) I altered some of the nonfunctional parts of the hive by adding some designer features that pleased me, and then deluded myself into thinking that the bees would also be pleased by my artistic touches. I put waterproof felt on the roof to make sure no rain *ever* got into that hive.

By early autumn I had completed my first beehive. I set it up in the backyard and lay down on the grass proudly looking up at my creation. From that perspective—with my eyes near the ground—the hive looked big and majestic. After all, that would have been the perspective of an incoming bee.

But I had no bees.

Not yet, at least. I would have to go back to County Mayo for these.

Late that winter I poured a concrete foundation for the hive. Unfortunately, it froze hard that night. I waited in vain for the concrete to set, but it didn't. The best it would do for me was to stiffen into a grainy cake that you could crumble just by squeezing the edges with your bare fingers. Of course, I *had* been told that you shouldn't mix concrete in very cold weather (the water will freeze up before it can react with the cement). In my unbounded boyhood enthusiasm and conviction of my personal exemption from life's difficulties (then and in the future), I had assumed that this rule was only meant for ordinary people, not for me. Sorrowfully, I dug out my first, failed concrete structure and threw the equally sorry lumps into the dustbin.

The bees had taught me another lesson, indirectly.

A few months later I had the hive sitting on a well-cured concrete base by the wall of our backyard. It happened that the neighbors on the other side of the wall were fond of playing badminton. Soon, there were concerns that putting bees so close to the wall might spoil the game for the bare-armed and bare-leggèd folks jumping around a mere twenty feet away or less. I fended off these concerns by explaining that, from my extensive field experience and my studies in the Barn Academy, I could assure them that bees were hard-working, peace-loving insects, and that they would *never* attack anybody unless they were attacked first. Unless, for example, somebody took a swipe at them with a badminton racket. A cautious détente was established.

The summer holidays finally came, and with them the anxiously awaited trip to County Mayo. This time I got off on the right foot and threw myself unreservedly into the farm work. Raking hay, gathering turf, helping to spray the potato plants against blight; nothing was a problem for me. The reward came soon. My dad visited one day to see how things were going. My uncle was smiling from ear to ear:

"He's working like a slave!" he beamed.

I was very happy. Getting up in the fresh morning air and willingly throwing myself into the farm work all day with my uncle and aunt brought its own rewards. I also got more out of my free time after work, when Cousin Tom came home from his day job on the railroad.

Another early lesson. Thank you, Miss Bee.

Social bees do not multiply in the same way that new families are reared by individual male-and-female couples. A queen and a drone do not fly off and build a new hive together. Far from it. Instead, the colony in a hive divides in two and the queen takes off with a whole swarm of bees to found a new hive. In the case of the domestic honeybee, when the hive begins to get too big, by some signal the worker bees begin to groom new queens. The way they do this is very interesting. First, some extra-large cells are built. The queen puts a fertilized egg into each cell—an egg just like the ones she puts in the thousands of smaller cells for the worker bees. When the eggs in the special cells hatch, they are given the "royal treatment" for six days—fed with royal jelly. This premium nutrition causes the eggs to develop faster and to mature into larger adults with fully formed ovaries. (In the case of the domestic bee, at least, nurture *does* make the difference. I often mused on the analogy in human life, how having the proper "space" and "nurture" can make a big difference to how one develops...) When the young "princesses" mature into queens, they fight among themselves until only one is left alive. (I suppose that's why queens have stings.) The last queen standing then attacks the incumbent queen, who leaves the hive with the swarm of follower-bees to find a new home.

So, it appears to me that emotion does not play a big part in a bee's life. They seem to be hardwired from birth to act instinctively, and without hesitation, to preserve the colony above all else. "All else" includes their own lives, the lives of the queens, and even the lives of the drones (at least until they have done their job).

Back to that evening on the farm when the bees swarmed and my cousin came running into the house to get me. The tail of the swarm was poorly defined, and it branched out into several strands. As the swarm moved, the bees at the tail seemed to be a bit "out of it," flying in and out of the main ball of bees, some circling around with no apparent aim. I mistakenly thought these were just stragglers, or indecisive hangers-on, but later I learned that actually they were scouts looking for a good place to build a new hive. The main body of bees then settled temporarily on the branch of a tree, forming a dense, heart-shaped mass around the queen to protect her until they all could move into their new home.

My cousin had placed a box upside-down in a nearby tree. I was amazed to see that the bees obediently gathered in a cluster underneath the box, covering the branches with their reddish-brown mass. Then they slowly crept up into it. They seemed glad to end their rebellion and find a new home. They were in for a few more moves, though, before they could get down to honey gathering and raising their young in the backyard of my home in Dublin.

At nightfall, my cousin put a white sheet on the ground near the tree. He had prepared another box—sturdy enough to take the bees on a four-hour car trip to Dublin—and he put this down on the sheet.

Then he brought out the "smoker"—a small barrel made of tin and filled with smoldering newspaper, a bellows to blow air through it, and a nozzle. When the bellows was squeezed, a cloud of fairly pungent smoke came out the nozzle. If you inhaled the smoke by accident you would quickly cough and gag. He aimed the nozzle at the box in the tree and gently puffed a light cloud of smoke into the opening. Then he removed the box from the tree and placed it on ground. The bees remained in the box throughout all this, except for a few who were still flying around in that apparently aimless way.

Not one bee was interested in stinging me.

Next, my cousin turned the box of bees on its side and placed it on the white sheet, opposite the empty transport box. The bees—in an effort to avoid the teargas I expect—slowly crawled out of their temporary box as if directed to do so by a traffic warden. To my surprise—and counter to all my boyhood impressions of bees up to then—they behaved with genuine docility and still made no attempt to sting or to fly off.

When bees swarm, my cousin explained, they are not in a combative mood. That is because they are not protecting any territory: they are just looking for a new home. Furthermore, they will have raided the pantry in the old hive before leaving and filled their bellies full of honey for the big move. In fact, the bees were so friendly you could let them crawl over your bare skin and they would treat it as if it were just a piece of old leather.

Soon all the bees had moved into the transport box at the head of the white sheet. I looked carefully for the queen, but could not positively identify her in the poor light. That was a shame, for I would have liked to see a bit of royalty.

The next day or thereabouts my dad drove us back to Dublin with the box of unsuspecting bees. There in my backyard, at dusk, I repeated the process, but in reverse, this time having the bees crawl into my handcrafted custom hive. They were wonderfully cooperative and friendly. Again I tried to spot the queen, but cannot honestly say that I saw her. Like good chess strategists, the bees had protected their queen very well. (That's as far as this analogy can go, since there is no king.)

In the remaining days of summer I watched the bees coming and going. On warm sunny days there would be a steady stream of takeoffs and landings on the alighting board at the hive entrance. Soon, this little board became stained from pollen-laden bee legs dragging over it, removing the Brand New stigma from my handiwork.

Now I was a true backyard beekeeper. Not just a theorist.

Autumn approached, the sun got lower and lower, and we turned our attention to indoor things. Bee traffic got slower and slower. Eventually there were days when only a few bees thought it worthwhile to leave the hive, and soon it was rare to see even one bee straggle out of the opening. But inside—I knew from the literature—they would be enjoying the comfy warmth generated by their own body heat. When I went out early one morning and found hoar frost on the grass, I had a snug feeling that I had done my part, and the bees would have just as cozy a home as I had for the coming winter.

I have always loved the Irish spring. Now, when people were straining to find proofs that it had come, I had my own clear sign: a few hardy bees venturing out of the hive. This, and a few brave primroses bursting out of the ground through last year's dead leaves, were all I needed. Now I could forget the lingering winter nights and take heart at the coming of fragrant new growth and long summer evenings.

Late spring was an active time for the bees, as there were lots of blossoms to harvest. In our own backyard two apple trees erupted in pink blossoms every May, like exploding fireworks. Chances are that the bees went much farther, to the overgrown fields beyond the railway, perhaps.

As the honey gathering (I mean the *nectar* gathering) got really frantic, there was the odd sting here and there. This was usually because somebody got too close to the hive. One day my dad got stung on the eyelid, causing his eye to close up like an over-ripe peach, leaving only a thin slit for him to see through. This made him look rather comical for a few days, and we had a hard time not laughing when he looked directly at us. He did not find it funny at all.

There were no attacks on the neighbors, for which I was glad. Or, at least, if anybody next door did get stung, the issue had been handled diplomatically between the adults. I now realize that the western honeybee is not as easily provoked as certain other species, and—more important—they do not gang up and attack you in great numbers. That was lucky for us, as we shall see later.

In late summer or early winter it was time to "harvest the honey," a nice way of saying, "rob the hive." Unknown to the bees when they moved into my handcrafted hive, the top was slyly designed so that humans could remove it very easily. Worse still—for the bees—the honeycombs themselves could be removed quickly by a few slick maneuvers. To do this, all you needed was a bit of teargas from the smoker. After the bees had settled down for the evening, you doped them with a few puffs of smoke directed at their front door. Next, a few more puffs into the hive from the top, letting the smoke circulate through the bee-ways. By this time *most* of the bees would be so groggy they would not offer any resistance. Then you removed one or more frames full of honey from the top of the hive, leaving the bottom ones for the bees. (Weren't we generous?)

The process of removing (stealing) honey was quite safe, both for humans and for bees. Nevertheless it was a bit scary for us humans, even armed with our narco weapon. Some of the bees would manage to dodge the smoke and fly around the hive in the attack mode. You needed a good bee bonnet, clothing that was free of openings at the collar, at the cuffs, at any trouser bottoms not tucked in, and at any buttonholes that were missing buttons. In short, clothing free of any opening that might admit the determined bee to some sensitive part of your body.

Again I have to give credit to my older brother: he was dauntless when it came to opening the hive, and with time I sort of acquiesced to letting him take my turn. I suppose that's what big brothers are for.

But what would happen to the bees in winter, now that we had stolen their provisions? Would they starve to death? By then all the flowers would have long since withered and, besides, it would be too cold and too dark to go out gathering nectar. Well, in return for their gift of honey, we would give them a large slab or "biscuit" of pure sugar. This we made ourselves, at home, by simply mixing sugar with tepid water until it became like medium-soft candy. Throughout the winter we would remove the roof of the hive and peek inside to make sure the bees had not eaten all their sugar. If they needed more, we cured some extra slabs for them.

I never questioned, then, whether the bees noticed that they had been shortchanged. Hadn't they worked hard all summer and laid in supplies of honey only to have it surreptitiously removed by humans? And replaced by plain, undigested sugar of inferior nutritional value? Well, we did provide them with a free house to live in, handcrafted with care and well insulated from the damp Irish winter.

We also protected them from roaming animals and badminton players.

* * *

Not too many years before I was learning how to manage bees in Ireland, somebody in Brazil was breeding African honeybees with European honeybees. They were trying to produce a hybrid bee that would have the best of both species—bees that would produce large amounts of honey *and* thrive in tropical climates.

The result was the Africanized Honeybee.

The new subspecies is smaller and not nearly as good at pollinating plants, but that piece of bad news is nothing compared with the next: it is much more aggressive. It is very touchy, and much quicker to attack anything it *believes* is threatening the hive. Although each bee delivers about the same amount of venom as her European relative, they go after their victim in a "pack" rather than individually, follow the victim to greater distances, and keep the attack up longer. As if that were not enough, it takes the Africanized Honeybee longer to calm down after an argument with an aggressor. It is not surprising, then, that this subspecies was dubbed the "killer bee."

In 1957, the hybrid bee was accidentally released into the wild (as indeed some people may consider to have been inevitable, given enough time). It began to move northward from Brazil, covering over a thousand miles every five years. By the 1980s it had reached Mexico, and in 1990 the first swarm was documented in Texas.

Since I started to live in Texas myself around 1981, I decided to take this threat seriously. I used to love going camping and hiking in the wild forests of Texas with my son and the rest of Boy Scout Troup 1659. Occasionally small groups of us went down to Big Bend National Park, in far West Texas. Once, we camped on a dry, gravelly terrace of the Rio Grande, a mere hundred feet from Mexico. (At that time, a local villager would row you across the river to the dusty little village of Boquillas del Carmen, on the Mexican side. Neither the Mexicans nor the US bothered about passports. In Boquillas you could sip coke and eat bean tacos in the colorful cantina. After 9/11, however, this unofficial crossing was shut down for twelve years.)

The campout that night—beside the gently flowing waters of the Rio Grande—was peaceful and quiet. The river did not flood, we did not see any killer bees, or any black bears either.

Instead, we awoke to the pleasant two-note tune of donkey bells as a Mexican cowboy rode along the other bank of the Rio Grande, probably checking on his ponies.

Nevertheless, sitting by the butane stove finishing our coffee and waiting for the first star to appear through the blood-red Texas sunset, we sometimes talked about killer bees. What was the *correct* thing to do if any of the boys or the adults were attacked? *My* first thought—I have to admit—was for all of us to jump into the Rio Grande. Or whatever body of water was closest. This would not have been very wise, however, unless you could stay under water as long as a pond turtle: the bees would simply hang around till you were forced to come up for air. Can you imagine breaking the surface of the water gasping for air and trying to gulp it down within a cloud of killer bees? The best advice, in short, is: "Run!"

But these matters are not trivial, nor are they merely abstract points to be made for passing the time around a campfire: the term "killer bee" is very apt. Six months after I started writing this story, a seventy-five-year-old man was viciously attacked and stung to death by killer bees, near the Mexican border at Nogales, Arizona. All he did was move an old tire while clearing some trash at the end of a dirt road. How could he have known that there was a nest of killer bees underneath the tire? How could he have known they would attack him so savagely? They stung their victim hundreds of times—on the face, neck, arms, chest and abdomen—some even came out of his mouth. Then they turned on his rescuers, forcing them into a survival mode of their own.[3]

By 2012 the killer bees had spread over most of the southwestern US, and had claimed all of Arizona. They are believed to have killed hundreds of humans.

But not all bees sting; some *bite*.

When we were living in Australia, we loved to go walking on Mount Coot-Tha, a forested hill rising above the suburbs of Brisbane, Queensland. This subtropical region is on the eastern coast of that fascinating continent. We were told that the name "Coot-Tha" is the Aborigine word for a stingless bee (or the honey from a stingless bee). The Aborigines probably liked the way the honey could be lifted from the nests without the annoyance of getting stung. Not that stingless bees are defenseless: they can take care of themselves very well against other insects by biting. First they bring the raider bee to the ground by clinging to its wings, then bite it to death. Stingless bees are still working on defenses against thieving by large animals, but then so are our backyard honeybees. This in spite of the stingless bee's close relationship to the honeybee, and her very long evolutionary path. (In fact, the bee mentioned at the start of this story who got stuck in the resin eighty million years ago, and left her fossil for us to speculate about her journey from Pangaea, was a stingless bee.)

We are used to thinking that honeybees need a social system to survive: no domestic honeybee can make it on her own. The young are completely dependent on the adults. The hive is protected by a collective air defense agreement. (It seems all this could be the envy of our trade unions: one bee for one job, undisputed. And of an Air Force general determined to win at all cost: squadrons and squadrons of kamikaze pilots.)

But now I know that my boyhood picture of the backyard honeybee's social way of life was by *no* means standard in the superfamily[4] to which they belong. In fact, most species in their group live *solitary* lives. Their way of life varies enormously, too. For example, in one species[5] mother and daughter stay together in the same nest, which consists of single-brood cells. Although each female takes care of her own brood cells, they build the nest together and defend it together. This is radically different from our western honeybee. It's as if they lived in a bee condo.

The orchid bee,[6] too, helped me discover that my accustomed model of backyard beekeeping is by no means standard among bees. (This bee almost exclusively spreads the pollen that is essential to our continued enjoyment of Brazil nuts.) The surprise was that in most cases only the *male* bees visit and pollinate orchids. Unlike the common honeybee, however, they are not driven by an instinct to gather pollen and nectar for the hive, but to gather *fragrances* for their own personal use. On the mating flight, it is thought, the queens prefer to dance with drones whose trailing whiffs boast many different perfumes, impressed by how many "foraging" trips these hard-working and long-living drones must have made. (It's tempting here to look for a correlation with human behavior.)

Growing up in Ireland, the common bumblebee was always of special interest to me, even before I became a suburban beekeeper. In my childview, this big hairy bee seemed less of a threat than the honeybee, possibly because of the way she lumbered slowly from blossom to blossom—apparently without much resolution—as opposed to darting in and out hurriedly, in decisive moves, like a UPS van doing its late-afternoon rounds. I also preferred its fuzzy black coat and bright yellow stripes to the honeybee's dull colors. And it was definitely better than the wasp's nasty stripes and scary sharp-pointed abdomen. To capture one, all you had to do was let her crawl into a foxglove flower, close the bell-shaped opening with your fingers, and nip the flower off with your fingernails. Lingering in a summer meadow, have you never felt your good mood tick up on hearing the low, droning hum–m–m–m of a passing bumblebee, her loudness rising and fading with her distance from you? And have you not looked around to spot her?

One species of bumblebee,[7] however, is a cuckoo bee. The queen lays her egg in the well-tended nest of a social bumblebee and lets that hard-working community rear her young.

Often, the cuckoo bumblebee looks very like the bee whose nest it enters. But it gets worse: one of these cuckoo bee species sometimes stings the host queen to death, to reduce the competition for her own offspring.

Coming back to the morality of how we treated our honeybees, it seems we struck a reasonable balance in mutual benefits, at least compared with bees in the wild: We gave them some ersatz honey till the clover bloomed again (even if the substitute was not as easy to digest). And we did not kill their queen.

* * *

Maybe I should have just kept my boyhood memories of backyard beekeeping, and not bothered reading about other bees at all. Because even this tiniest of tiny peeks at the solitary bee, the orchid bee, and the bumblebee has shattered my idealized picture of the well-organized bee society, and shown me that the social and royal ways of life are by no means the only ones that have worked for these insects on their long journey from Pangaea. There is good news, however: none of the bees I looked up have the callous cruelty of some of their cousins from the same Insect Order that came out of Pangaea: those that "raise" their young by injecting an egg into the body of another insect and letting the larva devour the unfortunate and unwilling host from the inside (and sometimes kill it).

Will bees be around when we are gone? In predicting the future you cannot rely too much on the past for guidance. When the League of Lizards had their annual meeting sixty-five million years ago they probably dwelled on ways to grow sharper teeth and stronger jaws. How could they have known that a Manhattan-size asteroid was silently gliding through space towards a cataclysmic crash with Earth?

Bees could probably survive a catastrophe such as a nuclear exchange engineered by our superior human intelligence. Or another hit by a really big asteroid.

But what about another event like the Permian Extinction? The one that killed off more than three-quarters of the marine and land species combined, brought the curtain down on the ancient era of life, and cleared the stage for the emergence of new forms. Given their record, the bees might survive that one, too.

And live together in a bee-loud world.

Backyard Beekeeping

SUBURBAN BEEKEEPING

The beehive that my brother and I handcrafted for our suburban backyard in Dublin. Some of the designer touches went beyond the needs of functionality. The bees worked hard for years and "gave" us more honey than we needed for our household. We ate the honey wax-and-all, that is, with the honeycomb.

None of the neighbors ever reported any stings.

Photo: Ca. 1962, probably by Louis Mullee (digitally altered to remove irrelevant detail).

THEY'RE LEAVING HOME…

The queen and her followers have flown from one of the hives and settled in a tree. She is being protected in the center of the heart-shaped cluster. Not shown here are the bee scouts who fly around looking for a good place to start a new hive.

Bees are very agreeable when they are swarming. They have left their hive (with a bellyful of honey) and don't have to defend it any more. All they want is a new home.

If you put a box over the swarm, the bees will crawl up into it. They will crawl right over your hand without stinging you. Still, it is best to do this in the cool of late evening, and to subdue them first with a few puffs from the smoker. And be careful not to crush any bees out of carelessness.

Photo: Dreamstime stock photos, http://www.dreamstime.com/

Backyard Beekeeping

HOMELESS BEES

This swarm of bees doesn't seem to know the difference between a tree and a bicycle. Luckily for the cyclists, bees are not aggressive when they are looking for a new home.

Photo: Posted by unidentified participant in the BP MS 150, a charity bike ride from
Houston to Austin, Texas, ca. 2006.

---

[1] This was a stingless bee. "Meliponiculture of Stingless Bees," Food and Agriculture Organization of the United Nations (FAO),ftp://ftp.fao.org/docrep/fao/012/i0842e/i0842e07.pdf, accessed 12th June 2015.

[2] Dennis Davis, United States Department of Agriculture, Forest Service Technology & Development Program, May 2000, 0067-2313-MTDC, 2400, "Working Safely in Areas With Africanized Honey Bees," http://www.fs.fed.us/t-d/pubs/htmlpubs/htm00672313/, accessed 28th May 2013.

[3] Johathan Clark, "Nogales man dies after being attacked by bees," *Nogales International*, 13th July 2012, http://www.nogalesinternational.com/news/nogales-man-dies-after-being-attacked-by-bees/article_a40a8ee4-cd00-11e1-8a6e-001a4bc-f887a.html.

[4] The superfamily is the Apoidae. *Encyclopædia Britannica Ultimate Reference Suite* (Chicago: Encyclopædia Britannica, 2011), under "hymenopteran," and under "bee."

[5] The name of this species is Halictus quadricinctus. *Encyclopædia Britannica Ultimate Reference Suite* (Chicago: Encyclopædia Britannica, 2011), under "hymenopteran," "social forms."

[6] The scientific name for the orchid bee is euglossine bee. *Encyclopædia Britannica Ultimate Reference Suite* (Chicago: Encyclopædia Britannica, 2011), under "euglossine bee."

[7] The "cookoo" species is Psithyrus vestalis.

9

SALLEY BRANCHES

The cows had been milked, the calves had been fed, and the hens had all fluttered up into their smelly roost. They had stopped their eternal clucking and begun to close their eyes. We locked the door to the roost so the farmyard hound dog could not go in and raise hell amid a cloud of feathers.

Now, finally, Tom had time for me.

"Come, Eugene, I'll show you how to cut salley branches," he said.

Tom was my first cousin, but while I was on my aunt's farm for the summer holidays he was more like my father. I followed him everywhere he went and learned to read his mind from the tone of his voice. Now it told me that he was finally free to choose what he wanted to do, after a full day's work as a ganger on the railway and then his evening's tasks on the farm. It also told me that he had read my mind, too, and knew that I had been hoping he would have an hour for me before nightfall.

The salley bushes grew in a watery spot along a ditch behind our farmhouse. There were about ten of them—fairly small, around eight or nine feet tall. The trunks were stocky and low, with lots of branches sprouting from knotty clumps where the growth from previous years had been cut off. Each summer would produce a nice new crop of shoots. Tom showed me how you could take a salley branch and bend it over double without breaking it.

"They're very supple," he said.

I took note of that new word—*supple*. (What better way to learn a new word than to experience it there and then, through the senses, before meeting it as a metaphor.) The salley branch provided a deeper metaphor, too: something (or someone) that bends under oppression, but does not break, keeping its toughness to spring back again when the danger has passed.

The new salley growth from the stumps had brownish skin of an unusual luster. The leaves were slender, about a few inches long (by the time I got there in summer), dark green on top, and furry underneath.[1] They were not nice to taste: somewhat bitter. I often tasted leaves and berries as one of the many ways I explored the world that was unfolding itself to me. I knew for example that you could safely eat the tiny leaves of the hawthorn bush (though it would have been a stretch to say they tasted good). Others put you off straight away, like the alder.

My cousin walked slowly down the line of salley bushes, pushing the branches aside to get a better look. He selected some that had especially bountiful growth and cut off the best shoots. I helped him strip the leaves and tie them into bundles. We removed the thin growth on the tips of the shoots because it was too soft and floppy to serve our purpose. The remaining parts had a nice even taper and were tough yet pliable.

The salley branch had lots of uses on our small farm, because you only bought things from the supply stores in Claremorris if you absolutely could not produce them yourself. First, it made an ideal switch, that is, a slender rod that can double as a crude whip. A gentle touch on the rump of a cow would quickly settle any question as to which way she should turn when you were driving her through the farmyard. And we always kept a switch in the kitchen to take a swipe at any chicken who dared come through the half-door to peck at crumbs on the floor. A switch could also deliver a stinging reprimand to our recalcitrant hound dog who continually threatened peace in the farmyard by chasing the chickens and scouring the henhouses for fresh eggs.

One of the handiest things on this earth is a basket. It is tough, and light. True, it can't hold water, but it can be used for almost everything else—for feeding chickens, bringing turf to the fire, arranging food on the table. A basket looks good, feels good, and certainly *smells* good (at least when it's new). Surely, then, the salley bush must have evolved especially to give small farmers a source of twigs for weaving baskets?

We had stored the branches in the barn to let them dry out a bit. After a few days my cousin took two chairs from the kitchen and set them down outside the whitewashed wall of the farmhouse. It was late in the evening (the only time he would ever be free to choose for himself what to do). We had about an hour left to enjoy the sun before it would slip over the western horizon to America.

"Now, Eugene, let's sit down and I'll show you how to make a basket."

"Oh great!"

Starting with nothing but the branches and a sharp knife, we formed the bottom with a bunch of rods radiating out from a hub, like spokes in a wheel. These we bound together by weaving a spiral through the spokes with some of the thinnest and most pliable branches. We had to hone our knife really sharp so we could make clean bevel cuts, as otherwise the ends could have splayed out and left stringy tags attached. We soon became quietly absorbed in our work, sitting amidst a pile of assorted salley branches in the last glow of the evening, few words passing between us. This let me savor the slightly pungent yet pleasing aroma of first-year salley growth.

When the bottom was wide enough we turned the spokes upwards to make ribs for the sides and wove some slightly thinner cuttings through them. I forget what this particular basket was to be used for, but its shape was now becoming clear. When it reached its intended height we turned the ribs sideways and wove them around the circumference of the basket to make the rim. We made this thicker and stronger by adding some extra branches, once again making use of their famed flexibility. All that was left now was to tuck in the ends and taper them flush.

"Now lad, what do you think of that?" said Tom, bouncing the finished basket on the ground to show me how robust it was. He was now showing his trademark smile of satisfaction at having once again captured my full, enthusiastic attention.

We had used nothing but raw salley branches and a kitchen knife to make our basket—no clips, no strings, no wires.

There is something inherently pleasing about a natural wicker basket—even more so when you have made it yourself, out of branches cut and trimmed yourself. It could be the simple harmony of form, the interwoven cross-hatches of the wicker—so often imitated in plastic and steel—or the slight "crookedness" of the rods left by the alternating leaf stems. The actual weaving is very satisfying, too; it induces a certain calmness of mind. Perhaps because there is only one single task to focus on, without any interruptions or distractions (the exact opposite to multi-tasking in a corporate office).

And one more very important thing: that calmness of mind can be brought back every time you catch the aroma of fresh salley branches.

EPILOGUE

My cousin Tom died about twenty-five years after we made the basket together. That was probably a good twenty-five years short of his "due" time, based on his ancestry and his lifestyle.

He had a full time job as a ganger on the railroad. In the evenings, after a meal and a short but relaxed break, he would start into his share of farm work—bringing the cows home, raking hay, feeding the calves. It would be well into late evening by the time we had finished, and yet he still had the energy and the enthusiasm to bring me out over the hills hunting rabbits. Sometimes we took the hounds with us; sometimes we set snares on the rabbit runs that led to a warren hidden among the furze bushes. It was usually dark when we returned. (That was before the myxomatosis disease was deliberately introduced into Ireland and left to wipe out most of the little furry ones; they had infested outlying fields and eaten some patches of grass down to stub.)

Often we went out again just after dawn to check the snares, leaving two sets of slurred footprints in the silvery dew.

Two sets: one large, one small.

Then Tom would leave for his day job on the railroad.

Never once did he say an unkind word to me, get impatient with me, or show any signs of distemper. In fact, I only remember him complaining once about *anything*, and then without pointing the finger at anybody:

"I don't mind working" he had said, "but when you don't feel well…"

That he often had stomach pain was just a simple fact.

In the end, Tom died from stomach bleeding.

---

[1] It was probably the common osier (*Salix viminalis*).

10

THE MESSENGER BOY

They say you get to fathom the depths of human nature just by working with people. I know that on *my* first day of work I got plenty of soundings. My last day of work fifty-one years later was not much different.

I started looking for work in 1959, when I was seventeen years of age. By then I had been in school for at least thirteen years. An eternity at that age. Our classes were very large, and it was difficult for teachers to set a pace that suited the crazy mix of abilities and attitudes that the boys came with. All in all, school was not very stimulating for me. At least not at that age: when I matured a bit, one outstanding teacher from the Christian Brothers would adopt me in learning and sow the seeds of knowledge. Luckily, those seeds would sprout just in time for me to stumble over the stile into the fertile field of higher education.

But that summer there were few seeds germinating in my intellect and I just wanted to meet life's realities face-to-face. Real things were happening out there in the world of the grownups. That seemed far more interesting than getting it secondhand from the classroom. Even more exiting, I would make some money of my own and be free to spend it on whatever I liked. (It would be years before I heard the term "discretionary spending.")

There was a chemist shop (a drug store) in the suburb of Ballsbridge, about ten minutes' walk from my home. (Later, the American Consulate would be built very close by, in Elgin Road.) The chemist shop needed a helper to deliver prescription medicines to their customers. Presumably these deliveries were for people who were confined to their homes and did not have anybody to slip out to the chemist for them.

On the face of it, that seemed like a suitable summer job for me. Medicines were clean and light; bringing them to people who really needed them was a useful job (and a good way to get some extra pocket money for the summer).

Dublin boys loved turning trade names and acronyms into irreverent rhymes and jingles. These would be exchanged on the street as a form of cultural currency. At that time most chemists proudly displayed the letters "MPSI" above their shops. The letters stood for "Member of the Pharmaceutical Society of Ireland." They were meant to give customers the comfortable feeling that all the medicines dispensed there were genuine sure-fire remedies. That they contained special, potent substances prepared in special ways known only to the pharmacy profession. But to us boys "MPSI" stood for "Monkey's Piss Sold Inside." We would sing this jingle while walking past a chemist shop whenever we thought of it. The custom was driven by the need for humor, only, because we knew little about the medicines sold inside and even less about the ethics of pharmacy.

But to get back to my first day on the job. I was hired at that chemist shop and soon afterwards I reported for work. When you left the street and entered the select precincts of a chemist shop, you were always hit by a trademark aroma somewhere between ladies' perfume and hospital disinfectant. That was followed immediately by a strong visual cue: a weighing scale with a huge dial and an iron pedestal sturdy enough to support the largest grownup you had ever seen.

Busy white-coated pharmacists met me on that first day in the Working World. I resolved not to let slip that jingle about the monkey, for I no longer had the group protection of my pals on the street. I was now part of the pharmacy business: this was my job, and I needed the money. I tried to suppress the memory of having bought a weedkiller in that same shop only a few years earlier. I had bought it from an unsuspecting young lady who obviously did not know that boys use weedkiller to make pipe bombs, that they have no interest at all in gardening, and that no sensible parent would *ever* knowingly consent to letting a fourteen-year-old boy go a chemist shop on his own to buy that potent oxidant.

The shop was quite busy: there must have been three pharmacists working the counter dispensing pills, elixirs, and potions of all kinds to cure the sick, placate the worried, and to complement or supplement nature's gift of beauty. In the back of the apothecary a youngish lady pharmacist was making up prescriptions. (Not the same one who had sold me the bomb-making ingredient.) She introduced herself and let me know that she would be preparing the packages of medicine that I would have to deliver. Her refined manners, neat appearance, and admirable bearing immediately singled her out to me as somebody I could respect and feel at ease with. She took pains to explain my job to me and to ward off any nervousness I might have had on this my very first day in the Great World of Grownups.

Most of the other pharmacists were busy running back and forth taking little bottles and packets off shelves and out of drawers. They did not pay much attention to me. There was a janitor, too. He was not so busy and had a lot to say to me, probably because I was the only one on a lower rung of the hierarchal ladder in that suburban drugstore. And, besides, I was the only other person who had time to listen. To my surprise he dug deep into his personal life, telling me that he had gone through a bout of depression; how the world clouds in on you when this happens and you can't enjoy even the simplest things that you used to enjoy; that depression was the worst thing that could happen to anybody. That left me wondering what the word meant, and why he was sharing this with me, a seventeen-year-old near-stranger. He must indeed have needed somebody to talk to.

I listened passively.

Meanwhile, the nice lady pharmacist was using a mortar and pestle to pulverize some concoction into a paste. Later in life I would see the mortar-and-pestle symbol used in connection with the pharma business so many times, and would wonder whether they actually still used them, or had machines to do all the pounding. She had prepared a stack of little boxes that were wrapped individually and labelled for various customers. I was about to set off on my delivery when I got a shock that sent my spirits tumbling. A trapdoor seemed to open beneath me and drop me into a dungeon of doom. It sent a chilling sensation through my body, telling me I should never have applied for that job. To explain this, I have to give some background.

At that time in Dublin, you could have staple foods delivered to your doorstep. Potatoes, bread, tinned food, etc. (This service was particularly important to our family of five, since our mother had passed away and we all had to go out during the day.) The groceries were delivered by boys riding the highly recognizable messenger bike with its huge wicker basket in front. It was a job that required little training, and was often done by boys who had only completed a minimum of schooling. Without going down the roads of enlightenment pioneered by learnèd sociologists, it was a simple fact of life that in 1950s suburban Dublin the messenger boy's bike often put a label on its rider. It placed the person riding the bike on a different side of a social dividing line established by tacit—though certainly not unanimous—agreement. Those delivering the groceries were on one side of that line, those receiving them at their doorsteps were on the other.

At age seventeen I just accepted this. I had not yet come to admire *any* person who did *any* useful task properly. Nor could I have guessed that eight years later I myself would be delivering newspapers to earn extra money (in Munich, Germany).

Or that about five years earlier, in 1953, a boy who left school at the age of thirteen to ride a messenger boy's bike—as a full time job—would become one of the most belovèd balladeers in Dublin: Luke Kelly. A man with a ginger beard as scraggly as used steel wool, a banjo, and "a voice to wake the dead and scare recording engineers."[1]

For sure, life does not deal an even hand. It asks with detached callousness that we use our wits and energy to get whatever we want using the cards we are dealt with, no use complaining. But life is generous in its compensations: those who leave the classroom early can become street-wise early. Messenger boys were often in that other classroom of life. But at that age I wore a filter and did not see past the label pinned on the messenger boy's bike by the only culture I knew.

Imagine my shock, then, when the janitor wheeled in *my* messenger boy's bike. Complete with the big brown wicker basket.

I composed myself as best I could and closely examined the addresses on my delivery list. I was immediately relieved to see I would only be going into streets where I was not likely to be recognized—the enormous houses along Elgin Road, those on the busy Merrion Road, and some of the cottages where Serpentine Avenue wound its way towards Sandymount. I made my first sortie with great caution and felt rescued when I got back to the chemist shop without having been spotted by any of my pals. And without having run into any gossipy neighbors.

Still, I was gripped by an uneasy indecisiveness. Should I quit? So soon? I was dismayed that this issue was preoccupying me when I should have been relishing the excitement of doing my first real job—and doing it in such a good clean environment.

But then the lady pharmacist brought me to one side and said:

"Eugene, you must have something to eat before you go back out. I've made you a nice sandwich and some tea."

"Thank you very much," I said, trying not to let the tension show. And, boy, did I need the release just then—the timing was perfect!

So for the next ten minutes or so I took a welcome respite to relish some tasty soft bread and tangy Dublin tea before venturing out again on my big-basketed bicycle. I could sense that it was the lady's thoughtful nature, and not mere duty, that was behind this. First impressions last, and I never forgot that act of kindness on my first day in the Working World, at the raw and impressionable age of seventeen.

But the next day my deliveries took me deep into home territory—to Sandymount Avenue and even Wilfield Road. Wilfield Road! That was only one street away from my own home. I could *easily* be spotted there by my pals. If caught, I would be put on the defensive and forced to live it down while my pals offered mock sympathy.

So I found myself nervously pedaling my messenger bike, furtively scanning my surroundings in all directions, ready to make a quick U-turn or duck into some side street if I saw anybody. As I neared my own house I took the reckless step of leaving the messenger bike leaning up against the granite wall of Sandymount Railway Station. The expensive medicines lay under the lid of the wicker basket, but without a lock. Then I set off on foot very quickly to deliver the packages for the houses in the street adjoining my own. Luckily the bike was still there when I got back, and nobody had touched the medicines. (Bike theft was rare back then.)

So once again I had made it back to the chemist shop without being discovered.

That did it, though, and I went straight to the nice lady:

"I'm sorry, but I don't like riding a messenger bike around where I live," I explained. "I think I would prefer not to work here anymore."

"That's all right, Eugene," she said, "We didn't know."

And that was the end of my first job—as a Dublin messenger boy. I had missed the irony completely: anxious to experience the real world beyond the classroom, I had walked away from a great opportunity to get a firsthand taste of it. Perhaps I might have bumped into a "real" messenger boy during my deliveries, and become a bit more street-wise.

The next job I took that summer was definitely punishment for being too proud to ride a messenger boy's bike. The location was okay—right next to swanky Grafton Street with its aura of high fashion and exclusiveness. But I wasn't selling haute couture to fancy-coiffed ladies with silken scarves, or even high-end socks to men: I was painting angle-iron frames for bedsteads, squatting alone on a stone floor in a poorly-ventilated and poorly-lit warehouse. The job was repetitive, and success did not depend very much on dialogue. It required little skill beyond judging how much paint thinner to use so your artless brushstrokes would apply a smooth coat of paint without leaving any sloppy ripples or sags. Instead of exotic perfumes I was now breathing turpentine essence.

And nobody brought me any tea or sandwiches.

* * *

A whole generation followed—marriage, children, career—without anything much ever happening to remind me of that first day at work. Then a truly extraordinary coincidence occurred. I had not been able to visit Ireland very frequently at the time (job, mortgage, etc.), but on that morning I happened to be riding into Dublin on a big double-decker bus. (Public transport gives you a more intimate encounter with a "strange" city than a taxi or a rented car.) I was sitting on the long bench at the back of the bus, upstairs. From there—with a little flexing of the neck—I could scan a complete halfcircle behind me and casually observe how a Dublin street had changed with the years. A street that I had once regarded as inalienable home territory.

The bus gained ground along Merrion Road in sudden starts and stops as smaller vehicles wove their way around it. (When it lumbered over the hump at Ballsbridge I glanced down at the River Dodder and a torrent of boyhood memories flooded into my mind.) I continued this casual reminiscing as the bus jerked and screeched its way past Herbert Park, just before the American Consulate. There was a knot in the traffic caused in part by a mobile crane set up on temporary supports by the side of the road. It was swinging a wrecker ball at a half-demolished building. Strewn on the ground were the defenseless remains of this once-proud building—jagged pieces of masonry, door frames, windows, splintered wooden beams. Just as the bus revved and swayed into motion again, the wrecker ball slammed into a naked wall of the building with a dumb thump and a mini-explosion of dust and bricks.

Then I saw it, still attached to a piece of wall: the MPSI sign. They were demolishing my old chemist shop.

THE MESSENGER BOY

I ventured out like an escaped convict on the run, scanning the street for anybody who might recognize me.

THE OLD CHEMIST SHOP IS GONE

In 1959 I rode my messenger boy's bike through the archway on the left; in the early 1990s I chanced to witness the dumb thump of a wrecker ball dislodge a pile of masonry, dust, and shards; in 2012 I found Bon Espresso & News, and Roly's Bistro, on (or near) the site of my old chemist shop.

Photo: Merrion Road at Clyde Lane, Ballsbridge, October 2012, (modified with Photoshop's ink outlines feature).

---

[1] Nathan Joseph, sleeve notes to LP "The Dubliners (with Luke Kelly)," 1964, Transatlantic TRA 116 LP.

11

THE CRYSTAL SPRING

I always loved filling a bucket of clear fresh water from the natural spring near the farm. The last few steps down to the well would take me over some flat stones half-hidden by summer grass and weeds. As I bent over the water, my reflection would suddenly shoot back at me—a dark featureless silhouette framed in bright clouds. The water itself was perfectly transparent, and you would not have known it was there but for the image mirrored off its surface and the quartz grains glittering on the bottom of the well.

We did not have running water on my uncle's farm in County Mayo, at least not when I started to go there for my summer holidays in the 1950s. At home in the city you just turned on the tap and pure, soft water from the Dublin Mountains would rush out. In the country you might have to walk several hundred yards or more to get good drinking water, but it was worth it to see the crystal-clear water welling up from the sand. And of course not having drinking water on tap in the farmhouse was never a problem for me. This and other contrasts with the big city—such as not having electricity—only helped to clinch this as one of the best childhood experiences of my life. A city boy let loose on a farm for a few weeks in the summer: what more could he ask for?

Companies that sell bottled water today use terms like "crystal spring" to invoke images of clear, sparkling water. The term is very apt. I learned its meaning long before I ever saw bottled water for sale in a store. One of the ways I contributed to my keep on the farm was to fetch drinking water from that little spring at the bottom of the stepping stones. The well was about three hundred yards from our farmhouse, at a spot where the road made a slight bend around a hill. A modest climb up the hill led to a little abandoned farmhouse under a stand of tall trees. The trees must have been planted long ago to shelter the farmhouse from the cold eastern wind, and now they were spread out and the branches interlocked like the beams of a cathedral roof. It was quite common to find abandoned farm buildings in the area; there was another one about a mile away, on another little hill surrounded by overgrown trees. This one was known as "Kennedy's Barn," and was being used an outhouse by those who still farmed the area. I never asked who the Kennedys had been, why they left, or where they went, but it's for sure that each of those damp moss-covered farmhouses would have had a good story to tell.

By the time I came ambling down the road to draw water from the well—and to wonder about the abandoned farm buildings—crows had long since made their noisy rookery high up in the branches—in the "rafters of the cathedral." You would hear their raucous "caw–caws" in full chorus as you approached. Except if you carried a shotgun (as I found out when I got older): they would see it long before you reached the trees, and take off in a feathery black cloud. (Crows are very intelligent, but they will probably never get credit for this until they stop bothering farmers.) Before I was allowed to use a shotgun, I would stand under the rookery, by the doorway of the old ruined house, and gaze up at them. My mind would build up a picture of farmers busy with animals and foul, and surely there must have been some children of my own age running around and having fun.

The small hill had probably been formed by sand and gravel carried by glaciers and dumped there when a global warming put an end to the last ice age. Our little well was probably the natural discharge point of the rainwater that had soaked into the hill and percolated down to the road. (And you could always count on a plentiful supply of rain in County Mayo.) The hill sloped away on all sides, so there were no streams or troughs to carry foul water from outlying areas into the farmyard.

By definition, a "mineral spring" is one with a noticeable amount of minerals such as calcium and magnesium dissolved in the water (and completely invisible). We never lab tested the water from our well, but it sure looked like the purest water there ever was: it glinted like Waterford crystal and refreshed your very soul with each hasty gulp. It must have been very soft as well—low in calcium and magnesium—because it would lather into a nice, rich foam when you washed your face with it.

The hill with the crows' rookery continued down past our little well until it leveled off into a soggy marsh. Sometimes, there, I would walk around the "pools among the rushes"[1] and let my bare legs brush past the tiny white blossoms on the rushes' stems. The water stood fairly still in the marsh, so it would not have been nearly as pure as that coming clean out of the sand higher up.

My cousin Mae was eternally busy around the thatched farmhouse: baking soda bread; peeling praeties to boil in the fat-bellied pot; stoking the fire with sods of turf; shooing away the pesky hens that stole into the kitchen through the half-door. Among these and a hundred other things she would be watching the skies for a good break in the clouds. As soon as it seemed clear, she would say:

"Go on down to the well, now, like a good lad, and get me a bucket of water. Here, take my bike."

So off I would go down the road to the well. I would hang the bucket on the handlebars of her sturdy, no-nonsense ladies' bike with the low crossbar. I would take the ride very slowly so I could check carefully for any wild strawberries that might have ripened on the roadside since the last time I had passed. If I was lucky I would meet one of the oldtimers I knew, such as Farmer Mark. He was one of my favorites. He always wore a long black coat with a thick piece of string tied around the middle for a belt. Mark always had time for me, and despite his being around eighty years of age, he always spoke to me with the enthusiasm of a boy ten years old at most. (A separate story in this memoir describes a little adventure I shared with Farmer Mark.)

Farmer Johnny was another good buddy I would hope to meet. When he came to our country store he always lingered awhile to chat. His face seemed to be permanently set with crease lines that came from habitually smiling, or at least grinning. Whenever he spoke to me, he would face me directly and give me his full attention—more than he gave to the adults, it seemed to me. I always listened intently because of his earnest enthusiasm and the way he tailored his subjects especially to my boyhood interests. He was at least fifty years older than I.

One summer my sister and I went to visit Johnny. He lived all alone on a small farm spread over a hill that had a commanding view of the neighboring farms. A patchy gravel road led up the hill to his house, and Johnny stood at the top beaming when he saw us coming. Then he invited us in with a loud, hearty welcome.

This homestead was definitely *not* abandoned.

His kitchen looked more like the inside of a barn than the inside of a home: farm tools were lying around everywhere—propped against the walls, hanging from the rafters, sticking out of the loft. It was easy to see that Johnny lived alone.

"Sure ye'll have a cup 'a tae now, won't ye?" he said, poking the fire to awaken the flames, and balancing a kettle on the glowing sods of turf.

He must have been fond of his own cup of tea, though not so fond of cleaning up after it, because his deal-wood kitchen table was completely covered with mugs, plates, saucers, and spoons. They all had little dried-up stains inside them. That was no problem for Farmer Johnny, though, and it was certainly not going to stop him from giving his young guests a fine welcome: he just swept his arm over a corner of the table, brushing the clinking dishes aside. When the kettle boiled he selected some cups from the table and swilled them out for us with hot water. Then we all sat down and enjoyed our afternoon tea while Farmer Johnny made us feel we were the most important people in the world.

If the skies to the west were very clear, I would be able to see the blue pyramid of "The Reek" on the west coast of Ireland. This was the local name for Croagh Patrick, a 2500-foot mountain overlooking Clew Bay. Every year on "Reek Sunday"—the last Sunday in July—thousands of pilgrims climbed this mountain. It is said that the practice goes back 5000 years to the Stone Age. That must mean that the custom had been adopted from pagan rituals after Saint Patrick converted the country to Christianity. Indeed, the path that winds up the mountain still looks like something out of the Stone Age, at least until you come to the little Christian church on top. My relatives in County Mayo often told me how some people made this climb barefoot; and how, inexplicably, they would not end up with lacerated soles after completing their spiritual journey. (I have spared you a very tempting pun here.)

Coming back to my trip down the road to the crystal spring: having finished my daydreams, eaten any wild strawberries that had ripened, and perhaps discussed some important ideas with Farmer Mark (like how to make a catapult), I would get off the big black bike and walk down to the well over the stepping stones. Clean fresh water flowed into the well continuously, because the sand beds held the rainwater and let it filter though relatively slowly. This was important, because you wanted a well that was not as temperamental as the weather—one that did not dry up during sunny spells or overflow with turbid water when it rained hard. So our little well with its steady flow of filtered water was free of frog spawn and green slime, tadpoles, long-leggèd spiders who can walk on water, and any of those suspicious little critters that swim around in stagnant pools. You would not hesitate to drink from it.

Dipping the bucket into the little well, I had to be careful not to knock loose any dirt from the sides, or to touch the bottom and disturb the silt, which would surely go billowing up into the water. When my bucket was full, daylight would glint off the galvanized-iron bottom and turn it into something strangely cheerful and satisfying to hold in your hands. Then I would rest it on the handlebars of Cousin Mae's reliable bike and walk it home. (Carrying it all the way home in my hand was not on: it would give me painful red creases on my fingers and a lopsided shoulder.) If I met a car on the way back—which I seldom did—that would not have been a problem at all: the country drivers were well used to people walking in the middle of the road as if they never expected to meet anything other than animal-powered traffic.

Back in the farmhouse the bucket of precious water would be set on the wooden wash stand. This water was only to be used for tasks "close to the body," such as drinking, washing one's face, making tea, etc. As soon as I appeared from my bedroom in the mornings, Cousin Mae would pour some of it into a white enamel pail set into in an opening in the wash stand. For those who needed it, there was a little mirror mounted at the back of the stand for beauty care. It was great to start your day by splashing that cool water into your eyes and dislodging the night-glue that kept your eyelids stuck together.

Farming requires a lot of water, and, where drinking quality was not needed, we collected rainwater from the roof of the hayshed. The barrels were always full when I was there (since there was no shortage of rain) and I put them to good use for experimenting with make-believe submarines. But the main use of the rainwater was for things like washing clothes and boiling potatoes. (It was certainly safe for that, because it was boiled almost to infinity on the big turf fire.)

There was actually a second well at the back of the house, beyond a stand of sally bushes. It was much closer than the one I just described, but it was on flat ground and the water was usually sullied with moss, algae, and bugs. In short, you had the feeling that it was *alive*. My uncle would occasionally put lime in the well to clean it up, but we were still very slow to drink the water seeping from those green walls.

Drawing water from the well was not the only way I lived close to nature during my summer holidays: I also learned how to milk the cows and make butter. My cousins Tom and Paddy had fulltime jobs on the railroad. When they came home in the evening, they would sit with the rest of us at the kitchen table, and after a brief rest, slide into whatever farm work needed to be done. Sometimes they would work till nightfall, leaving barely any time to linger in the kitchen before going to bed. In spite of all that was expected of them (or was it because of it?), I never knew my cousins Tom or Paddy to get uptight, get cross, or to talk to me without a relaxed smile at the very least.

Small farmers milked the cows by hand, then, sitting on a tiny stool and noisily squirting the milk directly from the cow's udder into a bucket. Always ready to pull a prank on a city boy, Cousin Tom gave me a little squirt of warm milk in the face the first time I came to help them in the cowshed. Occasionally they would let me have a go at the milking, if the cow did not rebel at my technique and knock the bucket over with a sudden kick of her hind leg. We would put the milk into a big wide basin and let it stand in the barn where it would cool down to an even temperature. After a while a layer of rich cream would form on top, which my cousin skimmed off every day and stored in a smaller basin with a heavy wooden cover. The cover kept out flies and crawling bugs, but it did not keep out humans—at least not this cream-craving young human from the city: sometimes when alone in the barn the temptation to nick a spoonful of cream was just too much. After about a week it was time to make the butter: You poured the cream into the little iconic wooden churn and began to turn the hand crank rhythmically. Inside, little battens thrashed the milk like a miniature paddlewheel. In about forty-five minutes you would be rewarded with little islets of butter floating on the cream. These would soon coalesce into big lumps of rich yellow butter.

Add some salt to that and you had the best butter I have ever tasted.

Digressing for a moment to the social customs on small farms during the 1950s. Whereas boys and girls with courtship on their minds will always find ways to meet up alone, in the country this often required some ingenuity. One Sunday after Mass, on retiring from the big kitchen table after the customary Sunday meal, the grownups were easing into that rare afternoon of leisure on a small farm that only a Sabbath can provide. My cousin Mae, then somewhere in her midthirties, told me with her customary decisiveness that we were going to spend the afternoon picking wild bilberries. A male neighbor around her own age had been visiting, and soon the three of us were on our bicycles headed for a small lake not far away. The weather was splendid. We sat down at a secluded spot among the thriving bilberry bushes, surrounded by young sapling trees and long grasses. After eating a snack and resting for a while, however, neither my cousin nor her friend showed any interest in picking wild bilberries. I took this as permission to wander off and explore the area on my own. In fact, I am quite sure that they even encouraged me to do this.

Having gathered as many bilberries as I could, and eaten as many as I could, I returned to our rest spot to find the pair sitting in a loose embrace. The incident was embarrassing and bewildering enough for me to let it pass completely. Now I know that I was probably taken along as a chaperone.

The rules were different for ten-year-olds. Down the railway tracks from our farm lived a girl about my own age, that is, around ten. We regarded each other with cautious neutrality, since (being of opposite genders) we did not have any common interests to share, much less to compete for. She did not, for example, go hunting rabbits. In my cousin Tom's eyes, however, she was the perfect girleen for me, and if I had any sense I would have been trying to draw her into a romantic relationship. (It was not clear to me whether this relationship was to start then, or could be delayed till I got older.) Both of us kids were very uncomfortable with the imposed social pressure, however, and it would have snuffed out any feeble flame of friendship that might have taken hold.

Now, back to the things I was able to handle well at that age. For our daily fresh eggs, we thanked the hens that roamed the farmyard from dawn to dusk, eternally scratching at the earth, jerking their heads forward, and making clucking noises as if to show how important they were. One of my jobs was to track down the independent-minded hens who insisted on laying their eggs in private nests outside the henhouse. I got very good at this and eventually was able to recognize troublemakers on sight. They were usually a bit bigger than their sisters, and they walked with a certain air of indignation. I would scour the bushes and other likely places for their illegal nests. Hens wandering away from the brood or suddenly appearing from outlying bushes aroused my greatest suspicions. I would raid the nests in the late afternoons and present the still-warm eggs to Cousin Mae. It was important for me to have finished doing this before Prince was let loose. Prince was our farmhound: he had to be tied up during most of the day because he was just as good at finding hens' nests as I was, he loved raw eggs, and he didn't distinguish between legal and illegal nests.

Geese were different: they always laid their big eggs in the wild. But they were easy to track, poor things. And the rewards were great: there is nothing like a big, soft-boiled goose egg with a blob of homemade, salted butter on top.

I did not like roosters. In fact I was always on their case and would chase them away whenever I caught them harassing the hens. I just could not see what good they did anybody. None of the adults on the farm seemed to know either.

* * *

The changes that began in Europe somewhere around the midsixties gradually moved people away from being locked into back-to-back work tasks just to meet their basic needs. Expectations rose in pace with the better economies, and of course the marketing people were always one step ahead in explaining to customers what they really needed.

Drinking water began to appear in bottles made of glass and plastic, large and small, simple and fancy. Here in Houston, today, every convenience store and even some hardware stores display stacks of bottled water near the checkout. Magazines display bottled water adorned with curving lines of pastel blues swirling with sparkling bubbles. All this is intended to build a picture of the purest water being taken from the purest spring.

The purveyors of bottled water have become quite sophisticated in their advertising texts, too. For example, the age of the water—how long it has been held in the ground—is termed its "vintage." One website states—correctly—that "wine needs time to smooth out its tannin structure, but the quality of mineral water is not determined by its age." But, the site continues, "the age of bottled waters should be noted as an enjoyable part of their backstories, which add to the epicurean pleasure."

The producers of bottled water duly test the spring for nitrates—an impurity that can leach through the soil from famers' manure pits or from septic tanks. This test is reported as the water's "virginality." Another advertiser promises that its "energy water" will bring a "feeling of emotional composure." (It doesn't say whether this emotional composure matches stepping down to a natural spring that is set among flat stones and summer grass.) Yet another seller hopes to "pardner with you in joining a prosperous tomorrow"—by selling you its bottled water, of course.

One might easily start to think of bottled water in the same way one anticipates the opening of an expensive bottle of wine in an expensive restaurant.

But, in fairness to those advertisers, bottled water can be tested *objectively*, since qualities like hardness and "virginality" are measured by quantitative chemical tests. Even "vintage" can be inferred fairly well from the surrounding geology. In fact, the perception-altering tricks in these ads are actually far less subtle than those used in selling beauty products, to take but one example.

* * *

A colleague of mine made a good living and brought up two fine sons selling Perrier bottled water. On a working trip to Paris, I bought him one of those very small cans of Perrier that apparently are sold only in Europe (probably because they are too small for Texans). I found it in a little convenience store on Avenue de la Grande Armée as I strolled near that big arch. It was within earshot of l'Étoile—the star-shaped intersection where brave drivers race around the arch bluffing incoming drivers to gain right-of-way. As I walked out of the store, I reflected on how different my surroundings were from those in County Mayo, even though my purpose was the same—to get some good mineral water. If I run out of money in my retirement, I just might go back and mine the clear gold from my crystal spring. But I guess I will probably never dash my sleepy face again with spring water scooped from the source with my own hands. Or have breakfast again on a vintage kitchen table, and let my thoughts blend idly with the soothing light coming in through the half-door.

Or eat stolen goose eggs topped with salted butter churned by my own hand.

EPILOGUE

My cousin Mae, and to a lesser extent one of my childhood housemaids, are the only people I can use to "live" the mother-child relationship. Mae never did marry. She lived alone on the family homestead after all the others were gone, although her brother and his family lived on an adjoining farm.

In the year 2000, at the age of seventy-nine, she was "in flying form," according to my sister Marie. That spring, she had dug and planted cabbage, onions, and potatoes. When my daughter and I visited her nearly six years later, at the age of eighty-four, her mental acuity was as good if not better than mine. She showed this by reprimanding me gently for being twenty minutes late. (I had got lost because the old roads I remembered had been erased in Ireland's fit of new construction.) Those twenty minutes were important for Mae, because she had carefully scheduled what we had to do that day.

Ten months later, she had a minor car accident and was admitted to the regional hospital in Castlebar. But complications led to the amputation of a leg, and soon afterwards, at the age of eighty-five, she died. The local newspaper printed a glowing obituary, highlighting her uncommon discretion, in particular.

The old farmstead in Murneen that had seen so much life and drama in the 1950s is now unoccupied.

CONVERSATION ON A COUNTRY ROAD

Farmer Mark always had time for me when I met him coming back from the well. He was far beyond the age where half-years are reported—somewhere around eighty—but he had the spirit and enthusiasm of a boy around my own age.

He wore a long black coat tied with a piece of sisal string for a belt. I suspect now that the coat was more for covering up his other clothes than for keeping him warm.

It was Farmer Mark who one day told me how to make a catapult, and this earned him a special place on my list of adults who understood children.

---

[1] Yeats, "The Stolen Child."

12

ALL THE FACES OF SNOW

The first person out of bed in the morning would run excitedly to the others and break the news:
"It's snowing! It's snowing!"
We would pull back the curtains and stand for a few moments to take in the scene. How could everything have changed so much overnight? The heap of jet-black coal had disappeared and merged into a oneness of white that had taken over the whole backyard—the pathway, the grass, the scraggly mess of withered plants in the flowerbeds. The apple trees that were so lanky and bare the day before now had their branches delicately traced in white, as if an artist had worked on them all through the night. (This only accentuated the well-proportioned shape given to the trees by my dad's eternal pruning and grafting.) The evergreen cypress at the end of the yard had put on a green-and-white overcoat, its branches sagging from the weight of snow panels clinging to its needles. Even the clothesline—the thinnest of all things—now stood out, profiled by a knife-edged accent in white.

Out front, in the streets, only smooth curves were left where yesterday there had been sharp angles and steps. The cars parked on the street had been transformed, too: big white cakes of snow lay on the roofs; windows had merged with bonnets; lamps and door handles had put on little white caps.

The lampposts had come into their own, with white crowns and caps all over. A plastering of snow on the main pole showed which direction the snow had come from.

Even the tar-filled cracks on the road disappeared, and for once we could see a continuous cap from curb to curb. Except where a line of footprints marked the careful route of some early-starter on their way to work. And across the front lawn the pawprints of a cat, on God knows what business. Best off all, the snow was still falling. Falling ever so lightly and gently, the snowflakes half-hiding the houses on the opposite side of the street like a semi-transparent drop on a theater stage.

The snowfall changed everything. Whatever we were planning to do after school was instantly forgotten and only one thing was important: getting the most out of that bounty of snow.

That is only one of the faces of snow that you may have seen if you grew up in a temperate climate as I did. But I find it fascinating to look at all the faces of snow—all the faces that this one simple combination of basic elements can put on for us, and how these can so easily affect our mood, even become part of our very culture. For it is, after all, only water.

Snow is a gift of nature—a form of crystal magic. The magic is worked by billions of water molecules, each nothing more (nor less) than two tiny hydrogen atoms tied to one of oxygen: H_2O. We take it for granted that our water goes through three phases—vapor, liquid, and solid—but the magic comes from the many different forms that these phases can take. For example when vapor starts to condense into tiny droplets of liquid water we can get mist, fog, clouds, steam trains, and saunas; single, double, and even triple rainbows. Even after vapor has coalesced into plain water we can experience it in many totally differently forms—from the raging, whitewater rivers we love (or hate) to raft down, to a gently flowing, fly-fishing river, or a stagnant pond covered with water lilies.

But it is the solid form of water that livens up our lives the most, for it gives us ice and snow. Ice brings hoary frost to freshen our morning walks, frozen canals (like those in Holland where one can glide between the Eleven Cities without touching a road), indoor skating rinks, and ice hockey games. Ice stores its coolness to keep our food and drink from going bad. Less useful, agreed, are the hailstones as big as golf balls—or even baseballs—that riddle our car roofs with dimples or even punch holes through our roof shingles.

Snow is "only" another face of solid water. It starts as vapor, which can be visualized as billions of very, very, *very*, tiny ping-pong balls jumping around and bumping into each other. They are of course molecules of H_2O. The show begins when they attach themselves to tiny specks of dust and build onto each other in regular six-sided patterns. Just as you could make many different shapes from a million pieces of play plastic, the tiny six-sided blocks build up to make all the different forms of snow that we see around us. The classic crystal star we see on Christmas cards and in ads for winter things is just one of the many shapes of snowflake that the water molecules can freeze into.

It gets even more interesting when we look at how different kinds of snowflakes build up to different kinds of snow*fields*—dry powdery snow, soggy wet snow, flaky snow, fine dusty snow, and so on.

In our part of the world snow usually fell silently—not in whirly, windy blizzards. Our senses were honed to detect signs that snow was coming: a subtle combination of factors such as a heavy, grey canopy of cloud, a weird sense of stillness, and even a distinctive smell in the air. Then we would go to sleep with images of soft fluffy snow falling outside. But along with the visual treat came the sense of *quiet* all around. Gone the distant noise of car and bus traffic on nearby Merrion Road. Gone, too, the droning of the distant power station at Poolbeg—muted out completely. No bird sounds, either, nor the sporadic sounds of human voices. Just quiet. Dead quiet. Snow absorbs sound like the foam rubber they use in sound recording studios to kill echoes.

When the snow did come we would spend hours outside making snowmen, with pieces of black coal for the eyes and the buttons, and colored scarves around their necks to keep them warm. We scraped snow off the ground with our bare hands (ignoring the numbness) and compacted it into snowballs between cupped palms. We staged pitched battles behind orange-boxes set up as defense lines and as ammunition magazines. Adults on their way home from work were tested for their tolerance to kids: often enough an adult who had never grown up would return fire and engage us in an animated but good-spirited exchange of snowballs.

But when the thaw came, we shuffled sorrowfully through the slush with leaky shoes and frozen toes.

After I left Ireland I was lucky enough to experience the wonder of snow in several foreign countries. That made me realize how many different faces snow can put on, and how they can affect the culture of the people.

Late in 1965 the snow was several feed deep in the Bavarian Alps. I was a member of an informal German-American friendship club, the *Columbus Gesellschaft*. (At that time—twenty years after the end of World War II—memories of personal experiences during war were on many people's minds, but rarely discussed, and then usually between trusted friends.) All my youth I had seen pictures and read stories of really deep snow blanketing whole mountainsides, covering gullies and scarps, even complete trees. I was eager to experience this kind of snow for myself so I signed on immediately when the club organized a weekend hike into the mountains.

Saturday finally came and I put on all the outer clothes I had. Normally, the native Germans would go skiing in winter, but I guess at that time the snow was not firm enough to make skiing enjoyable or safe. My colleagues explained that they would just be hiking over the snowfields. That was just perfect for me. I would learn to ski later; now, I just wanted to have my first taste of really deep snow.

A bus brought us to the trailhead and I kept up with my group easily on a well-defined hiking trail. Soon we arrived at a cozy mountain hut—a *berghütte*—the first one I had ever seen. Back home if we were going to stay overnight on a mountain in winter we had to bring our own snow tent, sleeping bag, cooking stove, and warm clothes. When you reached your highest point for the day you had to pitch the tent (and weight it down with rocks so it wouldn't be blown off the mountain), fumble around in the wind and dark to sort out your gear, and light your paraffin stove for a life-saving hot drink. That was before we could afford to buy fancy hiking clothes, so even in the best of times we would be dressed like a survivor from some wilderness trip gone wrong.

But in the Bavarian Alps they did it differently: when you reached the spot on the mountain that would be your resting place for the night, there was a cozy mountain hut—or even a small chalet. Once you stepped inside that hut you were immune to any threats from snowy blizzards or intense cold. The more popular huts even had central heating, warm showers, and food.

And wine!

That way you did not end up feeling like a pack mule or a Klondike gold digger struggling up the slope with the heaviest load your back could take without breaking.

There were other "firsts" waiting for me on top, though.

As soon as we reached the mountain hut my colleagues made for the over-heated common room and slid along the shiny benches one by one until they were elbow-to-elbow. A full-figured waitress in a colorful *dirndl* with a tight, low-cut bodice took orders for beer and *glühwein*. That's a drink made from warm wine mixed with spices; it protects you from the cold, damp mountain air. Nobody seemed to care about the white wonderland outside, visible as far as the generator-powered lights could reach. Beyond that, I knew, there must have been a spectacular scene of dazzling snow ridges and plunging, shaded valleys. These would surely reveal themselves in the morning. Nevertheless, I doubted I could wait that long, so I planned to slip out and walk around a bit before going to bed, even if it was dark.

However, after four or five glühweins and a native Bavarian meal of *bratwurst* (fried pork sausage), *sauerkraut* (shredded fermented cabbage), and *bratkartoffeln* (fried spuds), I realized that I would have to wait until the following morning to explore the white glory.

If I had recovered my strength by the morning, that is.

But there was one more surprise waiting for me before I went to bed.

Being used to Girls and Boys dormitories in the Youth Hostels, it gradually became clear to me that there was only one dormitory in this mountain hut. Would we boys have to sleep outside after all, in the howling wind and driving snow? No: You simply got into your sleeping bag, lay down on a long sleeping bench called a *lager*, and wriggled along it until you bumped up against another body, regardless of identity or gender. It was all perfectly logical: after the food and wine, everybody needed to find a slot on that lager fairly quickly, and this was the most efficient way to do it.

With my head swimming from the glühwein, my belly feeling full of lead from the fried potatoes, and drugged by the central heating, I slid into a dream world of soft quilts draped over hills and valleys. Everything was white, except for the inlaid patches of dark-green pines rising from the snow

…Z–z–z–z

That was yet another face of snow, one that had found a clear ingrained expression in the culture of the people.

It was 1965 and I was alone for Christmas and New Year in Munich. This town is so close to the Bavarian Alps that you can see the snowy peaks on a clear day. A work colleague had invited me to join his family as they paid their respects to their departed loved ones in the local cemetery. I was puzzled about the timing, though: we were to go at *midnight*. Why were we visiting the place of the dead at midnight, and in the middle of winter? I did not know this family all that well. It had not been all that many years since you could have been arrested on suspicion of body-snatching if you were caught wandering through a cemetery at midnight. And if body-snatching was on their minds, surely this was not the right season to try it, since we could have been tracked down so easily from our snowprints... But they reassured me that in the Bavarian culture it was perfectly normal to be among the gravestones on this night of the year, and promised to give me a special experience.

They sure did.

We drove along some narrow roads to a cemetery just outside Munich. There was about a foot of nice fluffy snow on the ground. To either side of the road, the soft stuff had worked its magic and reduced everything to a profile of gently curving mounds. Except for the road itself, that is, because passing cars had ground through the snow and squished it up into blocky windrows on either side. As we approached the cemetery I was amazed to see that the car park was almost full. The Dead would have plenty of company from the Living that night.

My astonishment grew even more as we pulled up and parked the car. *Dozens* of people were walking down the pathways of the cemetery; they were holding lighted candles and putting them down on the snow, by the gravesides. What otherwise might have been a ghostly, forbidding place, where nobody who was still part of this world would have dared to go at midnight, had been transformed into a congenial meeting place. Transformed by the magic of snow—and the culture of the Bavarians—even if there was no overt sign of participation from the other side. It was a veritable feast of light for the Departed and a wonderful way for the Living to bring them back to mind.

And a great way to take the superstition out of a trip to the cemetery in the middle of a winter's night.

Beauty often blinds us to its dangers, of course, and that can happen when snow puts on a different face. When the Bavarian winter was in full swing, the snow lay about two feet deep on the open fields, and much more in hollows and ditches where the wind had piled it up into drifts. The roads were nearly always frozen over—especially early in the morning. When the Authorities gave the OK, you were allowed to have your tires fitted with little steel spikes like sharp tacks.

One night I was driving out of Munich to a little town where I lived. The autobahn was not too busy, but the road was slimy and wet. Passing cars whipped up wet snow and lashed it across the road. I was stuck behind a car that was showering me with dirt and slush. Left and right, all I could see were piles of snow "flashing on and off" as they were caught in my headlights, like fast-moving TV ads. The rest was a black unknown, which I dared not look at anyway for fear of losing my tenuous fix on the road. The driver in front of me kept wandering back and forth across the white line dividing the lanes of the autobahn. I wanted to lose him but was afraid to make a move in case he drifted into my path as I was overtaking. Oncoming cars occasionally shone their headlights into my eyes and turned my windshield into a piece of frosted glass for agonizing seconds. I set my heating on low, to stay alert as I sped through the darkness.

After about half an hour reflective blue signs shone back at me marking off the distance to my exit for Moosburg: 300 meters... 200 meters... 100 meters. Good, I thought, I will finally be able to dump this guy. But no such luck: he exited too, and soon I was following his two points of red light along a much narrower road. Suddenly I saw a quick succession of white light, red light, and more white light: his car had left the road and cartwheeled into the snow. I rushed to the driver's window. He was able to speak, although his chest had hit the steering wheel quite hard. He looked at me with an anguished face, as if he owed me an apology for having driven himself off the road.

"*Eingeschalfen!*" he said: "Fell asleep!"

I could see that he was in shock, and not yet feeling any pain. (I knew that "non-feeling" before the pain comes.) As if to throw scorn on top of punishment for this slip, his upper body was plastered with broken eggs. The streaks of egg yolk and slimy egg white added to his sorry image. He must have been carrying the eggs in the back seat, perhaps back to his waiting family.

Now to a totally different continent and a totally different face of snow. If the atmosphere is *extremely* cold, ice crystals can grow directly out of water molecules, without needing any dust particles to "seed" them. For example, when damp air runs into much colder air, the water it has been holding freezes into crystals which themselves act like seeding particles. This produces quite a spectacular result: "diamond dust" raining out of a clear sky like micro-glitter. It must have been this kind of snow that I found in the Canadian Arctic when I worked there on a geological survey in the 1970s. We lived in a temporary but very comfortable camp on Melville Island, at 75 degrees north latitude (well within the Arctic Circle). It was around the beginning of May, and even at midnight the sun did not dip below the horizon for very long. When work was over, we had endless daylight to enjoy our evenings in the snow…

After dinner one evening the talk in the mess hall turned to how marvelous it was that people living in Arctic regions could survive the bitter cold of winter. An Inuit colleague explained that if you were caught out on the snow in a sudden storm, all you had to do was build yourself an igloo. And, he said gleefully, the materials for building an igloo were right there all around you. (No need to start looking for evergreen branches to hack down.) Delighted that we were so fascinated by his culture, he jumped up and said:

"Come on out and I'll show you how to build an igloo. It's easy! We can do it together—there's plenty of light!"

"OK man, you're on!"

We shoved our chairs back noisily and headed for the changing room to put on our boots and parkas.

The only tool we needed to build this igloo was a large meat cleaver. This we borrowed from the camp's cook, who eyed us very carefully before slowly handing it over with an "OK… I guess…" The snow outside was of the diamond dust type, very fine and compact. It had built up to about six feet during the arctic winter. Our Inuit friend showed us how to carve out large blocks with the meat cleaver. It was a bit like cutting through the stiff foam that holds flower stems together in the base of a bouquet. The trick in building an igloo is to lay the blocks in one continuous spiral rather than a series of horizontal rings. You have to cut the blocks with slight tapers so that they lean inwards to form a dome. If done properly each block is held in place by leaning against at least two others: the one directly below it and the one laid just beside it, "down-spiral." When you get near the top of your spiral the blocks should converge to leave an opening like a skylight window, which you close with a capstone cut to measure. When the dome is complete, you fill in the cracks with "mortar" made from powdery snow. All these materials can be found right there on the ground.

There is much more headroom inside the igloo than it might appear from the outside, because of the "cellar" left where the blocks of snow have been excavated. Around the inside of the wall you leave the compacted snow at the original ground level to form a circular "bench" about chair high. Now you can sit down, sleep, and unless you are a basketball player, stand up straight inside your igloo. As far as can I remember, it only took us about two hours to build it. Certainly not much longer.

None of us went so far as to sleep in our igloo that night, preferring our cozy survey camp with its well-stocked mess hall. Besides (we told ourselves) polar bears *had* visited the camp earlier that spring, and there was no point leaving warm meals out for them.

I had arrived in the Arctic around the time of the spring equinox, when, theoretically at least, every place on earth has exactly twelve hours daylight and twelve hours darkness. Although we would have to wait a few weeks to enjoy the bounteous daylight for which the Arctic is famous, we also had missed the utter cold of the long night, for which the Arctic is often feared. On a good day, without any wind, it would be around minus 40 degrees (where the Fahrenheit and Celsius scales happen to intersect to give the same value). At that level of cold you would start to lose the feeling in your fingers if you took off your gloves for even ten seconds. This is probably something folks living in northern Canada are used to, but it is frightening to lose the feeling in your extremities so fast if you have grown up in a temperate climate. (No more compacting snowballs with bare hands.)

At that time, around the midseventies, "streaking" was popular. It died out in later decades, possibly because nudity became blasé and streakers had shown all they had to show. They needed to move on to something else if they really wanted to stand out from the rest of us. But that was not yet the case for one chap in our Arctic camp who wanted to set a record for Furthest Streak North. Having made sure he had enough witnesses, he stripped down to his toenails, darted out one door, sprinted bare skinned across the snow, and looped in through another door. His streak lasted about ten seconds, after which he appeared reasonably jolly, though he did not mention how his fingers or toes felt, or whether he felt them at all. And nobody challenged him for his title.

Indeed, snow can show many faces.

Back to Ireland now. Growing up in Dublin, we were blessed to have the county of Wicklow on our doorstep. In a few hours by bicycle, or about half an hour by car, you could leave the bricks and concrete behind and find yourself in a veritable wilderness of shapes and colors. For the most part, the Wicklow Mountains have been washed down and rounded off into wonderful displays of suavely interleaved contours. And *never* boring: all of a sudden there will be a rocky crag or a cliff. If you forsake your rubber tires for rubber soles and hike the upper slopes, you will see deer cock their ears in the distance; you will come eye-to-eye with wild goats trying to decide whether you are a threat or not, before making an impossible descent over a crag; you will be compelled to pause and gaze at hidden lakes and cirques carved out by glaciers who evidently had great artistic taste.

But above all, it is the wide range of colors that enchants the visitor to County Wicklow.

For most of the year the landscape looks as if it had been painted by an artist determined to find all the hues that could possibly be made from the basic colors in a paint box. Many of the purple and reddish browns come from heather and bracken; accents in dark brown are kindly provided by peat hags—raw scars in the crust of peat opened up by the relentless battering of wind and rain.

This gets much better when it snows, especially when the crests high up are well covered, but the slopes below are only barely dusted with snow. Casting one's eye down to the valleys, the white begins to break up into the purple and reddish browns that the snow did not fully cover. If you are also blessed with a clear sky, the sun will bring out a full range of shades in the snow—bluish white, grey, hazy blue—depending on how the crests and valleys roll away from you.

All these, too, are the faces of snow.

Those of us who were compelled to feel the mountain intimately (most of my colleagues) used to head up at the first sign of the white stuff. Usually we hoped for a few nights of sub-zero centigrades so the snow would freeze into a hard crust. This was ideal for hiking, because the slopes effectively turned into "hardtop roads" that you could bound over without plodding laboriously and sinking up to your knees with every step.

Lugnaquilla, my favorite mountain, is in the south of County Wicklow. It reaches 3035 feet and is one of Ireland's fourteen peaks over 3000 feet. Yes, this is modest compared with, say, the peaks in Colorado, but massive compared with the highest points in some places I have lived, such as Houston, Holland, or Belgium (to name only some). But never mind the size: Lugnaquilla and the heather slopes leading up to it offer hikers a relatively easy escape into the Wicklow wilderness.

In 1972 we had a particularly good snowfall on Lug (as we call it). A buddy of mine in our college mountaineering club, who shared my love of remote snow-covered landscapes, proposed an overnight camp-out on the top, in the snow. He had a good all-season tent and an impressive range of high-level camping gear, including a compact primus stove for brewing up a hot drink on top. How could I resist?

I was in my final year of engineering school and I had student digs with a pleasant family near the Bellfield Campus. My landlady looked at me with an indulging smile that turned to concern when I told her I planned to hike up the highest mountain in Wicklow in the dark, in the snow, and to stay two nights on the top. Her husband was semi-paralyzed from a stroke and he discretely stayed out of this discussion. Besides, he was devoted to cricket. Their daughter, in her early teens, played civilized games too, like tennis and girl's hockey. (She did like watching rugby, although I suspected that was only because she had a teenage crush on a well-known Irish rugby player at the time.)

Now, sports like cricket, hockey, tennis, and even spectator's rugby, do not mix with hiking in the wilderness of the Wicklow Mountains (or any other wilderness, perhaps.) Up to then I was able to hold my own with my gracious hosts by relying on the one sport we had in common—spectator rugby—and by feigning interest in some key cricket matches. (I stayed clear of girl's hockey.) I also earned some points with the teenager by mentioning casually that I had had a few pints with her rugby player hero. Never mind that I stretched it here in an honest effort to be an interesting lodger: in fact I had just been with a few lads who knew the player and happened to be in the same pub at the same time.

I lost all those popularity points, however, when I was forced to reveal why I would be missing for two nights. I was just going to camp out in the Wicklow Mountains, I said. (When most guys would be socializing in the pubs.)

"You're mad!" was the simple and predictable reply.

Any chance I ever had of being accepted as a normal lodger simply vanished, but I was captivated by the magic of snow and could not be helped.

My buddy and I gathered up all the things we would need—a quilted down sleeping bag (dry), the paraffin stove, a lightweight kettle, and so on. After the last lecture on Friday afternoon, we packed our things into my Morris Mini and headed south for Wicklow. We took the easiest way up—Camara Hill—because it was dark, after all, and we had just come from a full day's classes. With our headlamps we were able to pick our way up the ridge with little difficulty. (That is, apart from getting tired of our boots continually breaking through the snow into some concealed hole—a common problem with soft snow.)

In about three hours the slope leveled out and we felt a brisk wind blowing in our faces: we were on the summit dome.

The top of Lugnaquilla was covered with powdery snow. It was firm enough to walk on, but pitching a tent in that wind took great care and patience. Anything that could fly would fly. After *borrowing* some stones from the summit cairn to hold the tent down, we crawled in, laid our foam pads over the freezing groundsheet, and rolled out our sleeping bags. Then we unpacked our cooking gear, set it up carefully at the entrance to the tent, and prepared to reward ourselves with a hot cup of tea.

Our primus stove was of well proven design—for the 1970s—though it would be some time before those compact butane backpacker's stoves came on the market. *Primus*, after all, means "first" in Latin. For decades this highly reliable stove had been used by mountaineers who might easily have tripped over our little mountain after the mighty peaks they had scaled. All you had to do was pressurize the fuel tank with a little hand pump, light a piece of kindling paper in a tray, and (with some coaxing) a hot blue flame shot out of a tiny fuel jet. The fuel jet was a critical part of the primus stove, and it was carried separately so it could be could be cleaned or replaced readily.

But we had forgotten to pack it.

So, as a penalty for not double–treble checking our equipment, we would not have hot food or a hot drink during our two-day stay on Lugnaquilla Mountain.

The next morning we awoke to a clear blue sky and a veritable wonderland of snow. The crystal magic had shown us another beautiful face of snow and we were able to forget about that tiny piece of brass that had come between us and our hot breakfast. At least until nightfall.

Unless somebody had camped overnight on one of the twelve mountains in Ireland higher than ours—very unlikely, we convinced ourselves easily—we were the only ones in Ireland to wake up that Saturday morning looking *down* on this soul-stirring scene of white. We pitied all the other inhabitants of Ireland, especially the hockey and tennis players.

Around mid-morning a group of hikers arrived after having set off early Saturday morning and climbed up by the same easy route. They knocked on our tent wall (for the fabric had frozen solid overnight) as we were having a late breakfast of cold soup. After some chit-chat we posed the inevitable question, to which they replied with genuine, heartfelt sympathy:

"Sorry lads, we're only up for the day. We didn't bring the primus."

When I got home to my digs and had cleaned up, I joined my landlady and her family in that most treasured of Irish traditions, the ten pm supper by the sitting-room fire. Cream crackers and cheese with a nice cup of tea. I was naturally expected to conclude the whole issue of sleeping on the mountain with some sort of a report that would rehabilitate me. To polite smiles I related our exhilaration on pioneering virgin tracks across snow-decked domes and ridges. How the scenes delighted us with their constantly changing hues of white tinged with blue reflected from the clear sky. (I secretly hoped it had been rainy and cloudy in the city while I was gone.) Finally, I tried to explain the unique feeling of lying in a warm sleeping bag listening to the wind howling outside (a really hard sell).

I did not tell them about the fuel jet we forgot to pack.

"When is the hockey starting?" I asked, cheerfully, as I reached for my first cream cracker.

It rarely snows in Houston, Texas, where I (mostly) raised my family. Even when snow does come, it is likely to turn into slush and disappear before midday.

One summer we took our Boy Scout Troup 1659 on a bus trip to Colorado. I had hoped we would get a taste of some snow high up in the Rockies, and some relief from Houston's steamy summer. Our highest hike was Mount Princeton, one of Colorado's 14,000-footers. Not only was there no crystalline

H_2O up there, but there was a lot less O_2, pure oxygen, than on the plains of Houston (which is about fifty feet above sea level on highway overpasses). Nevertheless, we were not disappointed: on a rest day the bus took us to the Continental Divide, where some patches of soft snow had survived near the road. The bus driver had barely pulled into the parking lot when the boys burst out the door in an excited frenzy.

"A snowball fight!" came the cry.

After pelting each other and the adult scouters for a while, the shout came up:

"Get the bus driver!"

Our driver had been fairly aloof up till then (probably because he was from the bus company, not part of our scout troop). Suddenly he was jolted out of his passiveness and had to defend himself against volleys of compact snowballs scooped up frantically by the boys.

Now he *was* part of our troop!

It was obvious he had taken it in the spirit it was given, because after that he opened up and began to find common ground with the boys, and with us.

The magic of snow had shown yet another one of its faces, yet another ability to affect culture.

Now to a place very famous for its snow: the Swiss Alps. The mountains there are geologically young and have not quite finished crushing and folding themselves up into peaks and valleys. This makes them a paradise for hikers, because the trails follow narrow ridges and traverse obliquely across deep slopes, giving you a stunning new perspective every fifteen minutes or so. Some of the trails are not much wider than your boot, and the slopes drop off so steeply that there is no need to speculate whether or not you would survive a fall. You just need to stay on the trail.

We often took the US scouts to the International Scout Centre in Kandersteg. Even in summer, this part of Switzerland's Bernese Oberland is prone to capricious snowfalls. Often you plan a hike only to wake up and see a white wall of snow where the day before there was a purple haze. In that case you would not go, because the snow may have hidden the trail and your foot could easily land on some weak "snow bridge" hiding a nice little gap ready to snap your ankle. Or worse.

But what if you go up in clear weather, on a clear trail, stay the night on top, and then find that the snow has come down during the night and hidden the trail back down? It just adds to the excitement, of course.

Hohtürli is a narrow pass through a nick in a ridge at the highest point of what must surely be the most spectacular hike in the Bernese Oberland. In Swiss German the word means "high little gate," or maybe "high narrow pass." If you only do one hike in the region, let it be this one. On our hike up there we arrived at the mountain hut near Hohtürli a few hours before nightfall. We were of course expecting to be spoiled by the luxuries usually put on by the Swiss Alpine Club. Instead, we found fully grown adult hikers sitting around all wrapped up in blankets and looking miserable. Other equally tough-looking hikers were cocooned in their beds under thick folds of blankets, reading books or dozing. Meanwhile, outside, erratic gusts of wind whistled around the corners of the building threatening to blast the anemometer off its mast. What was the matter with that place?

The central heating was not working.

We awoke the next morning to find that snow had fallen overnight and covered the trail we had planned to take on the way down—a trail we had never taken before and, therefore, one we were totally unfamiliar with. As it turned out the trail dropped down so quickly that the Swiss Alpine Club had installed fixed metal steps, like a fire escape. So we were spoiled after all. Even with the feeling of having "cheated" by using the steps, the descent through the snow with its stunning views of the valley below, and the encircling ring of distant peaks, was an unforgettable experience.

That, too, was another face of snow.

Finally, to the other end of the world: Antarctica. Nowhere have I seen the beauty of snow revealed in such raw, uninhibited, and revealing ways as in the Antarctic Peninsula. (Perhaps Alaska or the Norwegian Fjords can match it, but I have never been there.)

If you go to Antarctica in a relatively small boat, as I did, the two-day trip across the notorious Southern Ocean will put you in the right state of mind even before you reach the Antarctic. The early whalers had this to say about the Southern Ocean:

> Below 40 degrees, there is no law;
> Below 50 degrees, there is no God!

Still, nothing prepares you for the sheer beauty of the Antarctic once you leave the Southern Ocean and enter the protected waters of the Peninsula. Even in summer the sun does not rise all that high during the day, so, in effect, you have one long sunrise and one long sunset. As it slews slowly around the horizon, it catches massive snow slopes that blaze back in brilliant white, or it suffuses low-lying cloud banks with soft, almost mystic light. And as if that were not enough, these light plays change continually as you stand there trying to take them in: all of a sudden the sun will burst through a gap in the clouds and bring yet another stunning snow scene to life before your very eyes. It's as if the sun wants to remind you that it is the dominant and only force that brings life to this otherwise most desolate of continents.

The Peninsula has a violent past in terms of geology, and the snow does a great job in highlighting this: dazzling prisms of white perched atop towers of black volcanic rock; cavernous blue-green voids gaping from snow cliffs where calving has split off five-story blocks and sent them crashing into the sea.

You lose your identity in the overpowering and pervasive beauty of the Antarctic. You become utterly insignificant and humbled. Those around you appear to be equally powerless—and unwilling—to help themselves.

In the Last Continent, the faces of snow pass from beauteous to sublime.[1]

Growing Up in Dublin

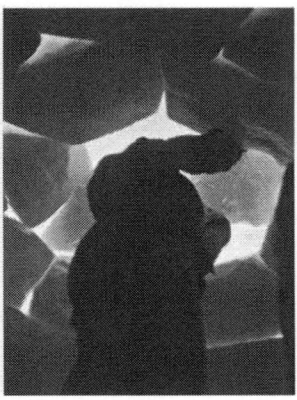

HOW TO BUILD AN IGLOO, CANADIAN ARCTIC

An Inuit buddy taught us how to build this igloo, for fun.

Top left: Cutting building blocks made of fine compact snow (not ice).

Top right: We let our Inuit teacher do the hardest part—fitting the last few blocks into the top of the dome without having it fall down on top of you. The sun skirted around the horizon most of the day, dipping just below it for only a few hours. Here, it is still glinting off the underside of our snow blocks late into the Arctic night.

Bottom: Nearly finished.

Photo: Rae Point, Melville Island, Canadian Artic, ca. 75 degrees north latitude, ca. 1st May 1974.

All the Faces of Snow

Winter: white-out at the summit

Fall: vivid brown peat, coloring grasses, washed rocks

LUGNAQUILLA MOUNTAIN, IRELAND

LUGNAQUILLA MOUNTAIN, IRELAND

Winter snow completes the hiking experience on Lugnaquilla Mountain, County Wicklow.

Top: My hiking buddy outside the little tent we shared for two nights. We were blessed with bright sunshine and spectacular views once the morning mist cleared. It didn't even bother us that we forgot to pack the little fuel jet for our primus stove and couldn't brew up any hot meals. If there is enough sun to melt the top of the snow during the day, and enough cold to freeze it into a crust during the night, you can bound over the snow "pavement" as sprightly as if it were a hard trail.

Bottom: Same mountain, but in different conditions. Most hikers in Wicklow will probably agree that Lugnaquilla likes to brood under dark, swiftly moving clouds as in this scene, painted on canvas. The brown patches on the left are peat hags—wounds in the peat layer opened up by the relentless beating of wind and rain. They are soft and mucky most of the year, making for some slippery hiking and the odd ungraceful plonk.

Sources: *Above*—photo near summit cairn on Lugnaquilla, elevation 925 m (3035 feet), winter 1972.

Below—oil painting by Amanda Mullee (detail) from a photo taken (in December 2001) on the Clohernagh approach to Lugnaquilla.

HOHTÜRLI PASS, SWISS ALPS

A capricious summer snowfall threatens to hide the trail as hikers descend to Hohtürli Pass, the straps of their backpacks flailing in the wind. A curtain of mist is coming up from the valley on the other side of the pass.

We found these hardy hikers sitting around the dining area of the mountain hut all wrapped up in blankets and looking miserable. Others had already given up and lay cocooned in their beds before the afternoon was out. Outside, the wind threatened to blow the anemometer off its mast.

The central heating was not working.

Many of these mountain passes were once the only routes between isolated highland valleys in Switzerland. This one goes from Kandersteg to Kiental, and has been turned into the most stunning hike in the Bernese Alps.

Hohtürli means "high little gate," or "high narrow pass," in Swiss German. Once we passed the base of the tortured rock pillar in the photo, the trail dropped almost vertically into that veil of mist. But the Swiss Alpine Club had spoiled us with fixed steel steps. The pass is at 2778 meters and the (normally cozy) hut is only about fifty meters higher. If you are an alpinist you can climb the majestic Blüemlisalphorn from this hut, as many of the locals seem to do.

Photo: Mark Mullee, from Blüemlisalphütte, 4th July 2004 (minor digital editing to remove clutter.)

SNOW CALVING, ANTARCTICA

My colleagues have left the (relative) safety of our steel vessel (the MV *Alexey Maryshev*) and packed into a zodiac (rubber dinghy) to look at this massive wall of snow up close. It is late spring in the Antarctic Peninsula and the winter snow is calving—splitting off and falling away from the cliff. The roof of that grotto looks like it could cave in at any moment.

Although the telephoto lens exaggerates how close they are to the cliff, a heavy chunk of snow crashing into the water would have created a wave big enough to liven up this photo for sure.

Photo: Antarctic Peninsula, 64–65 degrees south latitude, December 2007.

TOBOGGAN SLIDE, ANTARCTICA

Not the usual penguin-in-dinner-jacket shot, this scene of gentoo penguins with less-than-refined manners is actually very common during the breeding season.

The stains are what you think they are. The penguin with the soiled dinner jacket has probably fallen into it after doing an undignified belly slide. These birds are commuting between the water and their noisy, sociable nests among the rocks on top of the hill. They go down to the sea to feed (and hopefully to take a shower).

Penguins are comical to watch on land because of their waddling gait and unsure footwork. They are fearless of humans. It is fun to just stand still in the snow and watch them pass within a few feet as if you were not there at all. If they sense a leopard seal, though, they scatter *very* quickly.

Penguins are birds, but they do better as fish: once they hit the water their powerful flipper-wings propel them with frightening swiftness. For many fish and krill, that is the last thing they learn in life.

But don't try to cuddle those little penguin chicks when they appear: the mother will take your finger off with one chomp of her powerful bill.

Photo: Antarctic Peninsula, 64–65 degrees south latitude, December 2007.

A LONE EMPEROR IN ANTARCTICA

We came across this lone emperor penguin standing on a piece of floating ice. Our guides jumped up and down saying we were very lucky to see an emperor penguin so far "north" in the Antarctic (we were about 120 nautical miles outside the Antarctic Circle).

Emperors are the only penguins that never go on land. They nest on sea ice, and by the time their chicks are fully fledged the ice starts to break up and float away in pieces. Like this piece. The chicks start their fishing careers by rafting to sea on a chunk of ice. Perhaps this lonely penguin took the wrong ice bus.

Beautiful birds.

Photo: Antarctic Peninsula, 64–65 degrees south latitude, December 2007.

CONTRASTING FACES, ANTARCTICA

A dazzling prism of snow is perched atop a spectacular tower of black volcanic rock. Our guides told us that this peak and an identical one beside it were named after a certain "Eunice," well known to early sailors from port calls.

> Photo: Lemaire Channel, Antarctic Peninsula, around 65 degrees south latitude, at northwest point of Mount Scott horseshoe massif, December 2007.

---

[1] If you can't go to the Antarctic Peninsula yourself, and if photo-based accounts are not enough, this highly readable and erudite book will take you there: David G. Campbell, *The Crystal Desert: Summers in Antarctica*, ISBN 0-618-21921-8 (pbk.).

13

THE BLACKBERRY PICKERS

As the saying goes, "Be careful what you wish for: you might get it!"

In late summer we loved to pick wild blackberries. We would come across the sprawling briars laden with juicy berries as we strolled down public lanes, explored waste ground, or walked along the railway tracks. The berries were there for the taking—a gift of nature to be enjoyed by everyone. We would linger for a while to pick off the ones that had ripened, and sometimes—early in the season—we even ate the raw green ones in spite of their bitter taste.

So I pestered my dad to bring me on a *dedicated* blackberry pick—a trip with no other purpose besides picking blackberries in the wild.

I got my wish one day, but it wasn't what I expected.

Not that we were short of berries to eat, because we grew several species right there in our own backyard. Loganberries, for example; said to be a hybrid between a blackberry and a raspberry. They grow on long, thorny briars, like their blackberry cousins, but you can train them not to ramble all over the place by supporting them on wires, somewhat like grapevines. They are a deeper red than raspberries, and a bit bigger—about the size and shape of a sewing thimble. The succulent berries tasted best when dipped in fresh cream nicked off the top of a bottle of Jersey milk.

We also had two gooseberry bushes. One yielded sweet reddish berries that you could just pick and eat. The other gave us hairy green berries that you had to boil with a lot of sugar if you wanted to eat them without being forced to pull a wry face. So bitter were they. Gooseberries and loganberries were very easy to grow: the bushes just kept on pumping out berries year after year without much help beyond a bit of pruning.

Strawberries were different. We constantly battled against slimy voracious slugs who seemed to diet exclusively on our fruit. If you didn't spread Slugtox around the plants, you would find neatly scalloped half-strawberries in your patch, and long silver trails that petered out as they disappeared in the mini-wilderness of the summer garden.

But blackberries grew in the wild. They did not need any planting or tending.

And blackberries were obviously just as valuable as the berries that needed cultivation, because they sold jars of blackberry jam in the shops.

It was towards the end of a summer's day in the mid-1950s when my dad agreed to take me on a dedicated trip to the blackberry fields. That was only about a decade into the recovery from World War II, and many families were living at the barebones level. My dad had faced up to the unglamorous realities of those difficult years, and was keenly aware that they could easily have inflicted their heartless blow on our family—or on any family like ours—should the delicate scales of fortune have tipped against us and thrown us into dread need. So he quietly extended himself to his limits in order to keep those scales weighted in our favor, if sometimes only by one single gram. In the end, we never lacked the essentials—never even ran out of fun things to do. And of course we never really understood how difficult it was (and how easy he made it seem) until we tried it ourselves.

My dad knew a good place where blackberries grew in profusion. It was in Clonskeagh, where he had an "allotment" a few miles from our home. An allotment, also called a plot, was a small parcel of land leased by the city council at a nominal fee to anyone who wanted to grow their own vegetables. He grew an impressive range of vegetables in his plot: big white onions, scallions, lettuce, cabbage, sprouts, carrots, parsnips, peas, beans, and, of course, lots and lots of potatoes. This was a great idea in the mid-50s, and it could easily be revived if people get squeezed as much as they were then. But my dad's plot had its own special attraction for us kids. While he would be furiously spading the rich black earth, we would run off and play under a huge spreading beech tree that dominated a rise in the corner of the enclosure. There we would stay, romping on a carpet of three-sided beechnuts dropped from the tree's umbrella.

One of the effects of those languid years following World War II was that my dad had to downgrade from a car to a light moped. So off we went on his moped to pick blackberries. With my legs straddled across the narrow back carrier, I pressed my face against his back to stabilize our combined load so he could steer without swaying all over the road. Our faithful little machine labored up a small hill just past Donnybrook, close to where the River Dodder falls abruptly over some natural limestone steps. (This is where its sedate flow turns into a spectacular display of hissing cascades.) The moped's engine was overloaded and it rebelled by making a "bang–bang–bang" sound like a ram-jet engine, rather than its normal, contented "put–put–put."

We turned off Clonskeagh Road into a small driveway that probably led to a private estate. It was late summer and the blackberries were fully grown. Their thick, thorny brambles were sprawled all over the ditch line between the narrow road and an open field of pasture, aggressively smothering any long grass or other vegetation competing for sunlight. And the brambles were high: about as high as my chest was then. They had vicious, sharp thorns—like miniature shark's teeth—to make sure they ripped as much flesh as possible from the noses or paws of any animal that tried to penetrate their mesh. The thorns were of course very effective in drawing blood from the legs of boys with short trousers, too: Your foot would hook low-growing briars hidden in the weeds and draw the thorns across your shins leaving deep red scratches. Even if you only touched the briars without brushing past them, they would leave prick marks capped with tiny droplets of blood.

Nevertheless, the rewards of venturing into the thorny bramble seemed to balance the risks, for they were loaded with juicy blackberries. Most of the berries were either just right for picking, or a bit over-ripe, because it was so late in the summer. Few if any were hard, sour, or under-ripened. Before starting the work of gathering berries to bring home, I gobbled up my fill of the juiciest ones, on the spot.

Soon, big puffy clouds with silver fringes began to float across the sky, periodically blocking out the sun as if to remind us how chilly it could be without it. But between these little eclipses the sun transformed the scene completely and showed how vivid the colors really were. It highlighted the different hues and separated them very clearly: light green for young shoots, tinges of red for mature leaves.

My dad and I filled up a few buckets with blackberries until we thought we had plenty. Then we stopped and had a short snack in the open air, as the departing sun, for its last act, briefly grazed the highest treetops. Shadows became longer. The blackberry leaves were no longer contrasted against the lighter and darker greens around us. The different hues were quickly merging into a muted oneness that we knew would soon be completely drained of all color.

This fading spectrum seemed to trigger a little dip in my mood—that vague, tristful feeling that sometimes intrudes, uninvited, without our knowing exactly why. Perhaps making a special outing with the *sole* purpose of picking berries blunts the pleasure of coming across them by chance. Perhaps grasping at something one sees and wants requires more subtleness than I had realized, then.

I could sense from my dad's subdued mood that he was running a bit short on enthusiasm, too, although this could have been for any of several different reasons. Perhaps he had things on his mind that he could not share with me. Perhaps he had not been in the mood to go blackberry picking in the first place, and only went because I seemed to be so keen on it.

"I think it's time to go, lad," he said, "We have enough now."

I agreed readily. We quickly packed our things and left.

But there was another downer to come.

When we got home I put the buckets on the kitchen table and emptied the berries into an enamel basin. We would clean them and boil up a blackberry jam for winter. It was then that I made the discovery that everybody dreads: worms! Yes, the blackberries had worms!

With furrowed brows I speculated how many of the wiggly little things I had gulped down while I was filling the buckets, and before I had made that awful discovery.

That was the last time I pestered my dad to take me out especially to pick blackberries. I would content myself in future with those bonus finds that we enjoyed so much.

And I resolved never to eat wild blackberries again without making sure they were not maggoty.

14

BALLSBRIDGE LIBRARY

Books foster ideas. Ideas formulate beliefs. Beliefs are very strong motivators. But how can one even approach the problem of agreeing which idea is "right"? A text that moves one person to altruism may become a call to arms to another, in defense of some narrow personal interest.

I believe there is something in the human mind that drives it to seek out the pleasure of pure thought. Some prefer to pursue this pleasure after satisfying some more basic needs, such as a big meal followed by a good nap. By "pure thought" I mean the process itself, not necessarily what you are thinking *about*. If the subject happens to be purity of the soul, to take just one of a million examples, then so much the better; but it doesn't have to be, for the purpose of this argument.

It is easier to savor pure thought in a place that is carefully designed to lead you inwards, to the world of the mind. Such as a climate-controlled room with shelf-fulls of artfully printed book spines looking out at you, where like-minded people move with careful steps over hardwood floors, speaking in whispers.

And not speaking on cell phones.

My very first memories of this exhilarating experience are firmly anchored in Ballsbridge Library. This carefully designed little building stands on its own site between the Royal Dublin Society's show grounds and the right bank of the River Dodder. The proper name is Pembroke Public Library, but we always knew it as Ballsbridge Library, and this name still appears in some references.

Ballsbridge is a suburb of Dublin. I was born and raised there.

In the 1800s there used to be a separate community called Pembroke Township that included Ballsbridge and nearby areas, such as the seaside village of Sandymount. The former Pembroke Town Hall still stands on Merrion Road, a minute's walk from my old library. Judging by this bright and cheerful little building, it must have made a lively community even livelier when it was opened in 1880.

My home was so close to Pembroke Town Hall that I could hear the chimes of its clock giving us the time of day in Westminster Quarters. At least, I could hear the cheerful ding-dong, ding-dongs on a quiet afternoon when they were not deadened by the drone of suburban noise. Or, very early in the morning, when for some reason I floated up from a deep sleep to that no man's land just below full wakefulness, I would hear four lonesome notes saying "It's a quarter past..." But a quarter past *what?* What o'clock is it, actually? If I stayed in this half-wakefulness long enough, the hour that these jingles were building up to would be announced in the somber notes of their resolving tonic: dong–g–g–g; dong–g–g–g...

In the Irish language the bridge in "Ballsbridge" is called "Droichead na Dothra." Dodder Bridge. Nobody knows who or what "Dothra" was. As we Irish have trouble pronouncing the "th" as eloquently as the English do (or at all), we are exempt from even having to attempt it in our own language. Thus, "Dothra" drops the "th" sound and reduces to "Doh-ra," which is much easier. (The English never notice this omission, because they rarely try to speak Irish,[1] and have their own problem sounds when they do.)

Ballsbridge is a fairly upscale district in Dublin. Actually, the Dublin Post Office says my boyhood home is really in Sandymount, but in the 1930s when my dad bought our family home there, "Ballsbridge" must have sounded better to him. I had no say in this, of course, as I was still waiting in line to be born. But I would settle for having been raised in "Sandymount" anytime, because (however useless and vain it might be) I could at least drop the name of a famous person who also was born there: WB Yeats.

One often takes things for granted when they are simply "there." I did not notice the beauty of our library building in the 1950s. Nor did I ever take the trouble, then, to look at it when I was exploring the patch of wildlife on the left bank of the Dodder directly opposite. I never even thought of the library's architecture until, in 2012, I stood on that left bank and looked across the river rather than down into it. The façade was having a great time soaking up the last rays of a low October sun that was about to hide behind the Dublin Mountains. The architect must have been proud of his creation. Six well-proportioned windows on each floor, bordered in white masonry to contrast the dark brick walls and rusty terra cotta roof. In fact, all the building's features seem to have been very carefully designed to keep them in visual harmony. Today, the cupola and the flashing on the eaves have that sedate light-green color of weathered copper. They have proudly protected the tender insides of the building from the icy cold air, the modest heat of Irish summers, and the relentless lashing of rain hurled at it obliquely from the Dublin skies.

It was in that building—in the 1950s—that I discovered the expansive joys of reading, and the promise of limitless more implied by its warren of books. The ideas flew out from between the covers of the books. Books that had been protected so well by all that fine masonry and copper cladding.

Reading came naturally to us in the long winter nights of pre-television Dublin. I usually went to the library on a Saturday afternoon. It was a short walk from my home, and it took me past the well cropped shrubbery and majestic façades of the Royal Dublin Society. There probably were plenty of excellent bookshops in Dublin City then, but that was irrelevant to me, since *buying* a book was out of the question in that hand-me-down 1950s economy. This never caused me a single regret, however, because we had plenty of books in our cozy library.

I was fascinated by all those pages filled with print and bound between attractive covers. I was beginning to understand that the words and phrases stored on those pages were like "frozen ideas." Like food that waits cold and forgotten in a freezer until somebody grabs it, thaws it out, and releases all its juices and flavors. In the same way, in a library, stimulating ideas lie inert and unnoticed, hidden from direct view. There they remain, dead and meaningless, until human hands grab the book, open the pages, and human eyes focus the indented marks onto the retina (albeit upside-down). The retina turns the impinging light into the tiniest of electric signals and sends them to the brain. Then the fun starts. Like a room-full of bored people suddenly receiving a truckload of jigsaw puzzles, or chess sets, the brain gets to work putting all this together. But first, it has to combine the left and right eye-loads into a single, unblurred image.

It still fascinates me today, and for all I know it may still fascinate neuroscientists as they read the letters in their own theses.

But the wonder does not end there: it only starts. Starts with the cascade of neurons unleashed in the brain when the assembled images are passed on to it. The brain compares them to its own library of facts, emotions, and instincts before hurling its interpretation into the roiling cauldron of Consciousness. One can argue conclusively about what words the inky indents on the page mean—by comparing them to pre-loaded images—but two people, even two reasonable people, may *never* agree on their significance. They might have different intellectual paradigms.

For one, a call to arms; for another, a motivation for peace and altruism.

In the Children's Section of Ballsbridge Library, however, the information we got from the books was delightfully simple to interpret. We could build clear images in our minds from the marks indented on the pages. Sometimes the images were even as gripping and vivid as in the 1950s pictures, where Jim Hawkins climbs a web of rope ladder to the crow's nest in the ship's mast, crouches there in fear, and points his pistol at the ragged mutineer coming up behind him. The mutineer is trying to soft talk Jim into not firing the pistol, but only to gain time while he reaches for the knife in his leg band. Will Jack be fooled by the pirate's pretend friendship? Will he—a boy of my own age—have the nerve to fight back? Then we could breathe again and marvel at Jack's courage as he fires at point blank range, and we watch his attacker plunge into the tropical blue with a satisfying splash.

In this case at least, the message was clear: "Shoot!"

When not transported by pirate stories set in the tropics—or by Jules Verne's sailors straining their lungs to catch the last few molecules of oxygen in their submarine, beneath the Polar ice—you could wander through the maze of bookstands. Most of them were too high for me to see over, but I could still scan all the book titles and let myself be tantalized by what each might offer. The knowledge, ideas, thoughts, and the emotions they evoked could emulate experiences in real life, and of course transcend them in many cases. The better the writing, the easier it was to forget that you were "only" reading.

And what better environment to savor these experiences than Ballsbridge Library, in the middle of an Irish winter? The air outside was usually cold and damp, the skies often moody and unsettled. Inside it was always warm, and a bit humid, thanks to the zeal of whoever stoked the steam boilers. The tweed winter coats and woolen scarves of those escaping into the library helped build the atmosphere.

The distinctive smell of closely-stacked books in the library has remained with me to this day. Once again a little chip was implanted in my brain to shoot me back to Ballsbridge Library whenever I encounter that very same smell anywhere else in the world, suddenly reassuring me that I have not wandered too far. It is distinctly different from other paper smells: for example, the somewhat stale smell of cheap copybooks in the school supply store; the thick, fragrant ink embossed onto glossy brochures in the business world—all these are tied to separate feelings.

Voices were always hushed in the public libraries then, out of respect for other readers. That was simply taken for granted. Not even Jules Verne had a smartphone. At the checkout section two ladies sat behind a well-worn desk, backlit by whatever afternoon light was coming in through those nice windows I have described. The desk held the tools of their trade: dovetailed wooden boxes stuffed with library cards; date stamps with wooden knobs made shiny by many hands, and thumb wheels to advance rubber tracks with dies for each month and each day. A few stacks of returned books usually lay nearby. The slight gloom produced by the backlighting, the dog-eared cards, the mixture of human smells, woody smells, and radiator smells—all these seemed to conspire with the whispers and the supporting facial gestures to make it feel like taking part in some sort of a select ritual.

When you checked out a book, the librarian removed the card from the little pocket on the inside cover and stamped it with a due date. The quantity and timeline of old stamps on the card was a rough indicator of the book's age and popularity. If I did not return the book by the due date, I got a postcard from one of the ladies. My dad would then get actively involved. Keeping a book too long out of thoughtlessness was almost a venial sin. Other people might be waiting to borrow that book. If you ignored all this, you got a fine and had to face the opprobrium of the Library Ladies when you finally brought the book back.

Now I can see that all these images from the library would never have lodged so deeply in my mind had they not been tied to the normal stages of growing up: the books were widening my world beyond Ballsbridge and sowing the subtle seeds of wanderlust. They would grow into a compulsion by the time I was twenty-two.

The writer Frank O'Connor must have known every inch of the bookshelves in that library, because he was librarian there for the nine years ending in 1938. Too bad I missed that. I might perhaps have met this great short story writer, who was also "a poet, lecturer, novelist, linguist, critic, playwright, translator, broadcaster, librarian, managing director of the Abbey Theatre and self-taught genius."[2]

Ballsbridge Library—I mean Pembroke Library—overlooks the River Dodder at a point where Anglesea Road merges with the right bank, just before the bridge. The Bank of Ireland used to be on the opposite bank of the river, just after the bridge. Later, in the 1960s, the American Embassy was built a few minutes' walk away. I was living in Ballsbridge at the time and watched the embassy take shape. The unusual circular design reminded me a bit of a Roman amphitheater, like the Coliseum, but I had not yet read the newspaper articles about what it was supposed to remind me of. According to the US Government it is "a concrete expression of the close relationship between Ireland and the United States. Utilizing ancient Irish architectural features in a bold contemporary American design, it reflects the way Irish traditions have contributed to the socio-cultural scene in the U.S. today."[3] The shape does indeed evoke the image of an ancient Irish stone fort: a round structure, built without mortar, on a commanding site. Nevertheless I still see the Coliseum when I look at our embassy in Ballsbridge. But whatever it is supposed to bring to mind, it certainly takes full advantage of a commanding view from the apex of the triangle formed by Elgin Road and Pembroke Road.

It also appears to have been designed by the Democrats: there are no corner offices.

Let's turn for a while to the River Dodder itself. It is a river that only reluctantly follows human rules, but has itself ruled over some human culture, and some landscape, as it flowed down through County Dublin to Ballsbridge Library.

It begins very modestly on the crown of Kippure Mountain, where little streams have cut progressively wider channels into the peat that blankets the granite dome below. Incidentally, this cutting-away creates one of the area's signature features: peat hags. These slippery clumps of peat tufted with heather are great to look at but very tiring to hike on.

The little streams don't stay little very long, however, because once they get the feel of real gravity on the steeper slopes, they join forces with others to gouge out the flanks of Kippure Mountain. In fact, the Dodder lives a proud, splendid life before rendering itself to the Liffey at the Ringsend docks.

Winding its way through some quiet, secluded valleys in south County Dublin, the Dodder becomes entwined in Irish legend as well as providing more recent (and more believable) stories of settlers and their lifestyles. It flows happily alongside the roads that these settlers built, and gurgles under the bridges that, through the years, alternately crossed it, and were washed away by it. If the Dodder could speak it would tell you how the people used its steeply dropping course to power their watermills before steam power arrived, and how they abused it with noxious effluents long after steam power was gone. (Or maybe all that gurgling is actually river-speak.)

The pleasant little valley called Glenasmole is one of several that guide the Dodder down from the Dublin Mountains.

The word means "Valley of the Thrushes," in Irish. Once, in late spring, I was driving casually through the area when all of a sudden I was dazzled on all sides by wild furze bushes ablaze in vivid yellow blossoms. That alone would make a visit worthwhile.

In legend,[4] the warrior-giant Oisín must have had many bad dreams about that valley. Back then the country was ruled by Gaelic Celts, since the Romans had not bothered to conquer the land (or were still smarting from run-ins with Asterix and Obelix in the resistant pockets of northwestern Gaul). The Celts in Ireland had worked out laws and customs based on valor and honor. These were sometimes enforced by what are now called pagan rituals. Because the tribute system was strictly enforced, it really helped to be just plain *strong*.

Note that Saint Patrick had not yet arrived with the news from Rome, though he was soon to come.

Oisín the warrior-giant was living in Ireland at the time. He had everything going for him: a superb ancestral line, a handsome physique, a reputation for being a terrifying opponent in battle. His dad was Finn MacCool, leader of the formidable Fianna warriors. Not only did he have great strength, but he didn't have to fear losing it (or any of his other youthful qualities). You see, he had gone to a land where people never got old. It was called *Tír na nÓg*—the Country of the Young. And his place in Tír na nÓg was very secure, because he was married to none other than the King's daughter, Niamh of the Golden Hair. Niamh: A woman of impeccable virtue, arresting beauty, unfailing strength of character, and a heart that was altogether too warm for her own good. ("Niamh" is pronounced like "knee-av" in Irish; another reason the English would have trouble with the language when they came.) Furthermore, Niamh had actually sought out Oisín—not the other way around—and taken him from his brokenhearted father on her own white steed.

He must have been a real hunk.

And they would never grow old…

But there was a catch (there had to be). If Oisín wanted to leave Tír na nÓg for a bit he would have to stay mounted on his wife's big white steed; should he dismount, or be knocked to the ground, he would revert at once to his real age. As in stories of time travel between different regions of space, his "real" age was to be calculated relative to the ordinary world. (The one we live in, where people get rheumatism and arthritis, have yellow teeth or no teeth, become wrinkled with old age, and get afraid of catching pneumonia in February.)

Now Oisín was very happy in the Country of the Young, but he missed his dad and his old buddies from the Fianna. So he decided he would take a little wander back there to see them. His beautiful wife cried, begging him again and again not to touch the soil in that land lest she never see him again. But he left anyway (borrowing her horse for the journey).

He may have assumed that warnings like those were only meant for ordinary people, not for him. He was, after all, the strongest of the Fianna; his dad would be proud of him for becoming the first ever to return safely from Tír na nÓg.

Big mistake.

When Oisín arrived back in Glenasmole he looked all over the place for the lads, but couldn't find them anywhere. If he had read up on his Relativity Theory, however, he would have known that they had long since died out: at the speed his horse was traveling in Tír na nÓg (relative to the Land of the Mortals of course), in the ten years he had been there with his beautiful wife, a full *three hundred* years had passed in the land of his natural youth.

As he wandered around on his big white steed, he came across a few other mortals trying in vain to move a dirty big rock. Scornful of these "weaklings" (or perhaps because he was used to being gallant), he picked up the rock and threw it a distance of over a hundred feet (seven perches). Stooping to lift the big stone was not a problem for Oisín, of course, but it *was* a problem for the gold cinch strap holding the saddle he was sitting in. The strap broke, the mighty Oisín fell to the ground—victim of a neglected technical detail—and was instantly turned into a wizened old man.

He never saw his strong and beautiful queen again.

Indeed he would spend the rest of his days engaged in two popular Irish pastimes: commenting on the weather, and arguing about religion. At least he had a formidable partner for his theology sessions: none other than Saint Patrick himself. While Oisín had been playing about in Tír na nÓg, the saint had arrived to convert the Irish from paganism.

The rock that caused all this misery is still lying where it landed in Glenasmole, not far from the River Dodder. Its name gives merely a hint of the grief it caused Oisín: "Finn MacCool's Stone."[5,6]

There is an alternative explanation of how that "erratic" lump of granite might have ended up all by itself in that field. It could have been picked up by a different kind of giant: a glacier. The big slab of ice would have frozen the rock into its belly, carried it slowly down the valley, and dropped it when times got hot. But this story is not as spectacular as the one handed down in folklore, which is probably why it was favored by my strait-laced geology professor.

Nor do the stories woven around the Dodder end there. A lot of Dubliners will tell you that the water piped into the city from the Dodder's nearby reservoir at Bohernabreena is the purest and softest in the world. What the English call "the cup that cheers," the Irish call "a good cup 'a tae." Both will probably agree you cannot have this without good company and soft water. Dubliners will add that you simply cannot get a cup 'a tae as good as one made from Dublin water. But for whatever reason, the teapot never cools down completely in a Dublin home as long as there are people still awake (or already awake). You can always feel vestiges of warmth in the pot from the last session.

And *that* is no ancient legend.

An added benefit of soft water is that you don't need a whole bar of soap to get a decent lather, nor do you have to use a power tool to remove the calcium caked onto your kettle. Mind you, the Dubliners also claim that draft Guinness tastes best in their city, and that it deteriorates in proportion to distance traveled from the city. So far, however, the Dubliners have not tied the velvety taste of that draft to the softness of the water. Perhaps this is because brewing beer is more difficult than brewing tea: it relies more heavily on skill than on the raw ingredients.

But, to continue the Dodder's journey down to the Irish Sea. Near Rathfarnham Castle it picks up the Owendoher, a rather short little river whose name in Irish describes it succinctly: An Dothra Bheag, the Little Dodder. Little or not, it has cut its own steep-sided gorge, now flanked by suburban backyard walls that come as close as they dare to its edge. It surrenders itself to the Dodder at a point where its big sister is forced to make a sharp turn by a natural geological fault, at Shaw's Wood. (That name would not ring a bell had George Bernard Shaw not been descended from an original landowner. Never mind that Shaw fled Dublin at an early age to shake up British society with his acerbic wit.)

After passing through a few more suburbs and the obscure remains of some old millraces, the Dodder now enters the upstream limit of my boyhood territory: Clonskeagh Waterfall. This is a natural limestone scarp, not a manmade weir. You can imagine the river sliding over this scarp for thousands of years, ever since it cut through the gravel and clay dumped by the vanishing glaciers. It is really quite wide, with several separate steps—an absolute must for ten-year-old boys to explore. Who could resist the temptation to walk across that wide, flat top where the water was so calm (just before it tumbled over the edge into the frothy pools below)? As you gingerly stepped onto the rock, the river's continuous shhh–shhh–shhh got louder and louder until it drowned out everything else (including sensible voices telling you to go back.). We had done this several times, when one afternoon the force of the water on my legs was a bit stronger than usual, and the green slime a bit slippier (or so I rationalized later). In any case I quickly found myself kissing the flat stone of Clonskeagh Waterfall, though luckily I did not join the cascade down to the plunge-pool below. I got off with a split lip and a bloody mouth. At home, my dad was easy on me; he seemed to understand that I was learning to respect the hidden force of moving water. (More advanced lessons were to come later in life.)

From Clonskeagh, the Dodder only has to flow about five hundred yards to reach the Dublin suburb of Donnybrook. Now we are within a mile of my boyhood home. On Sundays, I often went to Mass in Donnybrook. Sometimes I even went to Confession there on a Saturday evening to clear the way for a guilt-free Holy Communion the next day.

In the early 700s a very holy woman named Saint Broc founded a convent near this part of the Dodder. It was given the name "Domhnach Broc," meaning "Church of Saint Broc." (The words for "Sunday" and "Church" are similar in Irish, in case one should forget the connection.)

It is nice to assume that Saint Broc founded the convent because she was inspired by Saint Patrick, the English bishop sent by Rome to bring Christianity to the Irish Celts. But that is pure speculation. It is not much of a stretch however to assume that the Viking invaders were *not* inspired by Saint Patrick, or by Saint Broc's contemplative life style, since they began to carry out savage raids in Ireland before the century was out.

In recent times the bodies of over six hundred Celts were found in a mass grave near where St. Broc had founded her convent. Not all had died of old age: the bones had grown to different stages of maturity ranging from young children to old men. A not-so-nice speculation is that a barbaric raid ended the convent community that Saint Broc had founded.[7]

But her church has not been forgotten.

About three hundred years passed: the English had wrested Ireland away from Scandinavian domination, and were anglicizing the land to render it more suitable for governing. First, those funny Irish place names had to go. So, for "Domhnach Broc," the Irish were given "Donnybrook." Centuries later the Irish returned the favor by giving the English language the common noun "donnybrook," meaning a free-for-all or a mêlée. This connotation is of course the exact opposite to what Saint Broc would have wanted for a church that bore her name. The perversion was brought about by six hundred years of Donnybrook Fairs. Judging by a popular ballad, this annual fair seems to have wandered a bit from its original charter to provide great food and lots of innocent fun for the ordinary folk:

Donnybrook Fair—a Jig[8]

There tinkers and nailers and beggars and tailors
And singers of ballads and girls of the sieve
With Barrack street rangers, the known ones and strangers
And many that no one can tell how they live
There horsemen and walkers and likewise fruit-hawkers
And swindlers the devil himself that would dare
With pipers and fiddlers and dandlers and diddlers

—All met in the humours of Donnybrook Fair

Brisk lads and young lassies can fill up their glasses
With whiskey and send a full bumper around
Jig it off in a tent till their money's all spent

And spin like a top till they rest on the ground
Oh Donnybrook capers to sweet cat-gut scrapers
They bother the vapours and drive away care
And what is more glorious, there's naught more uproarious

—Hurrah for the humours of Donnybrook Fair

Reading between the lines of this ballad, which are already quite explicit, it is not difficult to understand why the Donnybrook Fair was abolished in the mid-1800s when the standard of acceptable public conduct was being raised. One can imagine the "cat-gut scraping" fiddlers setting the pace on the dance floor and the dancers spinning like tops until they collapsed from a variety of overdoings.

Indeed, there must have been a lot of traffic in the confessionals around Domhnach Broc in those days. Or at least there should have been.

Continuing our trip down the Dodder, a short distance beyond Donnybrook we reach an important point: the upstream limit of the tidewater coming in from Dublin Bay. This occurs just before Ballsbridge. Rivers with a relatively steep incline for most of their lengths often find it difficult to decide which way to go when they reach flat land. No longer having the decisiveness that gravity forces upon them in the steeper parts, they often change course erratically in a sea of alluvium—the mud and silt that they themselves have carried down from the mountains. Up until 1751, people needing to cross the river at this point had to wait for low tide and ford it: there was no bridge. (The ford was near the spot where my old library now stands.) Finally, in 1751, the long waits and wet feet were ended with the opening of a bridge. It took the name of a Mr. Ball, who, long before, had lived in a house nearby. Over time his name had become a recognized landmark, and it still is today.

The Dodder has a history of disrespect for bridges. Once, as I crossed Ballsbridge in a bus on my way to work, I was astonished to see that the river had changed overnight into a furious, roiling mix of mud, sticks, and water—all desperately trying to squeeze under the constraining arches of the old bridge. Water was billowing up against the crown of the bridge—even above the keystones—protesting against being held up. All the more reason to respect those who conceived and built the present bridge, the last and most successful in the five generations since 1751.

Our pals told us that during the Easter Rising in 1916 the British forces then in power were prepared to destroy the bridge, if necessary, to prevent the independence fighters from entering the city via Merrion Road. To back up this story our buddies pointed to the holes drilled into the granite on the underside of the arches. Holes just the right size for dynamite sticks. But luckily it never came to that, and the biggest threat to this graceful bridge remains the river itself when it is crazed by heavy rains.

The name of the bridge morphed gradually over time, from "Ball's Bridge" (the one engraved on the 1904 structure) to "Balls Bridge," and finally to "Ballsbridge."[9] But the spoken version has hardly changed, and apparently it will always tempt aspiring adolescents to frivolity. Sitting in the upper salon of the Number 7A bus as it went over the bridge, it was not unusual to hear a chorus of teenage girls announce your location from the bench seat in the back, putting special emphasis on the first syllable: "*Balls* bridge" (giggle–giggle).

Just before a small weir adjacent to Ballsbridge Library, the Dodder used to well up a bit, at least when I was a boy. A slight curve in the river threw the flow of water towards the right bank—the Library side—and with it most of its erosive energy. Bypassed by the swift current, the inside of the curve enjoyed relative quiet. Eddies spun off from the main flow and scalloped out little shallow pools. When the river flowed full, it dumped more soil onto the bank, letting more plants take hold. Add to that the shade of the overhanging trees and you have a little haven for wild life. And now add some pre-teen boys with crude fishing nets and the picture of suburban summer life on the river is complete. We could easily wade out into the brownish water, enjoying the free foot massage given by the stones on the riverbed. The sun would project images of leafy branches onto the surface of the water. There we would fish for pinkeens—our name for small freshwater fish, mostly minnows. The unsuspecting pinkeens were scooped up into cheap plastic nets to spend the rest of their lives in jam jars.

While looking for pinkeens we sometimes saw eels, too, though we never tried to catch them. They swam almost motionless in shallow water dappled with sunlight—just holding their positions against a slight current—almost imperceptible in their silvery skins.

Later I was astonished to learn that these eels are not Dublin born, or even Wicklow born, but come from the warm waters of the Sargasso Sea, a huge gyre of ocean currents far closer to the subtropics of Florida than to our temperate isle.[10] Their sedate appearance in the Dodder belies their foreign roots: spawned by the millions in the Sargasso Sea, they hitch a ride to Europe on the Gulf Stream, do a complete make-over (a butterfly-class metamorphosis) to become elvers, and then swim up the rivers. They return to the warmth of the Sargasso Sea at the end of their lives for a one-time spawning fling of their own. How they find their way back is not known. My guess is that they slip south past Spain and catch one of the warm westward-bound currents back to that gyre. At least that's what I would do.

In a quiet corner of the Dodder, a mother duck would occasionally paddle by, followed by a row of little ducklings obediently weaving their way through her wake. Rats hurried along the river bank and darted into storm drains. We wondered how often they had duckling for lunch. There were otters, too, and we wondered how often *they* had raw rat steak for dinner.

The storm drains were big enough for young boys to walk into with only a slight stoop, so in we went of course. Sometimes you would see a rat scurry up the drain ahead of you and disappear into the darkness beyond, where even we did not dare to go. The drain just downstream of the bridge had a special attraction: it brought you directly under the Bank of Ireland. Now…what if we were to tunnel up into the bank vault from the storm drain…? Nothing came of that idea, though, and in time the Bank of Ireland would generate its own troubles, far greater than anything a few boys could have come up with.

Near where the savageries of nature were taking place—rats eating ducklings, otters eating rats (or so we imagined), minnows snatched from freedom to start life sentences in jam jars—there was a high wall that bounded the bakery of Johnston, Mooney and O'Brien. I still have never found such value as the cream buns sold from a little shop whose frontage broke the monotony of the brick wall in front of the bakery: spongy white bread with a thin light-brown crust—still a bit warm—sliced into two hinged halves bursting open with fresh dairy cream. No goo, no syrupy gel, no cinnamon: just fresh bread and fresh cream. And at a price well within any kid's budget. What have we done to the simple joys of life…?

That bakery gave us many other things, too, including this street rhyme:

> Johnston, Mooney and O'Brien
> Bought a horse for one-and-nine
> When the horse began to kick
> Johnson Mooney bought a stick
> When the stick began to break
> Johnson Mooney bought a rake…

"One-and-nine" meant one shilling and nine pence. Each shilling had twelve pence. To put that into perspective, half a shilling would buy you a "sixpenny wafer"—a special treat of rich vanilla ice cream sandwiched between two crisp wafers. This "sandwich" was so thick it would not fit into the juvenile mouth for the big bite.

We obviously did not give the bakery much credit for the value they placed on their dray horses. We were even less considerate in our street jingle for Kennedy's bakery:

Don't eat Kennedy's bread:
It'll stick to your belly like lead.

This mindless devotion to rhyme and meter had distorted the reality, of course, for a bakery is surely among the things most dear to humans. Yet another simple delight—this one entirely free—was the permanent whiff of baking that hung outside the high wall flanking the river. By association, the aroma brought to mind the warmth and promise that permeated a home kitchen. (I'm told that this whiff even crossed the Dodder to the RDS grounds near my old library, and that even the stylish patrons of the Dublin Horse Show had relished it.) Perhaps it was this pleasing sensation that led us subconsciously to the bakery's little shop.

And that was not all: At the top of the high brick wall there was a portal for loading sacks of grain. Immediately below—on the public street—there was a permanent heap of grain seed that must have blown free from the sacks as they were hoisted up. During my early boyhood, fairly soon after the World War II when times were *really* hard in Dublin, my dad hit on an innovative idea (no doubt inspired by his upbringing on a small farm in County Mayo): why not harvest this free seed to expand the lawn in our backyard? So, early memories of our backyard are very clear: The half that was seeded from a proper nursery had thick, rich grass that could be mowed into a splendid lawn suitable for any gentrified suburban family. The other half—grown from seed winnowed by natural forces at the bakery wall—appeared to be a hybrid mix of wheat and oats. It had a scraggly appearance, rather like a stunted crop of grain on a neglected farm, and it stubbornly resisted every attempt to refine it from its wild origins.

But, to a boy's mind, an unkempt lawn was okay (and could even be preferable): my summers on the farm in County Mayo have left me with a love of open fields and a corresponding aversion to compact, over-tended lawns. So when I had to leave the country and return to the miniature field in my Dublin backyard, I was grateful for that wild grass.

You can take the boy from the farm, but you can't take the farm from the boy.

On the city side of the bridge there was a British-style telephone box, the vivid red color long since painted over with multiple coats of government-issue, patriotic green paint. This was where I made my first-ever solo telephone call—yes, all on my own-i-o—inserting three big copper pennies, dialing the number on the shiny disk with the finger holes, and listening to my pennies fall into the moneybox—forever—as soon as my party answered. I believe that call was to my home, where sometime in the 1950s we became proprietors of a private telephone line.

Later my pals taught me how to "tap" numbers—make a call from a public telephone without paying. The numbers "0" and "9" were free anyway—because you were allowed to make free calls to the Operator (0) and to the Police (999); to get any other number—say the number seven—you gave the hook seven sharp, evenly-spaced taps, and so on till you were connected.

And not so long after that I would use that same telephone box for some very long conversations with my first girlfriend. It was worth making the short bike ride to Ballsbridge to avoid including my dad or my siblings in delicate exchanges that by their very nature had to be carried out in rarified company. It seems, after all, that a certain kind of experience can *not* be lived by deciphering images on white paper in a library. Or from secondhand reports, no matter how close the informant may be to you. They can only be acquired through one-on-one encounters—with no safety nets for your feelings. But while you can't find much help with these matters inside or outside a library, a good book will at least let you believe you have control over the other parts of your brain.

Returning once again to our river's path and the wildlife it contained: in summer, wild swans nested on the right bank, just downstream of the bridge (by Beatty's Avenue). Our relationship with those swans had nothing to do with their supposed grace and beauty; nothing to do, either, with feather-light ballerinas in flimsy dresses floating across a placid lake to the lustful music of Tchaikovsky. No: It was a standoff driven by mutual distrust and fear. Nor did their necks curve gracefully, as poets have reported: their necks were stuck straight out at us like bazooka guns ready to fire anti-tank rockets. It was indeed a *pas de deux* of an entirely different kind, one driven by the basic instinct of survival.

When it comes to ten-year-old boys of unknown intent but known destructive potential, wild swans do not waste time assessing the threat: they preempt any trouble by launching a direct challenge. We quickly learned to expect the big snow-white birds to ambush us as we stalked through the waist-high grass to their nesting place. Even if you only wanted to say "hello, swan," they would rush at you, grown to frightening size by having stretched their wings to full span. Then they would gimlet you with piercing eyes set in heads that were tellingly small in proportion to their necks, and go "chtha–chtha–chtha." All you could do was gape down their gullets and beat it back the way you came.

No, you definitely did not mess with wild swans.

Ballsbridge Library

As I entered my early teens, my focus shifted more and more from the natural playground around the Dodder Bridge to the rich world of thoughts and imagination to be found in Ballsbridge Library. This shift was imperceptible to me, of course.

One day I found a thick book printed in an elegant font. The paper was beautifully textured, with uneven edges simulating old-style binding. I had not yet ever read a *complete* book from the grownup section—one with many words and few if any colored pictures. I was eager to read it all—to make it the first real book I would read. I took it home and did indeed read it all, gaining praise from my dad, a self-educated person who had been able to read a lot before he got into the business of raising children. He had provided us with a tall bookcase at home. When you opened the glass doors you got a slightly musty book smell as you feasted on Emerson, Shakespeare, Jules Verne, Dickens.

With that book I probably passed quietly through one of childhood's one-way turnstiles; I had graduated from all those boyish things on the river banks.

At least until I would return to some of them later in life.

* * *

In the summer of 1986 a terrible storm caused the Dodder to overflow its banks in thirteen places. Water flowed down Anglesea Road, the site of the Ballsbridge Library. It created an unwanted lake on the well-tended lawns of the Royal Dublin Society, and soaked the books on the lower shelves of their private library. But my old library seems to have escaped.

And the bridge survived—again.

When I visited the library in 2012 (and "discovered" its harmonious architecture), I stepped inside briefly for old time's sake.

The little dovetailed boxes stuffed with dog-eared library cards were gone, of course.

Johnson, Mooney & O'Brien no longer baked the cream buns or sold them from the little shop in the wall. In the late 80s they abandoned the bakery. Gone, too, the whiff of fresh-baked bread floating over the Dodder, reminding us of the joys of home, charming the folks in the Royal Dublin Society, and adding to the joys of reading in Ballsbridge Library.

BALLSBRIDGE LIBRARY

The proper name is Pembroke Public Library, but we always called it Ballsbridge Library. It is on the right bank of the River Dodder, just upstream of the bridge.

Photo: October 2012.

US EMBASSY, IRISH STONE FORT

Above: The US Embassy in Dublin (42 Elgin Road). It is only few minutes' walk from Ballsbridge Library. It must have been designed by the Democrats, because it has no corner offices. Besides, the Republicans would never have put the flag on a tree.

Below: Irish Stone Fort, partially re-constructed, at Cahergal in County Kerry. Possibly from the Stone Age. "Cahergal" is derived from "An Chathair Gheal," The Bright Stone Fort.

Sources: *Above*: US Embassy, Dublin.[11]
Below: Photo 19th September 2013.

CLONSKEAGH WATERFALL

I used to love crossing the river on these huge stepping stones—until I slipped on the green slime and split my lip. The cascade's constant shisssh produces an ambiance that makes you want to just linger there. At least until the runoff from heavy rains comes thundering along.

The falls are a gift of nature crafted by the River Dodder where it drops over a fault in Dublin's limestone beds.

Photo: Tom Mullee, ca. 2000.

MR. BALL'S BRIDGE

The bridge in 2012. The friendly façade of the Ulster Bank would normally provide a very fine backdrop, but this has been left out in this sketch in order to focus on the beautiful stonework of the bridge. Some modern light poles were also removed, and the surviving ornamental light stands are shown against an unsettled Dublin sky.

The bridge is engraved with the date 1904, but the original crossing was built in 1751. It took the name of a Mr. Ball, who had lived in a house nearby. Before that first bridge you had to wait for low water, take off your shoes, and ford it.

The Dodder has no respect for weak bridges, but this one was built after that lesson had been driven home several times. Heavy rains can turn a few fickle streamlets on the heathery slope of Kippure Mountain into a roiling mix of mud, sticks, and the occasional tree trunk. This dangerous charge is forced under the bridges at a frightening pace. I have seen the water completely fill the arches of the bridge in this sketch and boil up against its crown. But the bridge has survived all these tests.

The river is stilled by the little weir just upstream of the bridge. This had created a little habitat for wildlife when I was growing up, and that wildlife got some unwanted attention from us boys. We caught pinkeens (minnows) in little pools that had been scalloped out by eddies, saw lots of rats and the occasional otter, and watched mother ducks proudly leading their ducklings through the riverside grasses.

Source: Sketch from photo taken in October 2012; the buildings behind bridge and the big willow tree on the right bank are omitted.

LET'S TUNNEL UNDER THE BANK!

This building just downstream of Ballsbridge used to house the Bank of Ireland in the 1950s. We could easily walk into the storm drain, at least until we saw the rats scurrying ahead into the darkness. It seemed like a big tunnel to us—ideally placed for breaking into the bank's vault from below. (Perhaps that's why they turned the building over to the Ulster Bank.)

As the Celtic Tiger went limp in the late 2000s, both banks faced worse threats to their assets than anything a few Dublin nippers could have come up with.

Photo: October 2012 (modified to remove graffiti from the brickwork, and to enhance outlines.

THE DODDER'S HUMBLE BEGINNINGS

The River Dodder rises behind this tussocked peat hag on Kippure Mountain. The eroded peat is often sprinkled with white grains of quartz worked loose from the underlying granite by freeze-and-thaw cycles. These parts are best hiked when "paved" with crusty, frozen snow, as otherwise it's too mushy for comfort.

In the background is Finn MacCool's valley, where Oisín fell off his steed, fast-forwarding himself past the remaining lives of his buddies. The Dodder's watercouse is generally steep, giving it a lot of energy as it flows down to Dublin Bay. This gift of gravity was a boon for watermills before steam energy arrived, but episodes of "unexpected" heavy rains caused disbelief and consternation as banks overflowed and bridges were washed away.

Photo: September 2013 (near TV mast, looking towards Ballymorefinn).

---

[1] One notable exception being the fictional British soldier in Brian Friel's play *Translations*.
[2] Jim McKeon, "Frank O'Connor," Ballsbridge, Donnybrook, and Sandymount Historical Society, Annual Record 2007, http://bdshistory.org/annual_record_2007.pdf.

[3] Website of the Embassy of the United States, Dublin, "About Us," http://dublin.usembassy.gov/index/embassy-news/about-the-embassy2.html, accessed 29th November 2012.

[4] Light-hearted interpretation of Ulick O'Connor's "Irish Tales and Sagas" (Dublin: Town House and Country House, 1996), ISBN 0-948524-59-1, which the back cover describes as a "...subtle yet glorious re-telling of the old Irish tales...."

[5] This version is from Christopher Moriarty, *Down the Dodder: Wildlife, History, Legend, Walks* (Dublin: Wolfhound Press, 1991, Colorado; The Irish American Book Company, 1998, ISBN 0-86327-286-X).

[6] Or it might be that Oisín got off the horse himself, overcome by having seen a stone trough that the Fianna used to put their hands in, and having "such a wish and such a feeling" for it; Book XI, Oisin and Patrick, *Lady Gregory's Complete Irish Mythology* (London: Bounty Books, 2004, ISBN 978-0-753723-22-7).

[7] Christopher Moriarty, *Down the Dodder: Wildlife, History, Legend, Walks* (Dublin: Wolfhound Press, 1991, Colorado; The Irish American Book Company, 1998, ISBN 0-86327-286-X).

[8] Irish Jig, "The Humours of Donnybrook Fair," and other titles.

[9] Christopher Moriarty, *Down the Dodder: Wildlife, History, Legend, Walks* (Dublin: Wolfhound Press, 1991, Colorado; The Irish American Book Company, 1998, ISBN 0-86327-286-X).

[10] *Encyclopædia Britannica Ultimate Reference Suite* (Chicago: Encyclopaedia Britannica, 2011), under "migration," catadromous fish."

[11] Website of the Embassy of the United States, Dublin, "About Us," http://dublin.usembassy.gov/index/embassy-news/about-the-embassy2.html, accessed 29th November 2012.

15

THE CARBIDE LAMP

Prince and Beauty were two hounds my cousin Tom kept on his small farm. Prince had sleek, jet-black hair, and bright blue eyes that always seemed to be anxiously sizing up everything and everybody around him. Beauty had reddish brown hair; he was older than Prince, and a lot less aggressive. Prince had to be kept chained during the daylight hours, when the hens and chickens were around, as otherwise he was likely to take one of them. Beauty was allowed to run loose around the farm all day, and would always go with us to the fields when we were making hay, digging potatoes, or bringing home the cows. Both dogs went wild at the sight of a rabbit.

Tom was always very busy on the farm in summer, when I was allowed to stay with him for three or four weeks. However, he always found the energy to go hunting rabbits with Prince and Beauty, and me. The rabbits were plentiful. They had eaten some of the outlying oatfields down to bare stubs, which naturally made the farmers very angry. Tom really hunted the rabbits not in the hope of solving this problem, but because I was fascinated by the experience, being a boy condemned to live most of my life in the big city.

We usually went hunting in the evenings, an hour or two before sunset. There were certain places where the rabbits had their warrens. You would have to approach them very quietly, and from the downwind direction, otherwise they would all have disappeared underground by the time you reached the warren. They never strayed too far from their burrows; as you crept up on them you would see them hop quickly to the nearest one, their white tails bobbing up and down. Sometimes they would stop just at the entrance to the burrow, as if to make sure it wasn't just a false alarm. Then, after first cocking their ears straight up, and turning one wide eye towards you, they would quickly dart out of sight.

The hunting was cruel. But somehow I didn't think of that side. At least not at first. If the wind was right, and we could hold the dogs long enough to get near the rabbits, Prince and Beauty would sometimes beat them to the entrance of the burrow. This only happened when the rabbit was unlucky enough to be surprised too far from his home. With rabbits, the chase was always short: either they made it to the burrow in a matter of seconds, or they ended up in the jaws of the hound.

With hares it was different. Hares did not have burrows for refuge, but they did have long, powerful hind legs that that could carry them as fast as the hounds. More importantly, perhaps, they had the ability to make sudden, sharp turns in the middle of a full-speed chase, leaving the hounds tumbling over one another in confusion, trying to retrace the lost scent. We knew that when the hounds rose a hare, we would probably not see them again for an hour or so, when they straggled home exhausted—and still hungry!

At least this type of hunting gave the rabbits and hares some chance. With the carbide lamp, though, the odds were not the same. The carbide lamp was made for carrying while walking. A small canister strapped to your waist contained the carbide to generate the gas that burned fiercely in the handheld lamp. The light it produced was much stronger than an oil lamp; only an electric lamp could match it.

We went hunting with the carbide lamp in the dark pre-dawn hours. The lamp sent a long, straight shaft of light out

The Carbide Lamp

in front of you, making everything you aimed it at suddenly spring to life in vivid detail out of the surrounding blackness. Needless to say, the rabbits were not prepared for this. Startled and shocked, they would first stand motionless, paralyzed by the dazzling light. Their eyes became reflectors that immediately gave their positions away. Before they could gather their senses enough to start the dash for the burrow, vital seconds were lost. Easy prey for hounds.

After the hunt, Tom, the hounds, and I would walk the last few hundred yards home along a narrow, winding asphalt road. Occasionally, an early-morning motorist would suddenly round a sharp turn behind us, pinning us all against the roadside fence with two piercing headlights approaching at frightening speed. Then, as often in years to come, I would think of the rabbits caught in the beam of our carbide lamp.

Author's note: By exception this and one other story in this book were written in 1989, over twenty years before the others.

16

THE WINDMAKER

I stood still and watched in childhood awe: jets of air were blasting into my face causing me to scrunch up my eyes, and swishing past my ears as if I had stuck my head out the window of a car. Only far louder. It was coming from a row of big fan blades staring at me from the wall of an enormous brick building. There was a loud roar coming from inside the building, too, as if something big, powerful, and angry was in there trying to get out. I was puzzled: The huge metal blades whipping up the air, the roar from inside the building, the wind blasting at my face—all this was new. I turned to my dad and asked excitedly:

"What's *that*, Daddy?"

My dad had taken me for a walk along a seawall in Dublin Bay and we had come to this strange building. Dublin Bay is shaped like a horseshoe, with rocky headlands guarding the openings to the Irish Sea. Sand builds up inside the bay, so when the tide goes out it uncovers a varied landscape of sandbanks, pools, and channels. This was a treat because you could walk out for miles at low tide. You could take a friend, leave the city behind, become lost to the rhythm of your feet splashing through the pools of salty water. You could leave toe-prints on the sand ripples, to be erased by the next tide. You were never really alone, because even if you were alone, the seagulls always seemed to be staying with you, their forlorn cries muted by the expanse of echoless, open air.

The Windmaker

Indeed, the tidal flats were ideal for the casual walker, but in the old days boats trying to get in and out of Dublin Port dreaded running aground on the shallow sandbanks, and there were many shipwrecks. So, in the 1700s, two seawalls were built—the North Wall and the South Wall—one on either side of the channel that takes the River Liffey out into Dublin Bay.

I grew up fairly near the South Wall, which starts at Poolbeg Peninsula in Ringsend. The South Wall was the best for Sunday afternoon walks, because it was more exposed to the sea, and you really felt that you had left the city behind. It reduced to a narrow breakwater as you approached the Poolbeg Lighthouse at the very end. From there you could see the whole of Dublin Bay and the mountains that framed it.

A most beautiful sight.

On the day in question—when I was accosted by that mysterious, roaring gale—we were on the South Wall. It must have been in the late 1940s, when I was around six. At that age one takes things at face value and believes everything one is told. We had passed an old building called the Pigeon House. There were never any pigeons nesting in that house, but there *was* a Mr. John Pidgeon who lived there around the year 1760.[1] Mr. Pidgeon was caretaker of a storehouse used in the building of the "Great South Wall" to keep the port free of shifting sand banks. At that time the wall would have looked a lot different than it does today: you would have seen canvas sails filling up with wind as the ships serving Britain and Europe arrived and left. Given that it could take a whole week to get to and from Wales—in good weather—it was not surprising that the passengers embarking and disembarking on the dock near Mr. Pidgeon's storehouse were tired and gaunt. Mr. Pidgeon saw how raw the weary passengers were, and he figured they would jump at the chance of buying some tea and cakes to refresh themselves. And they did—once he started selling them from his storehouse. Later, the "d" was dropped from "Pidgeon" and that's how we got a "Pigeon House" with no pigeons, to confuse later generations of children.

Strolling past the site of Mr. Pidgeon's old store that day, my dad was evidently in a lighthearted and carefree mood—a bit frivolous, in fact. That walk was very popular on weekends, and my dad would almost certainly have treated me to an HB ice cream as we mingled with the other strollers. (I kept that tradition alive for my own kids, substituting Texas's Blue Bell ice cream for the brand I grew up with in Dublin.)

Not far beyond the Pigeon House there was a power station that used to make electricity for the city, and this became known as The Pigeon House Power Station. That's where the howling wind and the loud droning noise were coming from. The plant stopped making electricity regularly in 1976, but its two tall chimney stacks still dominate the skyline of Dublin Bay. They are hard to miss because they are painted with wide red-and-white bands, making them look like giant candy sticks. Although these contrasting color bands are probably there to help low-flying airplane pilots, they have turned the chimneys into undisputed icons of Dublin Bay. And for many first-time visitors in regular airplanes circling to land after an overnight flight from the US, their first impression of Dublin may well be the stark red-and-white bands of the candy-stick chimneys, caught in the low early-morning sun. This visual is no less striking for the returning emigrant, especially when the tall chimney stacks are topped by stark-white seagulls floating lazily over the bay.

But today, in 2013, the candy sticks are big ghosts of the power station they once served. Even so, they are part of the city's soul.

But back to that strange, roaring wind: to me—a small boy—it was totally new, and my dad obviously caught the wonder in my eye. We had passed the Pigeon House and were standing under the candy-striped chimneys. The row of exhaust fans on the wall of the power station looked as big as the side of the hayshed on my cousin's farm in the country. It was then that I asked my dad what it was:

"That's for making the wind, lad," he said, in a quiet, matter-of-fact tone. Then he continued (in case I had not caught the full importance of the Windmaker):

"This is where all the wind for Dublin comes from—the wind that we have in our back garden and the wind that blows down our road."

I was grateful for this revelation and pondered the magnificence of a world in which people would build such a machine. Otherwise we would not have had any wind. I visualized the Windmaker roaring and blowing all day so the clouds would move across the sky, our clothes would dry in our back garden, and the chestnuts would be blown down from the trees where we could get at them. After that day I always thought of the windmaking machine whenever I saw a small cloud move across the sky like a lost sheep, or watched the roiling billows in a cumulus cloud. I would think of the Windmaker every time I saw fallen leaves scurrying along a footpath and swirling up into little vortices, chased by the blustery Dublin wind. I may even have shared the important knowledge with some of my pals (if I did, they did not question it).

If I had thought deeply enough I would have figured out that the Windmaker had helped give us the Pigeon House; it had bulged out the sails on the masts of the old wooden ships and brought all those weary passengers to Mr. Pidgeon's tea shop on the Great South Wall.

---

[1] "The Pigeon House, Ringsend," Dublin City Public Libraries, http://dublincity-publiclibraries.com/dublin-buildings/pigeon-house, article submitted by Your Library, 3rd August 2010.

17

GOING TO THE ROW

A steam engine is by nature a small explosion of power. It claims most of your senses—not just your eyes and ears—especially if you are standing on the edge of the railway platform as it thunders past without stopping. Even standing close to a steam engine when it is only *starting* to move is an exhilarating experience.

Until I was about ten years of age, I used to take a steam train to school every day. I never got tired of watching the huge pistons and levers groan and strain as they coaxed the iron monster out of its inertia. It was like trying to move a big old dog who was determined to stay lying down. First, steam hissed and puffed from jets and nozzles on the engine's belly; then the giant wheels started to turn—slowly and reluctantly—inching the whole train forward; the first thunderous puff from the chimney shot a blast of steam and smoke that billowed up under the glass roof of Westland Row Railway Station; then the huge chain links tying the rail cars together started to clink one by one as they took up the load. That first labored puff was followed slowly by another, slightly less strained, then another and another, until they began to come quicker and easier. If you stood real close to the engine (as I always did) you could *feel* the thrust of energy within your body.

But once in a while a string of railroad cars refused to yield to the brute force of steam. Something had to give: the wheels lost their grip on the rails, and all hell broke loose. A thunderous explosion shook the very guts in your belly and vibrated your rib cage (making you suddenly aware that you had one). The wheels now spun free in a paroxysm of epileptic convulsions, while the train stood still. Pistons, levers, and rods jerked in and out rapidly, hissing and blowing hot steam. The chimney belched out black smoke in five or six rapid-fire shots. All through this you could smell the heated grease and oil from the pistons, and you even had the sensation of *tasting* it. Now the steam engine had got to all five of your senses.

Maybe even a certain sixth sense.

Eventually the steam would win, of course, and the carriages would crawl forward obediently. As soon as the engine cleared the cavernous roof of the railway station, there was a sudden quieting. Only the jerking and squealing of steel scraping against steel remained, and soon this was gone, too. There was what passed for quiet in the station, while the smoke and steam trapped under the big glass roof found its way to the two gable ends of the station, and escaped into the indifferent Dublin sky.

Then the sound of human voices could be heard again, at least until the next train suddenly thundered in.

In Dublin, if you said you were "going to The Row" it meant you were going to Westland Row Christian Brothers School. Starting in 1950, I went to The Row for ten years—ten very formative years. Our school was right beside the railway station I have just been talking about, which is how I got to know steam trains so intimately. For those born after these old trains were retired to the railway museum or the scrapyard, the best way to feel what it was like to ride one routinely may be to watch an Agatha Christie mystery set around 1930: Watch Detective Poirot as he stands on the platform of some quaint English railway station and steps onto the train, passing unconcerned through little clouds of steam escaping from the tamed beast. Watch how calmly he reads his newspaper as the train whistle-screams through green embankments, and squeezes under stone bridges causing the windows to rattle and thud in protest.

Our school was somewhat famous because one of the leaders of the 1916 uprising, Pádraig Pearse, had attended it. Some mementos from Pearse's short life were displayed in a simply carpentered cabinet on a wall: his military tunic, a lock of hair. From time to time our teachers would mention Pearse, and we regarded him with a mixture of vague curiosity and dutiful reverence. After all, those events had taken place some 25 years before we were born—an eternity for anybody under the age of ten—and we tended to class them along with stories from Ireland's prehistory.

We started our train ride to school at Sandymount Station, a few minutes' walk from my home. In 1937 this train stop had been adding features to make it a *real* railway station, and not just a halt. It got a station-master, a book stall, and—sure to be welcomed by passengers who got bored easily—more advertisements. According to an *Irish Times*[1] report, passengers taking the early train to Dublin one morning were surprised to find an iron footbridge over the tracks that certainly had not been there the night before. To add to this feat of moonlight construction, the station-proud residents of Sandymount considered their new bridge to be fit to take its place beside Sydney Harbour or San Francisco Bay.

When I began to use the station (about thirteen years after the sudden appearance of the Golden Gate-class footbridge) there were two waiting rooms on the city-bound side and one on the outbound side. The city-side waiting room was the liveliest, because most people waiting to board a train were headed into Dublin, and most of those using the outbound platform were getting off the train and hurrying home. You could tell the mood of the people from how they walked (or ran) as soon as they stepped off the train onto the homecoming platform.

There was a level crossing at Sandymount Avenue, a fairly busy road even then. It was attended by a gatekeeper in a little house overlooking two heavy wooden gates. When a train approached you could hear one or two sharp dings of a bell inside the gatehouse. On this cue the gatekeeper would look both ways for car traffic, grip the handbars of a huge wheel, and start yanking it furiously like a helmsman desperately steering a ship away from a reef. In response, the two big gates would start their lumbering swing across the road, powered by human muscle. Unlike most of the railway crossing barriers of today, there were none of those light-weight booms that rise up into the air. After a minute's herculean effort by the gatekeeper, the gates would complete their swing and lock noisily into a well-greased latch on the other side of the road.

The crossing was now closed to all cars, bikes, and horses. But not to foot traffic, at least not necessarily: the little pedestrian gate may still have been open. This gate had a sturdy deadbolt on the bottom so it could be locked open or closed independently of the main gate. It was controlled by the gatekeeper—from his watchpost—so *he* had the final responsibility for deciding how close the train could come before it was too risky to let anybody dash across in front of it. His decision might depend on whether the aspirant was a nimble schoolboy or an old age pensioner. (Sometimes you had perfectly legitimate reasons for dashing across in front of a train, for example if you were stopped by a train while running late for a bus.)

After a train passed, the gatekeeper would reverse the process. Occasionally we went along for the ride, standing on the lower beam of the gate as it swung back across the road. The gatekeeper didn't seem to mind this, probably because he was just glad we had survived the bigger dangers.

Riskier by far was the habit of dashing across the tracks *inside* the railway station, after all the gates had been locked. This was necessary when you lingered at home too long after lunch and arrived on one side of the tracks just as your train was about to stop on the other side. By this time it would be far too late to clamber over the Golden Gate Bridge (grandstanding in full view of all the punctual passengers waiting snugly on the platform). So you were left with two options (apart from being late for school): risk hopping across the tracks in front of the approaching train, or wait until the last carriage had clattered past, nip across the tracks, and run up onto the platform after it. Neither could be done with any dignity.

It seems, in life, no matter how well defined the criteria are for making a decision, some split-second choice will fall so close to the borderline that you will lose whatever self-possession and calmness of mind you had claimed to have.

At some point during my school years, they began to replace the steam engines with diesel engines. More precisely, they were diesel-electric engines, meaning that the wheels were actually turned by electric motors, which in turn were powered by enormous diesel engines. A lot of people only heard the word "electric," however. After all, it was the 1950s, and we were used to machines that burned coal and puffed smoke. Then somebody spread the rumor that there was electricity running along the rails, and that we could be electrocuted if we touched their silvery surfaces. But in fact there was no electricity in those rails, of course, and no risk of gaining unwanted fame on any "third rail." Nevertheless the *belief* that we might have fried on the rails had the needed effect, at least for a while. In fact, I suspect it was the gatekeeper who had spread that rumor, and I would not blame him if he had.

All of this had an incidental effect, too. In summer the level crossing would be bathed in the smell of grease from the levers and rods that drove the gates, implanting yet another smell-trigger in my youthful brain, one that on cue brings me back instantly to swinging gates and nervous moments judging the distance of an oncoming train. I sometimes think that our brains come with a free, built-in recorder—not only for video, but for smell, and hearing, and even emotional effects.

Passengers on the railway were separated into First Class and Third Class depending on how much they paid for their tickets (not much has changed since then). I never wondered what happened to the Second Class, or if there ever had been one. Probably, that was a bit of early "perception management," as the term "Second Class Passenger" is too close to "Second Class Person."

We were Third Class Passengers. (The downgrade from First to Third was not nearly as difficult to swallow as with today's Economy Class air tickets—there were no leg cramp or elbow-in-the-rib issues, and nimble Third Class passengers could beat the sedate First Class passengers onto and off the train).

In Sandymount Station, the First Class waiting room had steam heating and doors that could be closed to keep it nice and cozy inside. At times we would peep in, and, if there was nobody there, just stay for a while inside to savor the experience.

On the first schoolday of every month we went to the Ticket Master's office and bought a "seasoner"—a season ticket. This was a pass to travel freely on the train every day. The Ticket Master always basked in warm, stuffy heat in winter, and we figured there must have been a boiler somewhere generating steam for his office and for the First Class Waiting Room. (Not that we envied him: I never felt the cold in winter as a boy.) After our visit to the ticket office we would walk out and look at our nice new cards printed with the new month's date. It was a good feeling to have our seasoner—we felt a bit special.

On the train, the First Class passengers had their own carriages. I never traveled in one of them, but we knew from secret investigations that they had nice velvety seats. Some well-dressed ladies on our street rode in those fine carriages. We were okay with this separation, however, because we had a diplomatic standoff with these ladies over "canted" balls. (If you canted a ball you threw it wild, for example into somebody's flower bed). The entire train was heated liberally by steam radiators. Judging by how hot it was in our compartment, I doubt if we had any less steam than the First Class passengers. Occasionally, a small wisp of steam would escape from the radiator under your seat and rise up past your legs and arms. Steam has a smell, and this was quite a pleasant experience, a bit weird and unusual but strangely agreeable.

Westland Row Christian Brothers School—The Row—is less than a mile from Dublin's city center, just south of the River Liffey. Trinity College is to the west, the Irish Parliament buildings to the south, dockland and industry to the east. The commute to Westland Row railway station was fairly short—about 15 minutes. There was only one intermediate station, Lansdowne Road (where the international rugby games are played). The train route passed a coal-fired gas works with enormous tanks called gasometers that rose and fell inside a circular iron lattice.

An old wooden boat lay half-sunken in the Grand Canal Dock, overshadowed by a tall, drab building (as if some guardian of visual aesthetics was trying to keep it out of sight). There it rested, decaying peacefully—never to float again—its wooden beams sticking up like the ribs of some skeleton-beast rotting in the wild. Over the years we gazed at the pitiful wreck indifferently for a few seconds as our train passed by. One day, on returning from the long summer holidays, we noted without any emotion either way that the old wreck had passed some critical stage of rotting and had squatted down completely on the bottom of the sluggish canal—a ghostly green skeleton fading down into the murkiness.

The view as we approached Westland Row station was not pretty, but we accepted it without complaint, as we accepted everything else in this city that had mothered us. If we were going to complain, it would have not have been about what we saw, but about what we smelled. It would have been about the choking sensation from the sticky, acrid air hanging over the streets. It was more than a smell: it was a *taste*. It seemed to catch in your throat, invading your taste buds and probably your tonsils too. The weather people blame this on "inversion"—hot and cold layers of air getting flipped upside-down and ending up with the cold layer on the bottom. There it hangs, the cold layer, sometimes staying close to the ground for days and days because it's too dense and morbid to vent up through the hotter air above it.

And with it stayed the city's dust and smoke—millions and millions of tiny specs of that solid stuff belched out by the city's coal fires.

The only thing missing now was fog, and all that needed was a slight temperature drop—to below the dew point. No problem for a city like Dublin.

Smoke + fog = smog.

That pungent-smelling and bitter-tasting air even followed me into the schoolrooms sometimes. This of course planted yet another childhood "memory chip" in my brain that still brings me back instantly to Boyne Street whenever I taste that particular flavor of smog anywhere in the world. But it has not happened again in Dublin since the city bravely got rid of its coal fires.

Now, be it clearly noted that completely different memories will surely be evoked for some who grew up near the slow-moving Grand Canal, the stodgy gas tanks, and the drab brick walls. You can possibly invoke these feelings for yourself by listening to this English dockland song from 1949, which many Dubliners would love to claim as their own:

> I found my love by the gasworks croft
> Dreamed a dream by the old canal
> Kissed my girl by the factory wall
> Dirty old town, dirty old town.
> —Ewan MacColl[2]

It was all part of the city that mothered us.

Nor did the smoke and fog that hung in the air seem to slow down any of my classmates who lived right there in the middle of it, near Fenian Street, in red brick houses that must have been over a hundred years old. (I had a lot in common with that area: my life began a few blocks away in Holles Street maternity hospital, and two years later my mother's life ended in that same building.)

When a school pal invited me to his home one day I found that most of the available space on the living room wall was taken up by sports trophies that he or his family had won. There were silver cups and bronze-like statuettes of footballers sliding in for the triumphant kick, or players with their hurley sticks held at the level of their athletic shoulders, looking down intently at a little ball they were about to blast through the goalposts. The family tree seemed to be written on black Bakelite trophy stands.

Not only that: The narrow allowance of living space in the tiny front room did not constrict in any way the warmth I felt when I was invited into it. It was normal then for the ma to produce a huge plate overflowing with soft, fresh sandwiches. These came with steaming hot tea served in bottomless cups. But more important (I realize now) was the way you were made to feel part of the home—the ma's smile beaming across her healthy, rosy cheeks—those alone would convey the message very clearly.

No: We did not complain about the city that mothered us so well.

In Primary School—around the age of six or seven—the City of Dublin provided milk and sandwiches for us kids. When we arrived in the morning the huge metal crates would already be sitting on the floor. The milk came in squat bottles, smaller than the usual pint bottles. At lunchtime the teacher would open the crates and distribute a bottle of milk and a sandwich to each boy. The sandwiches were always soft and fresh, having been made that morning for sure. When eaten with the creamy milk they made a satisfying snack. A bit soggy and bland, perhaps, but enough to fill our little bellies.

I cannot recall what was in the sandwiches, but my guess is that it was cheese. That would explain why one day a mouse ran out of a box when the teacher opened it. The mouse was probably enjoying *his* lunch in the dark crate (in spite of the racket created outside by over fifty schoolboys) when suddenly he found himself in the spotlight, the giant form of a fully grown human looming over him. Then he darted across the floor in a mad, bewildered dash for cover. The teacher gave immediate chase and brained him with one well-aimed swat of his stick.

Poor guy. He should have known that teachers always kept a hard wooden stick at the ready, and were very dexterous in its use.

Sometimes, in winter, it would already be getting dark when we went into Westland Row Station to take the train home after school. Whatever daylight the heavens still had to offer was heavily filtered by years of soot layered onto the enormous glass roof of the station. The walls, the platforms, the people walking along them, all seemed to merge into a oneness with little distinction between form and color. It got even darker when you boarded the train, if the gas lights in the carriages had not yet been turned on. As the feeling of enveloping gloom grew, a man would slink through the train, reach up to each gas light, and put a little flame to it. The result would be a brilliant white light—enough to bring on that nighttime feeling, enough for the adults to read their newspapers as the train slid out of the station and passed those big gas tanks.

* * *

In autumn 2013 I took the train along my old school route with my son, who is a good two generations removed from the time of my school runs. The footbridge over the railway tracks was gone—the one that had moved the proud citizens of Sandymount to compare it to the Sydney Harbor Bridge in

1937. It had been replaced by a modern underground passage (no more close calls dashing across the tracks in front of approaching trains).

My forehead was up against the windowpane as the train reached the spot where I used to pass the big gas tanks and the boats rotting in the canal dock. Some things had not changed at all, others had changed radically: the old boats were gone, but others had taken their place. They all seemed to be in good condition. A man with short, wind-roughed hair and a weathered face was washing some of them down with a hose. A splendid new building had risen out of the water on piles, where I remembered only murky green and rotting wood. Officially it was called the Waterways Visitor Centre, but Dubliners would never accept such an uninspiring name for a stocky little block sitting on the water, so they had dubbed it "The Box in the Docks."

Inside The Box I found some very inviting exhibits of Ireland's canal system (which, in its time, was a great way to travel the country in style). A sign in the hall bore the words "Watterweys Airlann," and my (Texas-born) son asked me to translate them. Clearly the two words just meant "Irish Waterways," but they did not match their respective English or Irish counterparts exactly. We asked the young curator, who sprang from his desk and answered our question with great enthusiasm, then going on to answer several other questions we had not thought of asking. It was Scots Irish, he explained—the language spoken by the people of Scottish descent who had settled in Northern Ireland. Since the canals covered all of Ireland—not just the Irish Republic—the signs had been designed to cover all of the languages spoken on the Green Isle: (in random order!) Irish, Scots Irish, and English. (Though my Scottish friends would always give me at best a mocking side glance whenever I said it, Scottish Gaelic originally came from Ireland. Either that, or both countries had the Internet in the fourth century, so close are they.)

The iron framework that used to girdle one of the rusty-colored gas tanks was still there, but the tank itself was gone. In its place was a shining new apartment cylinder—not an apartment "block," because it had to be shaped like a tank to fit inside its girdle. Cast into an iron plate on the base of the stanchions were the letters "London 1885." All the apartments had good views from their curved windows. (They are probably occupied by bankers and lawyers—certainly not retired civil engineers.)

Some of the buildings that used to flank the Grand Canal Dock in my school days were still there, at least in principle. A tall, apparently derelict building bore the words "BOLANDS FLOUR MILLS" in huge letters, the "L" and the "A" being hidden behind a nice little crop of trees growing from the gables.

But here is the most dramatic change of all: Where I remember drab railway lines, Dublin has built a new station from which young, well-dressed people stream out over green landscaped pathways to various new office buildings. Right beside the new train station is a posh new building decorated inside with large patches of vivid red, green, blue, and yellow: Google's European headquarters. On one of the upper floors is what appears to be a large gym full of hard-pushing yuppies. Facebook is not far away, but a plate on the wall of Google's colorful new office building says it all: "Google Docks."

* * *

Back to my school days in the 1950s. When we stepped off the train in Westland Row station we flashed our seasoner cards at the inspector manning the exit gate. He usually looked somewhat weary, was fairly short, and had a well-worn uniform with shiny cuffs and shiny sleeves. Nevertheless, these were offset by an acceptably near-white collar and a cap with a black plastic visor. Then we trotted down a sloping ramp, using most of our energy to resist gravity and to avoid bumping into slow-moving grownups. That brought us out on the street level beside the iron bridge that would take our train on towards the city center.

In the mornings the narrow passageway between the railway station and Saint Andrew's Church was always open to the public, so we used it as a shortcut to school. Later, when the morning Masses were over, the big iron gates would be closed, because it was actually on church property. But of course the church did not maintain this property for boys to take shortcuts to school: it was for making it easier for people to get into the church.

And the Christian Brothers had told us we should not pass so close to the church without dropping in on the way to school. So, dutifully, we ducked quickly into Saint Andrew's Church through the side door, dipped our fingers into a little holy water font, and shuffled quietly to a small altar. For a few moments we left the temporal world outside, gazed into the flickering votive candles, and passed ever so briefly into the abiding calm of meditation. Prayer, that is. We asked little rehearsed favors of those in the spiritual domain, such as getting help at being "good" and at not missing out on the joys of learning. Occasionally we dropped a big copper penny into the money box (noting with satisfaction the noise it made), lit a candle off someone else's wish-flame, and placed it on the rack. We often knelt close to some adult—typically a woman past middle age with her hair covered by a scarf—but we never asked ourselves what *their* world might have been like, or what favors *they* might have been asking from the other domain.

The Christian Brothers must have been glad that we had started our day off in such a positive way.

We definitely *needed* a good start, because we were still boys. Just outside the door of the church there was a wide wrought iron gate guarding the entrance to a flight of stone steps going down to a lower level. At the bottom there was another big gate guarding what appeared to be a passage under the church. How interesting! Better still, the entrance gate at the top was sometimes left unlocked…

Soon we were wandering through the dusky vaults under Saint Andrew's Church where some of those in the spiritual domain had left part of their temporal belongings behind.

Coffins!

What a surprise. The coffins were laid out in side vaults closed off from the main underground passageway by iron gates. Peering through the bars, we could see that some of the coffins were open. On testing the gates, we found that some of these were unlocked. That was too much to resist: Soon, we were inside the vaults staring into one of the open coffins. Staring at… *bones!* What else, you might say—since that's what coffins are for.

At the end of the main entrance there was a T-junction where passageways branched off left and right. We were afraid to enter these because the lights had not been switched on, and anyway we felt we were getting a bit too far from the entrance—too far from daylight and our familiar surroundings. But we did wonder how much deeper these tunnels went into the underground, and whether they led perhaps to some big labyrinth beneath the city. Usually, however, when we got this far we turned and ran quickly back to the exit.

Then we went to school.

One night, after one of these visits down into the vaults, Saint Andrew's took its revenge: I had the devil of a nightmare. I had gone in with some of my school pals when, to our horror, we found that somebody had locked the main gate while we were exploring the side vaults. We pressed our bodies up against the locked gate and curled our fingers in vain around the iron bars. We were trapped, and nobody knew we were there. Then the rats came. Their short, shrill squeals terrified us as we waited for them to start nibbling on our ankles. They were coming out of those dark passageways beyond the T-junction, the ones we had always been afraid to go into…

That was the last time I went down to the vaults on my way to school, but I did continue to offer a morning prayer at the little altar on the way to class.

I needed that.

It really is a minor wonder that *any* boy ever reaches the age of twenty-one without some disfiguring accident.

One day I was in the train on my way home for lunch. The train was slowing down for its stop at Lansdowne Road, and was just passing behind the rugby playing field. At that time they were building a new spectators' stand very close to the railway tracks. It was so big that the train actually had to pass through a temporary tunnel made of construction beams and shrouded in scaffolding. The steel bars of the scaffolding came very close to the windows of the train.

Now we have all read the signs (in Irish and in English) warning passengers not to stick their hands or their heads out of train windows. But those signs were for others, not for me, of course. I had been playing with a little brass weight attached to the end of a cord, salvaged from some old window frame. I had stuck my head and arms out the window and was playfully swinging the brass weight around in the air, with the cord wrapped around my big finger so it wouldn't fly away. I had completely forgotten about the scaffold-tunnel that the train was about to enter. The cord snagged on the scaffold and in a split second was violently whipped away, leaving me staring in astonishment at the big red circles marking where it had been coiled around my finger. This quickly turned to shock as I realized how close I had come to having my big finger brutally ripped off.

The lunch break was long enough for me to make a return trip home on the train every day. When we returned to Westland Row for afternoon classes, our shortcut between the railway station and the church would always be closed, so we walked along

Pearse Street and then under the old railway bridge that dated from 1834. It was a very sturdy bridge, and quite long—it had to be, since it supported an entire railway station with all its platforms, and the trains themselves when they rolled through. By the 1950s over a hundred years of rain had leached calcium from the joints between the limestone blocks, and this trickled down the walls like chalk scribbles on a blackboard. The acoustics were impressive: when a car or lorry entered the cavernous arch, there was a veritable explosion of road noise. The echoes seemed to answer each other as they bounced wildly off stone walls and roof, making decibel highs matched only by a modern teenager's car stereo.

At that time we classed any adult over about forty as an "aul'fella." The term had a very mild tinge of disrespect, but it was not derogatory. For example you would not use this term for an adult you knew and respected, such as a kid-friendly neighbor. (The corresponding term for those of the complementary gender was "aul'one.") We got used to sharing the footpaths around the old railway station with hardcore aul'fellas of the city in well-worn grey suits that one day had been their Sunday best, shirts without the detachable white collars, and baggy trousers. They were often bandy-leggèd and walked with an uneven gait. Nearly all had chronic smoker's cough. As soon as they reached the cover of the dimly lit arch, they would disgorge what was bothering their throats, right there on the footpath for all to see. (I am hoping the slang word for this product has lapsed out of use by now.) They could often be heard muttering to themselves as they passed—lost in their own world, a world so different from ours.

Occasionally you would come across an aul'fella talking to himself, that is, having a conversation with a person who was invisible to the rest of us. Dubliners had a fitting term for such a character:

"Ah yes," they would say, "he's gone natural."

That, too, was part of the city that mothered us.

Some of the most impressionable lines we had to learn by heart in English class were from Tennyson. They sang of a land where one could live effortlessly in peace among sea breezes and aromatic spices: the Land of the Lotus Eaters. A band of sailors on a very long trip, weary of battling the sea, give themselves over without a fight to the soft music they find in Lotos Land. We memorized their song:

> There is sweet music here that softer falls
> Than petals from blown roses on the grass,

Better still, there was free food and water there for the taking:

> Round and round the spicy downs the yellow Lotos-dust is blown.

Soon they start to forget why they went to sea in the first place, and ask themselves why they should not just stay there, on firm ground, instead of going back to sea and getting lashed by salt-laden spray as they pitch and roll in the waves beside the spuming sea-monsters:

> We have had enough of action, and of motion we,
> Roll'd to starboard, roll'd to larboard, when the surge was seething free,

Seduced by the spicy aromas, the gentle sea breezes, and the free food, they resolve to stay in the Land of the Lotus Eaters:

> Let us swear an oath, and keep it with an equal mind,
> In the hollow Lotos-land to live and lie reclined
> —Tennyson[3]

* * *

Going to The Row

On the 16th of June 1904 a man walked down Westland Row past the railway station where the steam trains puffed their plumy blasts of smoke and steam. He had plenty of time on his hands, and indeed his mind had been wandering much further than his feet that morning. He crossed over from Westland Row onto Lincoln Place and went into a chemist shop. His wife had told him to buy her some face lotion.

Immediately, he finds the atmosphere inside the shop very relaxing: sweet-smelling oils and scented soaps of all sorts, shelves stacked with little tins and boxes promising remedies for all the common discomforts of the body. Gee's Linctus Pastilles; Boric Acid Ointment; Sloan's Liniment. The chemist looks up the recipe he had filled for the customer's wife the last time.

"Sweet almond oil and tincture of benzoin," the customer says,[4] while his mind wanders to a pleasant memory evoked by those sweet aromas, "and then orangeflower water…and white wax also."

Like the sailors in the Land of the Lotus Eaters, he is overwhelmed by all the pleasurable thoughts and sensations around him and starts to forget why he went into the shop in the first place. He tells the chemist to hold the face lotion for him until later in the day, buys a bar of sweet lemony wax soap on a whim, and heads out of the shop to a local place where he can take a bath. The thoughts unleashed by the seductive sensations in the shop have now taken over his mind completely and he visualizes: in the hollow bath to lie, reclined on white enamel, soap-scented in lather under a gentle stream of tepid water.

I visited that same chemist shop in 2012. Over a hundred years had passed since that Dubliner was overcome by the sweet-smelling aromas inside, and fifty years since I had gone to the school only one street away. It was a sunny but cold October afternoon. A sign over the shop read:

Chemist | Sweny | Druggist

Inside, the shop appeared to be just as it was in 1904. They still sold lemon soap. The wooden shelves were stacked with colorful tins and bottles. The chemist stood behind the counter in a white coat and a red bow tie. But there *were* changes: the chemist was holding what appeared to be a glass of champagne in his hand—not a pestle—and beside him a young man was dispensing words—not drugs. Another thing: The countertop was covered with secondhand books.

Although the chemist shop in Lincoln Place is very real—made of bricks and mortar and wood and glass—the man who bought the bar of lemon soap there never had a real body made of skin and bones, for he is of course the prince of Dublin fiction, Leopold Bloom. And the face lotion was of course for that other fictional darling of Dublin, Molly Bloom.

Though Sweny's is only a few minutes' walk from my old school, I never even knew of its existence during the ten years I walked or cycled close by. Not that our English teacher was likely to explain Bloom's thought-wanderings throughout that long day. And for sure he was not going to have us memorize Molly's unguarded neural chatter in the last chapter of the book.

Sweny's stayed in business until 2009,[5] and, at least until 2013, when I visited it again, was kept open by volunteers. So it seems that the pure spirit of fiction has saved the pure bricks and mortar from the formidable forces of economics.

A nice triumph for art.

* * *

Around the age of ten we were taught how to sing the Mass in Latin. That was long before we started to study the Latin language, however.

We met around mid-afternoon in a big classroom, where about thirty of us stood in rows with our hands clasped safely behind our backs. We had a good music teacher—one with the skill and the will to capture the attention of a bunch of boys trapped in a classroom with one eye on the fast-disappearing light outside. He would first teach us how to memorize the Latin text, syllable by syllable. The Nicene Creed starts with:

Credo in Unum Deum
I believe in One God

Patrem omnipotentem, factorem caeli et terrae
Father almighty, maker of heaven and earth

Visibilium omnium, et invisibilium
And of all things visible and invisible

Lines learned by heart at age twelve tend to stay around for a long time, even if you hadn't understood them completely when you engraved them into your young brain. (And even if you had no understanding at all of how people fought and died in the 400s either to defend or to deny the tenets of this Creed.) But now I am glad we were taught this hymn because I can recall it fairly well whenever I hear a beautiful Credo by Palestrina or Mozart.

To help us memorize *invisibilium*, for example, our teacher would say:

"*'in-visi-bili-um;'* think of your friend Billy…*bili*…same thing."

Then he would rap his tuning fork on the stool and give us a "do" to get us all on the same key. The truth is we enjoyed singing this simple Gregorian chant together once the multi-syllabic Latin text came to us naturally.

All this was of course building up to a big occasion: High Mass in Saint Andrew's Catholic Church, Westland Row. We filed into the pews in the center nave and sang our guts out to a packed and devout audience. Any musical sins we committed were surely forgiven and absolved by the rich tones reverberating through the church from the pipe organ.

Religion has to be *lived* before it can be reliably understood. It cannot be learned from a book, or (as they say about a love affair) by having a trusted friend go through it for you and then tell you what it was like. To escape this treacherous ground, I invite you to decide for yourself on which level(s) religion is actually "lived": the physical, the rational, the emotional, or the one that is supposed to keep these three in balance—the conscious sprit (for want of a better definition).

Ireland was around 98% Roman Catholic in the 1950s. I was part of this majority—dunked in the holy water font as soon as possible after my first breath. After that we seemed to live our religion with every breath we took: at home; listening to the good lady down the road; with our country cousins; at Mass on Sundays. And in school: no less than a half-hour lesson on religion every day (that's two-and-a-half hours a week, a rigid schedule for any subject). The Christian Brothers painstakingly explained how to discern the different shades of right and wrong we might encounter in our everyday lives, a vital study in ethics for which I am still very grateful. But there were commercials: we had to accept on faith that our church was the one and only true church. This dogma was delivered with the same matter-of-factness as, say, the location of Australia on a world map. The Brothers took pains to assure us, however, that people from the other religions could get to heaven, too, if they lived just lives and followed the rules of their own religion. Nor did any adult outside school ever even suggest otherwise. *Et in terra pax hominibus bonae voluntatis*—and peace on Earth to men of good will. We certainly did not need to be told this last part: our daily lives outside school had left us with enough common sense and intuition to know that our non-Catholic buddies and neighbors had the same chances of getting the nod from *their* gatekeeper as we did from Saint Peter (all else being equal).

Going to The Row

How then did the idea circulate among us boys that if you walked around a non-Catholic church seven times you would see the devil? As shocking as this may sound at face value, we somehow managed to place it on a "parallel track" in our minds, as if it were some sort of a tale from medieval times or earlier and had nothing to do with our own lives.

But who was going to *test* it?

Nobody, it seems.

A few of us tried, once. We made one lap around a selected church, but soon into the second lap we spontaneously and unanimously gave up and ran off.

Mostly, I disliked school, and sometimes I thought it disliked me, too. Sitting in the train on the way to school I was always a bit uneasy—even anxious—numbed by the thought of leaving my delightful, free world and entering a classroom disciplined with dispassionate rigor. It's not surprising then that I was not much of a scholar, at least until my last two years, for a reason I will explain later.

November was always a tough month. Our long summer evenings were gone, we had enjoyed the delights of autumn, and now we had to face up to short, sunless days and—worst of all—the dulling reality of school. But two brilliant comic books came to the rescue: the *Beano* and the *Dandy*. As far as I can recall, the *Beano* came out on Tuesdays, the *Dandy* on Thursdays. My sister remembers that every week a friend from down the road would come to our house and swap one comic for the other, so each household only had to buy one of them.

The characters jumped out of the pages of these comics in vivid images: Dennis the Menace, with his untidy mop of hair, thick eyebrows sloping inwards above his riveting eyes, menacing smile, and his signature red-and-black sweater that spelled "DANGER." He was forever disrupting those around him, but always came out the worst himself in the end. Now I know that Dennis is your quintessential nightmare kid who can unhinge any otherwise peaceful and caring parent, teacher, or scout master.

We were all familiar with Dennis's tools: the catapult, the water pistol, the pea shooter. We made good use of the pea shooter ourselves, in fact: If you removed the ink refill from a ballpoint pen, you got a hollow barrel of just the right bore for propelling a hard grain of rice with a blast of air from the lungs. Better still, you could shoot in rapid-fire mode by keeping a small supply of rice grains in your mouth. Then, if things got slow during class, you could pick out a schoolmate and land a single, well-aimed grain-pellet on the back of the neck.

Desperate Dan was another regular—a giant of a man with a lower jaw like an anvil and a chest as big as an industrial boiler. He got this strength from eating pies made of one whole cow at a time, and he could pull a steamroller as easily as he could pull a child's pram. But poor Dan needed every bit of strength he had, for he was forever getting himself into a jam.

Roger the Dodger was an altogether different character: instead of brute force or blatant troublemaking, he focused on cunning to avoid doing his share. Alas, Roger, too, always got his just reward in the end.

How profound it is that Dudley Dexter Watkins and a few other creative artists in an English publishing house could have enriched our childhood so much.

One day something happened that radically changed my attitude to school. I was sixteen and we were all assembled back in class after a good summer holiday. I had gone on a week's bike ride to the southern city of Cork with two buddies. It had been my first major trip outside Dublin without my dad or any of my siblings.

Things were changing.

On that somber day back in class, after a summer of unprecedented freedom, the teacher was handing out envelopes with the results of an important exam (the Intermediate Certificate). He was a Christian Brother, that is, a member of a religious order dedicated to teaching, as opposed to a secular teacher. He walked through the rows of boys with a stack of envelopes in his hand, reaching out to each one as their name came up. He looked down at the pile, then at me, took a few steps forward, handed me my little white envelope and said:

"Congrats, Eugene."

I had achieved modest success in the exam. I was glad of that, though I had not realized its value when I had been preparing for it. (I had been much more focused on my first long-distance bike ride to Cork.) But something very unusual had happened that day: the teacher had called me by my first name. That was a big change. Up until then most teachers would simply call you by your surname. In my case they never bothered to ask for the correct pronunciation, and always got it wrong. This teacher was *different*—this whole thing was different. I took note.

He was our math teacher. When he introduced us to calculus, he did so with such passion that for the first time I began to feel that philosophy and mathematics were not so far apart after all. Calculus is probably the most powerful tool for solving problems in physics. But it cannot always be dished out to students with the same air of unassailability as, say, Euclid's geometry. That is because it relies on the theory of limits—what happens in that mysterious zone close to the "infinitely small." From the passion our teacher put into his calculus lessons it was obvious that he was saying "I know you will find this hard to believe, but trust me, it'll be okay." There would be an unusual quiet in class, as if the students needed more time to decide whether they would accept this guy or not.

Indeed he had good reason to caution us about this trap. Supposing a very mean person were to tell you that your life depended on determining *exactly* how fast you were driving right now, at this very instant (and the person who sold you the car had fiddled with the odometer). It would be no use measuring how far you had driven in the last ten minutes, say, because you might have stopped for a red light. (In Houston of course you would have sped up for that red light.) Measuring the distance traveled over ten minutes would only give you an average speed. To get your actual speed right now, you would have to measure the distance traveled over a very small "instant" of time. (The person demanding the answer is a stickler for accuracy, and there is a lot at stake.)

But how small a time step must you use to "get it right," and satisfy this guy? Our math teacher tried to explain the problem:

"I can keep making the step smaller and smaller. Forever, if I like. But no matter how small I make it, *you* can always make it a bit smaller. But not zero. You can't make it zero."

What does it mean—philosophically—that you can continue making something smaller and smaller *forever*, yet it can't become zero? Won't it ever come to some point where it just can't get any smaller, and then give you the "right" answer? Well, no, it won't (at least not yet), but the theory of limits will give you a fantastically accurate answer, one that will satisfy all but those probing the frontiers of theoretical physics. (With a bit of luck, that mean guy will not be into particle physics.)

Besides, it would probably not be wise to reduce any time step to zero even if you could: the present would vanish, leaving you with only the past, which you cannot change, and the future, which you cannot rely on. Thus a true instantaneous present is a bit of an illusion.

In the early 1700s the German philosopher Leibniz pondered this issue very carefully.[6] He poured his limitless energy not only into patriotism and statesmanship, but also into pure thought. One can imagine how this extraordinary man—broad-shouldered and bandy-leggèd—sank into a chair for several days or—just as easily for him—bumped along the roads of Europe in true "coach" class, to ponder these deep questions. Today Leibniz is probably best known for being one of two contestants for the honor of having developed calculus, the other being Sir Isaac of course.[7] (One could be forgiven for assuming that Leibniz owes his fame to the butter cookies that bear his name, the ones we love to eat at supper.) Perhaps not having had a steady income had something to do with his constant striving and his bottomless energies.

A devout Lutheran, Leibniz believed that when you had atomized matter as much as possible—and could not split it up any more—you would find "monads"[8,9] there. The substance of Leibniz's atoms, or monads, was much more spiritual than material. Each monad had its own soul. It had no extension—so it didn't have to worry about what would happen if its space shrank to absolute zero—yet it did have energy, and was capable of action. Although monads were free to act independently of each other, according to their own "perceptions and appetites," they lived in a perfect state of harmony with one another, a harmony that was pre-established from the beginning.

The source of the ideal harmony among monads was the Omnipotent Father—*Pater Omnipotens*—maker of heaven and earth...

Visibilium omnium, et invisibilium
And of all things visible and invisible

This brings to mind my old friend Billy who helped me learn how to articulate that creed in Latin.

Indeed, our math teacher successfully sowed the seed of intense curiosity in my mind. Today, over fifty years later, I have a pile of fascinating books[10] on my side table written by brilliant cosmologists trying to nail down that last bit of "essence." The bit just before you reach absolute nothing.

It is profound to think how Leibniz must have sat for days in his chair pondering his monads, not knowing that two hundred years would have to pass before the sacred independence of time and space, so rigidly guarded by Newton, would dissolve as quickly as a sugar cube tossed into a cup of hot coffee. And that quantum theory would walk on stage so slyly from the opposite wing to shatter any hopes of finding certainty for a long time to come. Even worse: That the physicist in Bern who stunned the world by showing that time and space were inextricably related, would soon get into hot water himself over the idea that physics was subject to the laws of probability. Was it really all just a gigantic throw of dice?

In 2015 this story is by no means over: in fact it appears to be just beginning. If you are looking to the far edges of the universe to find out how it works, you may be looking the wrong way: the secret lies in the "infinitely small."

Getting back to my high school math class. My teacher must have smiled secretly to himself when he saw that I had taken the bait for the mystery of infinite smallness. He eventually lent me his own textbook so I could study at home and get all this straight from the source.

Now I felt like a human being: I was in some way equal to this person—since he seemed to be implying I could understand the book as well as he could—yet I still had an idol to look up to. Thank you, Brother Collins.

One afternoon we had a little problem in class: the clock on the wall had stopped. What can a school class do without a clock? The teacher tried to get it going a few times, but each time the pendulum swung slower and slower until it came to a stop. The boys were of course in no hurry to get it going, and would have been glad to spend the rest of the class watching the teacher fiddling around with it.

Then one of my "pals" helpfully suggested that I might have been able to start it, because I was known for having a compulsion to takes things apart and put them back together again. But I had no idea how the classroom clock worked, my dad having wisely put our living room clock off limits and confined me to dismantling old alarm clocks. Nor did calculus with its fantastic theory of limits help me understand why time had come to a *complete* stop for our classroom clock.

Nevertheless I was in a spot to come up with something, because of the confidence the whole class had put in me: my schoolmate had set me up nicely. I reasoned that if I shortened the pendulum it would not have to swing out so far, and that the force thus saved would overcome whatever obstruction was causing the works to hang up. Adopting the demeanor of the master clockmaker guarding his professional secrets, I said I could fix it but kept everybody in the dark about my method. The teacher stood on his high stool again, stretched to his full length, and carefully lifted the clock off its nail. I tried my remedy—moving the big brass disk a bit higher up the pendulum—and the clock kept going. The teacher put it back on the wall. He was very curious to know what the secret was, so I explained that I reduced the pendulum's swing.

"Won't the clock go faster now?" he asked.

I was taken aback, because I really had not thought of that. I managed to wriggle free of the question somehow, possibly because we had spent enough time on the clock and we needed to get on with our lessons.

He was right, of course. Physics is kind to human intuition, and may smile indulgently upon it sometimes, but not to the point where it will exempt us from any of its rules.

Nor can I remember getting out of school any earlier that day. Or any other day, for that matter.

Another day in English class, it was my turn to recite poetry out loud to the whole class. At that time you had to memorize certain stanzas of poetry for your "eccer," short for "exercise," your homework. For some reason the teacher and most of the class had got distracted while I was reciting from "Gray's Elegy." Speaking of simple people who never had the chance to be educated, and were marked by simple gravestones, Gray says:

Full many a gem of purest ray serene,
The dark unfathom'd caves of ocean bear:
Full many a flow'r is born to blush unseen,
And waste its sweetness on the desert air.

When the distraction in class ended, the teacher saw that nobody had been listening to my recitation. He tuned to me for a few moments. Then, to bring the class back to attention, he borrowed Gray's last line above and said, with a smile:

"You're wasting your sweetness on the desert air."

This casual incident had the unintended effect of anchoring Gray's famous poem firmly in my mind. I still admire Gray's earthy assessment of those who are locked out of life's opportunities—opportunities for doing right as well as for doing wrong—by simply being poor:

Chill Penury repress'd their noble rage,
And froze the genial current of the soul.

His choice for how he would like his own epitaph to read is also loaded with meaning, though it took me some years to realize it:

He gave to Mis'ry all he had, a tear,
He gain'd from Heav'n (t'was all he wish'd) a friend.
—Thomas Gray[11]

For me, at least, the pearl of wisdom in the last line resonates with the central theme of Beethoven's Choral Symphony. This work jolted audiences and became the new axis of revolution for the Romantic Period in classical music, if of all music (if not of all art). Beethoven must have thought his urgent humanist plea could only be expressed by a full chorus of human voices as well as a full orchestra. Then he had the huge chorus give full vent to his theme using the words of Schiller, a

German poet and dramatist who had inspired him very much: "If your best shot in this life wins you [just one] true friend... [then you can join us in our heavenly joy]."[12] Schiller's actual words to describe true friendship are very catchy: "To be a friend's friend."[13]

The teacher's remark about my recitation actually had a subtle but charitable motive: acute shyness had often impeded me to the point where it was better—for everybody—that I wrote out my lines on paper. I had only got through the recitation so smoothly because nobody was listening.

When my dad was widowed and left with four kids, he hired a housemaid until he judged that the youngest child would be able to stay out of trouble at home while he was at work. I was that youngest child. By the time I was going to primary school we no longer had a housemaid (that is, I was no longer a threat). I have vivid memories of taking warm shepherd's pie from the oven when I came home for lunch; my dad would bake it and leave it there on low heat before going to work. Sometimes he would prepare a small snack to perk me up right after school was finished for the day. The essentials in any wintertime lunch box were hot tea and a soft, spongy sandwich. He would put these into my school case, which was made of pressed cardboard finished with an embossed faux leather design. It came complete with a tiny one-tooth key, to keep other boys out, so it really could have passed for an attaché case used by somebody working on a low-budget diplomatic mission.

I would welcome that little snack as I sat in Westland Row railway station after school. The waiting room was warm and cozy, with rows of long hardwood benches kept shiny by the constant traffic in sliding backsides. The benches seemed to beckon you to flop down on them and merge into the quiet anonymity of the common room. (Even schoolchildren get a dip around three thirty.)

On one of these dreary afternoons I was about to pick my spot on the communal bench when my school case slipped from my grasp. It fell onto the concrete floor with a sickening smack and, of course, when I opened it I found a soggy pulp of school book and warm tea. Vacuum flasks were made of glass back then.

This scene comes back vividly whenever I get that specific sickly smell of milky warm tea: the sadness about wasting my dad's caring effort; the lost lunch; the soggy, distorted pages of my school book; the disfiguring stains; tea dripping from my attaché case. Early sensations of smell do indeed appear to lock fast in your memory and remain there permanently hardwired to the emotions they came with.

In my school, "corporal punishment" was the norm in class. For us that meant that you got a stinging "biff" on the open palm of the hand, delivered with a wooden stick or a piece of stiff leather. This was your punishment for not doing what you were supposed to do, or for *doing* what you were *not* supposed to do. There were variations on this form of correction, such as turning the leather sideways so the hard edge would strike your hand—thereby delivering a more concentrated blow—or partially missing the palm and hitting the inside of the wrist—where the skin was much more sensitive. To be fair to the teachers, the last variation may have been caused by fatigue, or a bad aim, but the effect was still the same.

A certain very well-known teacher developed a method for delivering rapid-fire biffs: he simply swung his arm in circles from the shoulder, delivering a whack every time it landed on the boy's outstretched hand, like a Gatling gun.

Arguably, the worst punishments left no corporal marks at all. One day, when one of the boys fell short on learning some lesson, the *head teacher* had him stand up in his place, with fifty of his classmates watching in silence. After a studied pause, looking down at his own feet, and with an expression of disparagement on his face, the teacher said to the boy (and of course to the whole class):

"It must be terrible to be an eejit."

That, too, was part of the city that mothered us.

On another day in English class, the teacher was explaining the merits of a poem. Almost casually, he pointed out the poet's masterful use of contrast—as a figure of speech—to make a strong and indelible statement. Yeats was speaking about the "excess of love" that led our most famous former student, Pearse, and his colleagues, to shove a Declaration of Independence in the face of the British Empire. It was Easter 1916. Their rifles were no match for the gunships that sailed up the River Liffey to shell their positions, but in the end the big guns were no match for their excess of love:

> And what if excess of love
> Bewildered them till they died?
> I write it out in a verse—
> MacDonagh and MacBride
> And Connolly and Pearse
> Now and in time to be,
> Wherever green is worn,
> Are changed, changed utterly:
> A terrible beauty is born.
> —Yeats[14]

The contrast in the last line was so powerful that it stuck in my mind there and then. I had no inkling at the time how often I would meet those two words again long after I left school, and left Ireland. In fact I grew up (by sheer coincidence) in a house only a few minutes' walk from where Yeats was born, and I walked past it to my bus stop about a thousand times. I admit that this is only a vain attempt to claim something in common with the poet, but the fact is that I was not even aware of the coincidence at that time. And even if I had been aware, I certainly could never have imagined how often I would find others resorting to Yeats's words to describe ideas that transcend the superficial. Or how deep and how wide he probed into human nature, and how finely he distilled its essence. (As for how Easter 1916 could have stunned ordinary men and women into leaving their ordinary lives so readily, one need only read the sensitive and literate account left by an ordinary young man who walked through the debris field himself, and was changed radically: Ernie O'Malley.[15])

* * *

Somewhere around the mid-1980s, on a visit home from the States, I walked into Dún Laoghaire railway station, with the feigned confidence of somebody who had never left Dublin, and asked the clerk for return tickets to Westland Row Station. My composure was soon shattered:
"Do you mean *Pearse* Station?"
"Oh…is that what it's called now?"
It seems Pádraig Pearse had got due recognition since the days I walked the platforms of former "Westland Row" station. Well, good for him: that's better than having a little wooden cabinet on the wall with a soldier's tunic and a lock of hair.
As I re-acquainted myself with the city, I discovered that Connolly, too, had a railway station named after him, the one we used to call Amiens Street Station.

* * *

In my final year of English, I suddenly "discovered" Wordsworth (meaning I suddenly woke up to what the English teacher had been telling us about him.) There was something in one particular poem about the English countryside that resonated perfectly with my own love of the Irish countryside. That evening I dissected the poem word by word, phrase by phrase, and wrote a flowery appreciation. At the next English class the teacher singled out my write-up as being especially good. But my moment of classroom fame was short lived, for he added quickly:

"Did you do it yourself?"

I was surprised, but not discouraged, because Wordsworth was all that mattered to me.

The old desks in our classroom bore the evidence of heavy usage. The wood was heavily "distressed" by cryptic carvings, names of past pupils, scratches, scrapes, hacks, and ink stains. They had ink wells with sliding brass covers, so we were forever messing with the ink and sticking the pen nibs into the wood.

As an alternative to giving all my attention to the teacher, I would divert some of it to making a few marks of my own in the desktop with a penknife. Or I would embed some pieces of a discarded razor blade into the wood, varying the lengths so when you "plucked" them you got a tiny "do–ray–me." Then I would play crude little tunes, hoping not to draw too much attention.

This fidgeting was one of the reasons I did not get the most out of my school days, though it was mild by comparison to some others. The desks were built with strong cast iron legs and hinges. If addressed directly by the teacher, you had to stand up by flipping the seat so it wouldn't dig into the back of your straightened knee. If you didn't mind the discomfort, you could simply leave the seat in the down position and bend your knees slightly around it, being careful not to slouch. But in addition to responding adroitly to the teacher you had to keep your mind on the guy behind you. When the teacher had you in the spotlight, this fella might flip your seat up so when you sat down again you sat on nothing. You could not retaliate immediately because that would surely provoke an even greater disturbance, and anyway there was no guarantee that justice would favor either one of you.

Actually, if you sat on "nothing" you got off easy, because all you had to do was grab the desk on your way down and hold fast: by far the worst was when the very tip of your tailbone—the coccyx—landed on the cast iron hinge of the upturned seat. That *really* hurt!

One day, (let's call him) Cassidy was put on the spot to show his knowledge of some issue. When poor Cassidy tried to stand up, however, he found that he was severely handicapped: his legs had been chained to the desk. This was the work of the boy behind him, who had found a good use for his bicycle chain while waiting to get out of class.

These pranks usually went unnoticed, again because nobody wanted to attract any more attention in class than was absolutely necessary. But one day the sharp crack of a gunshot brought all work to a sudden stop. There was stunned silence as everybody turned their heads towards the end of one of the center rows. Gradually one boy emerged as the focus of all the stares. The teacher brought him up to the front of the class and demanded he hand over the weapon. It was a starter pistol. The type that fires blanks. He just wanted to liven the class up a bit, and he did.

That begs the question of whether our behavior was influenced by Dennis the Menace. A suitable question for a sociologist, perhaps, but my guess is that it was the other way around. That is, the writer of the *Beano* had probably been influenced by boys like us (maybe he *was* like us).

In The Row, the teachers were tested, too.

It was all part of the city that mothered us.

THE TUNNEL

The cavernous railway bridge under Westland Row station always made me feel like I was in a tunnel. Whatever daylight entered the tunnel was quickly neutralized by dark limestone walls streaked with calcium seeps. These reminded me of chalk scribbles on a blackboard.

In the 1950s we would meet some real Dublin "characters" here on our way to school. Some of them seemed to blend right into the character of the tunnel—people who were more at ease outside the glare of common daylight.

Nevertheless, when I revisited the tunnel fifty years later, my old school building was contrasted in stark sunlight, as shown in this photo. The railway station had been re-named Pearse Station, in honor of our most famous past pupil.

Photo: September 2013; digitally modified to show outlines.

SWENY'S CHEMIST

The Chemist shop famous for the imaginary purchase of a bar of lemon soap. Sweny's was only minutes away from the school that I attended for ten years. Neither Leopold Bloom nor his wife Molly was on our English curriculum, however.

To left and right of "SWENY" are the words "CHEMIST" and "DRUGGIST," respectively. "Sweny" rhymes with "Penny."

Photo: Lincoln Place, Dublin, 27th October 2012.

DISPENSING WORDS IN SWENY'S

A young writer[16] dispenses words to a little group of visitors packed tightly inside Sweny's. The Chemist looks on, holding a curious vial.

Volunteers have preserved the Chemist Shop as it was on the 16th of June 1904, when it sold lemon soap, Gee's Linctus Pastilles, Boric Acid Ointment, and Sloan's Liniment. (The Champagne came later.)

Photo: 27th October 2012.

THE OLD BESIDE THE NEW

This façade looks over the Grand Canal dock, only a block away from the new Google building. It has not changed since I used to cycle past it on my way to school in the 1950s, except for the fine crop of trees growing out of the gables.

Photo: September 2013.

---

[1] "Sandymount Halt," *The Irish Times,* 11th September 1937.
[2] Ewan MacColl, "Dirty Old Town" (1949). Refers to his birthplace, the town of Salford, near Manchester, England. The song was made popular by the Irish folk group The Dubliners, then recorded by many others as folk songs became popular again in the 1960s.
[3] Tennyson, "The Lotos-Eaters," *Poems,* 1842.
[4] Joyce, *Ulysses,* Chapter II, The Lotus-Eaters.
[5] Geraldine Gittens, "Ulysses chemist shuts after 100 years," 20th June 2009, http://www.herald.ie/news/ulysses-chemist-shuts-after-100-years-27915641.html, accessed 16th December 2012.

[6] *Encyclopædia Britannica Ultimate Reference Suite* (Chicago: Encyclopædia Britannica, 2011), under "Leibniz, Gottfried Wilhelm."

[7] There was much controversy over whether Leibniz co-invented calculus independently of Newton, or had seen Newton's work and borrowed from it. This caused a damaging gulf in the exchange of scientific information between British and Continental mathematicians.

[8] *Encyclopædia Britannica Ultimate Reference Suite* (Chicago: Encyclopædia Britannica, 2011), under "monad."

[9] Ibid., under "atomism."

[10] Among which my most cherished are by Brian Greene, such as "The Hidden Reality."

[11] Thomas Gray, "Elegy Written in a Country Churchyard," this version (with old spelling) from The Poetry Foundation, http://www.poetryfoundation.org/poem/173564, downloaded 17th May 2015.

[12] Schiller, "*An die Freude*" ("Ode to Joy"), second verse, (author's interpretation).

[13] *Eines Freundes Freund zu sein.*

[14] W.B. Yeats, "Easter, 1916."

[15] Ernie O'Malley, *On Another Man's Wound.*

[16] Denis Kehoe, reading from his novel *Traces of the Flood*, on 27th October 2013.

18

ETHICS IN MARBLES

We had a name for them: "useless grownups." I can still hear the sickening crunch as some useless grownup stepped on a chalk marble in our play ring. Or he would hit a glass marble with the toe of his shoe and knock it clear out of the game, off the footpath, and down the road. Maybe they had been lousy marble players in their own boyhood, we thought, and they still had some hang-up over that. They were men, usually around 30 years of age, but not quiet "aul'fellas"—our name for grownups so old that no further breakdown in age was necessary. They killed the mood quicker than an angry schoolteacher. When they saw us playing marbles on the footpath they would put on that air of adult superiority and pause ever so slightly (if we were lucky) as if to say "Make way for me, I'm an adult." Then they would stride right through our game without making the slightest effort to avoid scattering or crunching the marbles.

If nothing else, this prompted us at an early age to judge adult behavior and to classify grownups into "useless" and "friendly."

Marbles is an easy game to set up. All you need are the marbles, a smooth surface, something to draw a circle with, and some free time. The aim is to take your opponent's marbles and not to lose your own. The reward for a good shot was immediate: that colorful glass marble you knocked out of the ring became yours. Another reward was that you quickly learned some basic strategy and risk-taking skills, especially when you had misjudged those of your opponent and watched him pocketing marbles that had been yours just a few moments beforehand.

We played the game a lot when we were youngsters growing up in Dublin. At least when we were going through a certain phase, roughly the years after hopscotch and before the teen hormones arrived. A game of marbles could be started on an impulse, whenever we had some free time, for example on Saturday mornings or on schoolday afternoons before teatime. We would play on the concrete footpaths outside our homes, or on the hard clay surfaces of secondary access lanes. As the marble season progressed (usually in spring), a good player would carry around a big pouch of marbles and show them off to his pals.

Not all marbles were the same, though. The glass ones were the best. We called these glaziers (obsolete slang for "eyes"). At the other end of the scale were the little brown marbles made of chalk. I can't remember if we thought highly enough of these to give them their own name in boyhood slang. The glaziers were usually bigger than the chalk marbles—and considerably more expensive. I still remember the joy of getting a small plastic bag full of colored glass marbles. They were smooth and glossy, and the colors blazed into life when you put them in the sunlight. Inside each of these little orbs was a hidden world of twisted whorls and streaks. If you looked at them from a different angle, they would put on a different display.

On the other hand, the chalk marbles were soft and dull. They scratched very easily and would crumble without the slightest resistance when pressed between two hard surfaces. For example between the pavement and some grownup's boot. But of course the decision to spend pocket money on a bag of chalk marbles caused far less analysis and doubt, so cheap were they.

Over time, however, rough handling would reduce those nice smooth glaziers to little balls of frosted glass. Some even had small craters in the shape of convex shells. (Later I learned to use this (conchoidal) type of fracture to identify glassy minerals in the field, such as volcanic obsidian.)

The largest glaziers were about an inch in diameter, though most were only about five-eighths of an inch. We used the big ones as "shooters" to knock other marbles out of the ring. This is probably how they got so many craters.

Your ranking in the hierarchy of marble players was set by the size and quality of your collection: shooter-glaziers, normal glaziers, chalk marbles, sometimes even enormous steel ball bearings. You carried them around in a coarse fabric bag with a drawstring to prevent spillage from rough handling. At home, if things dragged, you could take all your marbles out of the bag, spread them on the floor, and make endless drives and shunts with them. This would preferably be done on a carpet rather than on linoleum or wooden floorboards, as otherwise they would roll away in all directions and with so much energy that you could never corral them. There was always a danger of getting into trouble with the adults, too, because they felt insecure sharing their walk spaces with randomly dispersed marbles.

You started a game of marbles by drawing the circle, which should be about three feet in diameter. If you were on a concrete pavement, you did this with a piece of schoolroom chalk. On a clay surface, you would use a sharp stick or piece of stone to inscribe the circle. Each boy placed a marble somewhere within the circle. The players shot as close as possible to a line to see who got to play first. The player shot his marble into the ring and tried to knock out somebody else's. If he succeeded, he kept the marble and got another shot.

The proper way to shoot a marble is to "knuckle down," that is, place the knuckles of your favored hand on the ground at the exact point you are allowed to start from. You hold the marble in your up-curled fingers and shoot it off with a flick of your thumb. But in our games we allowed an alternative method: press the marble to the ground between thumb and forefinger and propel it forward with a somewhat inelegant swish of your hand. This sort of shooting often led to accusations of "fudging"—letting the hand actually guide the marble the first few inches from the starting point before the fingers let go of it. Competitors would be especially watchful if the shooting distance was very short, because the opponent might try to illegally control the marble's course by hand almost all the way to the target. Looking back, this was not a very fair or ethical way to play marbles, and I wish we had not gone along with it.

As far as I remember, none of the neighborhood girls ever joined in our marble games. I cannot remember whether we ever invited them to play, either. It is most probable that they were not interested in playing marbles and, besides, they had more than enough games of their own.

Footpaths are for people to walk on, of course, so playing marbles on them brought challenges not related to the skill of the game. We needed all the width of the footpath to draw a decent-sized circle and still have room to deploy our marbles at strategic locations. Also, we needed to crouch or lie on the pavement ourselves to line up a shot. This did not leave much room for other users of the footpath, such as adults on their way home from a hard day's work. When a grownup walked up on our game of marbles, some sort of tacit agreement had to be reached. Ideally this would have been voluntary on both sides—adults and boys. Some grownups, however, were just not interested in negotiating *anything* with boys who were blocking the footpath. This taught us how to discern the key character traits that determined how to handle the various grownup types who intruded into our lives.

Age and gender appeared to be the two best factors for assessing the threat posed by grownups. (Yes, we practiced "profiling.") Other, more subtle factors were probably at work also, but these would have been hidden to us. There was one gentleman I will never forget: over six feet tall; spine upright like a back door; elegant posture; long, black overcoat. Rumor had it that he was an unimaginable eighty years old, and that he walked every day. When he approached the little knot of boys crouching on the pavement, he *always* had a hearty greeting for us. This was an instant signal that he was one of us—that is, he had never lost his boyhood, despite the seven decades between us. Then—as naturally as you could imagine—he would walk clear of our game and our strategically-placed marbles without putting a dent in his graceful rhythmic stride. Naturally, he ranked high in our grading of useful grownups. For all we knew, he could have been the marble champion of the year 1880.

Ladies would usually greet us with an indulgent smile, and either detour carefully around the marbles or step gingerly through them without knocking any out. They always had a telling smile on their faces stating that they were happy we were having fun. The ladies also scored high on our list of useful grownups.

Then there were the useless grownups—like the one described at the beginning of this story.

One Sunday morning I went to have a game of marbles with my pals in the clay-covered laneway. It was a crispy autumn morning, shortly after we had started another year in school. I was wearing "longers" for the first time, our name for long trousers. One usually made this transition at about age thirteen, and my pals were making the customary big deal of my passage into the longers phase of life. I can't remember how I played that morning, but my memory of that ribbing over my new longers placed a bookmark in my mind. It brought me over another little threshold on the road to adulthood, another piece of lost boyhood; another step closer to leaving marbles behind forever.

Ethics in Marbles

* * *

Now, well into my adulthood, I have to face a paradox: I will not let my grandchild, or any child in my care, play with marbles; I will not let marbles of any kind into my house, even under lock and key. This is because of a terrifying moment I lived through watching my own son nearly choke to death while slowly swallowing a marble.

So I will not pass on whatever marble-playing skills I learned crouching on the footpaths and laneways in Dublin.

But I will pass on the other lessons: Don't walk on children's toys. Walk a lot, with poise, and at a measured pace. *Never* miss a chance to relive your childhood.

19

THE SIXTIES—ALL CHANGE HERE!

It was 1964. That date meant nothing to us—just the next number in the calendar we used for counting the passing years. How could we have known that we were only a year away from the zenith of a revolution? A revolution that would not only shake up popular culture, but threaten the very matrix of society by rattling the pins that held it together, and then removing them altogether. This revolution was called The Sixties.

Anybody who was over twenty years of age in 1965 will remember how the value of money suddenly began to change in the early 60s. We who were still growing up in the 1950s never had to question the worth of a shilling or a pound—we trusted them as we trusted the sun to come up in the morning and to go down in the evening—and we had a very keen sense of what they could buy us in a shop. Prices were so stable that they could be factory printed on wrappers without fear of having to put new price stickers over them.

But the inflation of the 1960s went far beyond the value of money: it soon began to eat away at the very core beliefs that motivated us. For many, this turn in the road came up unexpectedly and without any warning signs. Long before the 60s were over, however, most people had to face the reality that things were changing all around them—things they thought never needed to be changed, or never could be changed.

We were having a great time that summer in 1964. We had been blessed with fine weather in Dublin and were taking full advantage of it. We hung out together in the city until the last vestiges of light had faded, then walked home in the warm night air. We were in our early 20s. It was nothing to spend all Saturday night playing vinyl records and doing party pieces. But, having been dyed Catholic at birth, before going home we would go to the six o'clock Mass on Sunday morning. It did not seem illogical to go straight from a party to a church and slide along the shiny pews behind demure middle-aged women in headscarves and men with creased, hard-worn faces. They probably got up that early every morning. For us it was fairly simple: We *had* to get a good sleep after the party. We *had* to go to Mass. It would have been un-Christian to expect us to get up at 11 am to catch the last Mass. So we went to the first Mass, and then we went to sleep.

After disbanding from the Mass, some of us agreed that it would have been a shame to waste all the sandwiches and soft drinks left over from the all-night party, so we regulars would meet again on Killiney Beach around mid-afternoon.

Yes: soft drinks, sandwiches, and Sunday Mass; that was the culture many of us still lived in then.

At that time I had no money beyond what I earned at a low-paid, white-collar job. My fiscal year started when I came back from my annual two-week holiday, broke, and it focused entirely on saving enough money over the next fifty weeks to go hitch-hiking in Europe again, for the remaining two weeks of that year. I would not have understood what the gold standard was, even if some Nobel economist had given me private lessons on it. And it wouldn't have meant anything to me if that economist had predicted that in 1965 the gold standard would begin the wobble that led to its historic collapse around 1968. (Besides, some equally famous economist would surely have confused me by predicting the exact opposite.)

The midsixties was a turning point in popular culture as well as in world economics, and in 1965 I was of course much closer to the world of popular culture than I was to economic theory and its predictions. But, even in the world of pop, when

I first heard Mick Jagger's pile-driving beat protesting his frustration at not getting no satisfaction, how could I have imagined that half a century later learnèd people in "serious" fields would still be using those pop lyrics to make crucial points? Crucial points in economic theory, even.

One Monday morning in 1963 I was settling down to work with my colleagues in the office. To ease into the new work week, we always started off with the ritual of telling each other what we had been up to on the weekend. This often fell flat, because, for example, I would get indulgent smiles at very best when I told them I had been hiking through frost and snow in the Wicklow Mountains. I, in turn, was bored to death listening to why Manchester United *should* have won the soccer game, and it would only get worse when I pointed out the cold fact that they had *not* won it.

But on this Monday morning one of the girls quickly cut all this short. While arranging her desk for work, she irrupted boldly, knowing full well that her story was going to trump everybody else's:

"Ah sure wait'll I tell yous what happened to *me*," she said, still looking down at her desk and arranging things, "I lost me shoe in the Carlton!"

"Your *shoe*? How'd ye do that?"

"We went to see the Beatles. The crowd went wild at the end and started pushin' and shuvin', tryin' to get up front. I was just lifted up and carried along. Me shoe came off and I never saw it again."

"Yer lucky that's all ye lost!" replied one of the soccer fans.

Beatlemania had come to Dublin, from just across the water in Liverpool. By that time there could hardly have been anybody under thirty who was not familiar with the "Yeah, Yeah, Yeah" refrain in "She Loves You." And for some over thirty or forty years of age those Yeah, Yeah, Yeah's were inane cries that caused them to shudder in fear of losing their values. Those same values that had produced the world that the newcomers were now enjoying.

The Sixties—All Change Here!

For me personally it was John Lennon's riff on the chromatic harmonica in "Love, Love Me Do" that had won me over. This was earlier—around 1962, I believe. Those hand vibrato and rolled tongue effects—as if John needed to prove he could do *that*, too.

Our troubled and rebellious hero James Dean had sped to his death in 1955. Buddy Holly had left us, too, in 1959. We took these losses personally, but also with a certain bewilderment, for we never thought anybody of our age could die.

I had still been combing my hair backwards—against the grain of the follicles. This was a vestige of the tabletop crewcuts we had got in an attempt to identify with our idols of the 50s. But now my admiration of the Beatles led to an almost unconscious move to comb my hair forward and let it grow. That was before everybody started to do it, and I was glad that it went down well.

The barbers began to worry.

In the afternoon of the 22nd of November 1963, I was plodding away at my accounting job in the same office where we heard about the Beatles having been rushed on the stage. About six of us, mostly in our 20s, shared the big office, which was brightly furnished and brightly lit. A colleague and I were especially prone to making quips to relieve the tension during work, and we always had one ear cocked to catch some unguarded word that might be turned into a good-natured joke.

But the break we got from work that afternoon was of an utterly different kind: the boss appeared in the doorway and announced that President Kennedy had been shot. (Kennedy, a Catholic, was revered in Ireland. Not long before, I had seen his handsome tanned face smiling from an open limousine passing slowly through a sea of admirers in Dublin's city center.) The boss in our office was a highly intelligent professional, and one of the best managers I have ever had, before or since. After we had settled down, he announced that we would say a Rosary. Still somewhat stunned, we all agreed without hesitation, for this was a perfectly reasonable suggestion (though it might be denounced today as religious discrimination). Soon we were all kneeling on the floor, resting our elbows on turned-around chairs, offering Our Fathers, Hail Marys and Glory-be's to help the unfortunate Kennedy find peace Up There.

In the meantime, one of the truck drivers was waiting outside in the loading bay, looking for somebody to sign off on some paperwork. Not finding anybody, he peered through the window only to see everybody down on bended knees. Later—quite pensive and subdued—he came into our office and told us that he admired how we Catholics had reacted to the tragic event. He was Protestant.

It was against all this cultural background that we met on a Sunday afternoon on the beach in Killiney—after one of those all-night parties (and after going to Mass early that morning). We always brought a transistor radio and had it playing away, the music blending with the endless squealing of seagulls, the sloshing of surf, and the sound of small children playing in the sand. Nobody had—or needed—any other means of playing music: cassette recorders had not yet arrived, at least not for us.

Looking back now, it is clear that one of the most extraordinary upheavals that "rocked" the popular culture of the 1960s in the UK had just begun: pirate radio.[1] This revolution had everything: loyalty and betrayal, political sabotage, old-fashioned sabotage of the sledgehammer kind, hijacking on the high seas, shipwreck, white-hot business rivalry, promotion of love and tolerance tinged with eastern mystic philosophy. It also had that ingredient critical to the success of any revolution: popular support.

Ronan O'Rahilly, a businessman and promoter of unpopular popular music, had created his own record label because the established labels would not record one of his protégés, Georgie Fame. But the government-regulated BBC would not play Georgie Fame because he was not an established artist. Radio Luxembourg was broadcasting popular music to the UK from mainland Europe—and therefore outside the control of the BBC—but it refused to play O'Rahilly's label because their time slots had all been bought out by major labels.

Something had to change; this *was* the 60s, after all.

O'Rahilly had seen a photo of the then young Caroline Kennedy cavorting in the Oval Office, and, he imagined, disrupting the government of the most powerful nation on earth by distracting the man who headed it (her dad). He liked this image, because he was planning to do some disrupting of government himself. On Easter Saturday 1964, following the leads of Scandinavian and Dutch pirate radios, his Radio Caroline started broadcasting from a ship moored off the eastern coast of England. Its first live deejay record was "Can't Buy Me Love," by the Beatles.

Radio Caroline was Britain's first commercial radio station. After only three weeks of broadcasting, a Gallup Poll showed that it had nearly *seven million* listeners in the United Kingdom.

The BBC was forced to change.

The vessel MV *Caroline* had been registered in Panama and was operating in waters outside the territorial limits of the UK. So, by design, it was also operating outside the laws that regulated the ears of those for whom its broadcasts were especially tuned: the maturing 1960s young.

No surprise, then, that Radio Caroline did not get much love or tolerance from the BBC, or from the British Government: a piece of grit had been slipped into their comfortable oyster shell and was grating against their tender insides. But that same gritty grain quickly became a lustrous pearl dearly cherished by almost everybody I knew around my own age, in that tumultuous year of 1964.

Until then we (in Ireland) had relied on the popular music broadcast by Radio Luxembourg to fill what we saw as an obvious, gaping hole left by The BBC and the Irish national broadcaster, Raidió Éireann. This missing "sustenance" probably resulted from too much entrenchment in the pre-'60s culture. But it wasn't that we didn't value the excellent broadcasts that the national stations made in *other* areas of culture: the traditional folk music recorded by Raidió Éireann in farmers' kitchens; the BBC's hilarious Goon Show; its chilling Journey Into Space (where astronauts get lost in time travel, make a desperate landing on a strange planet, and with their last few gulps of oxygen, open the hatch of their spaceship: Can we breathe the air on this planet?).

And much more: the BBC had opened my mind with ponderous discussions hosted with beguiling ease on its Third Program. One night its distant AM radio signal brought Beethoven into my kitchen and caused me to stop in wonderment at that new sensation. These are only some of the programs that had us glued to our kitchen radios in the 1950s.

It was just that our world was changing, and the state-run radio stations were not.

Nor was Radio Caroline the first[2] to recognize that things were changing—not by any means: Radio Normandy and Radio Luxembourg broadcasted popular music to England before World War II; Radio Mercur had broadcast from a ship off Denmark in 1958, and several other transmitters had cranked up in Scandinavia. In 1960—four years before Caroline—Radio Veronica sprang to life off the Dutch coast from an old lightship with the wonderful name *Borkum Riff.*

There was nothing new about young people trying variations on their parents' beliefs and culture, but why was it so intense this time? Perhaps these parents had put so much of their life force into home and family after World War II that they simply had nothing left to spend on taking care of a revolution. But, whatever had caused the breakaway to be so intense, it's clear that when the government tried to silence Radio Caroline some years later, it miscalculated or ignored the power of pop when combined with the power of the vote: eighteen-year-olds had got the vote in 1968...

And no government can regulate against popularity.

That Sunday afternoon in the summer of 1964, on Killiney Beach, we were getting a good AM signal from Radio Caroline. She had left her spot off the eastern coast of England and was now right beside us in the Irish Sea. (On the way to her new mooring off the Isle of Man she had caused a lot of buzz by sailing close to Dublin and playing requests from Irish listeners.)

One song dominated the airwaves that afternoon. Its chords seemed to go straight to your inner private feelings like a friend who had permission to enter without knocking.

It was "The House of the Rising Sun."

Eric Burdon's strong vocals seemed to be rising and falling as if they were being carried on the capricious sea breeze. An open beach tends to swallow sound, because there are no echoes to amplify it, no resonating objects to color it, but the song was still sharply punctuated by the crisp guitar picks of The Animals. I was not conscious of Eric's slight British accent then, nor would I have been able to place New Orleans on a US map.

Looking back, it's possible that the song's popularity with the deejay was boosted a bit by Caroline's founder Ronan O'Rahilly's close acquaintance with the lead singer Eric Burdon. But even if it was, then more power to O'Rahilly, because so many artists' works might never have reached us through the miracle of radio without Caroline in the UK and her sister pirate ships in Holland and other countries.

A year or so earlier I had passed through London on one of my hitch-hiking trips to the Continent. A big poster dominated the window of a record shop near the youth hostel where I was staying. It showed water splashing down a sinewy mountain stream quite typical of the region. A thick coating of moss covered the bed of the stream, turning everything into a restful dark-green evenness. Except for a few well-rounded stones that stood out bright and clear: The Rolling Stones.

The faces arranged around the image of the stream bore those then new expressions designed to set the pop singer clearly apart from the old mold: an ever-so-faint trace of a self-satisfied smirk, not a bit boastful, but disarmingly admirable. The poster said that those guys had no intention of staying put and gathering moss.

They didn't.

But, to further date these events, Mick and the boys had yet to blast their way onto the pop scene and into pop history with that now legendary "I Can't Get No Satisfaction."

Nor was it only in popular music that the spirit of the young was breaking through in bolder forms of self-expression: the bikini had arrived in Dublin. (This was only six years after 1958 when the nuclear bomb tests on the Bikini Atoll[3] had ended, leading us into the Nuclear Age, and—from the fashion salons of Paris—the Age of the Two Piece Bathing Suit.

In fact, one of the girls in our beach group was wearing a bikini that day. The lads pretended that it was normal, not wanting to be accused of being old-fashioned enough to even comment on it. Much less to be caught glancing slyly.

After listening to the ballad of New Orleans five or six times and loafing in the sun until we felt we were natives of the Riviera, it was time to go for a dip. Even in the best of summers the water is colder on the east coast of Ireland than on the west. (Warm water does indeed reach Ireland from the Gulf of Mexico—where I am writing this—but it is diverted up the west coast. Thus it warms her belly without quite taking the chill off her back, the eastern seaboard.) Although Killiney Beach lies somewhat sheltered in its little cove, I suspect that the water is kept cool by a longshore current running not too far off that cove. None of this geoscience would ever have kept us from swimming there, of course. At least not in the summer: Did men not swim all year round at the Forty Foot in Sandycove, after all?

So we ran across the pebbles, splashed through the surf, and started leaping over the waves. We must have looked a bit like dolphins. The girl in the bikini looked a bit like a mermaid. The waves were not very large—just high enough for us to frolic and throw a ball around. After the initial shock of hitting the cold water, I got that pleasant rebound where you actually feel warm. This is relative, of course: you *are* warm, but only by comparison with the shock on first entering the water. Then suddenly, with no warning whatsoever, both my legs locked tight: a cramp. I was no longer able to stand on the bottom, or swim, because my legs had become dead weights. Luckily, the water was only up to my chest. I treaded my arms rapidly through the water, propelling myself towards the shore like some strange fish-animal. I yelled to alert my friends. They were not far away, and soon were gripping my arms and torso to stop my legs from dragging me down. It was not far from the shore, but that little stretch of water looked much different now. As soon as we reached the surf line I lay face down on the sand to get some strength back. I stayed there motionless for about twenty minutes until the cramps died away—still face down, my mouth digging a small hole in the watery sand like a flounder.

I guess that put a damper on our little gathering for the day. Eric Burdon kept on singing about the house in New Orleans, and the guitar chords kept clanging. But we headed home. As we stood outside the changing booths waiting for our buddies to come out, a woman who happened to be waiting there too, said:

"Isn't that awful now. Did ye see that lad they pulled out of the water…lyin' there on the beach. He must be drowned."

I quickly let her know that I was that lad, and that I was OK.

"Oh…! Well thanks be to God!" she said, her eyes rolling up to God, too.

Then, as we were walking back up the steps to Vico Road, one of my mates told me with a badly concealed smirk that the girl with the bikini had lost her top in the grapple to pull me ashore.

"Oh?" I said, "I didn't know that."

How could I have noticed that, lying face down on the sand?

* * *

In spring 2013 Mick Jagger was still performing live, still tryin' to get some satisfaction. The Stones still ain't gathered no moss. Out of the four lads from across the water in Liverpool, only Ringo Starr and Paul McCartney are still with us. I heard Paul chatting on NPR recently and he was doing great, still making music.

    I still get that same thrill when I hear the harmonica riff in "Love, Love Me Do."

    I still don't understand the gold standard.

EPILOGUE

Today is the 9th of April 2014. Fifty years later, Radio Caroline is still playing pop music. While writing this I paused for a few minutes to tune in, and caught Joan Osborne singing her hit "One of Us."

This brought me back to a much earlier event that I now realize is strongly related to the 1960s revolution in popular music. I was casually listening to a radio quiz on the BBC—probably in the early 1950s—when the young contestant was asked to name a new electronics device that had recently been invented. It offered a powerful new method for controlling the flow of electricity: it could either speed it up, or slow it down—transmit it, or resist it.

"The *transistor*," came the correct reply.

The transistor was also very small, and it used very little energy.

So, just as it was undreamed of in 1950 that transistors would reduce the size of the kitchen radio to that of a portable lunch box by 1964, in that same year Ronan O'Rahilly probably never dreamed that fifty years later the transistor would allow me to listen to his Radio Caroline five thousand miles away, live, on the Internet.[4]

No more searching for 199 meters on the AM dial, as we did on Killiney Beach in 1964.

Editing this on the 20th of April 2015, and listening to NPR, I heard Paul McCartney induct Ringo Starr into the Rock and Roll Hall of Fame.

And on the 24th of May 2015, The Rolling Stones kicked off their latest tour with an energetic show in San Diego, California.

RADIO CAROLINE

This is the MV *Ross Revenge*, Caroline's third ship, in 1983. The unbelievably tall radio mast shows how determined the founders were to keep Caroline on the air. Unfortunately, Britain's 1987 hurricane mortally wounded this mast, and a few weeks later it went crashing into the sea. Caroline was silenced, but not for long. The radio engineers strung copper wire from the funnel and jury-rigged a spindly tower on the stern to restore a signal.

A new fiberglass mast caught fire, broke in two, and fell into the sea as soon as power was switched on. Volunteers solved these problems by bolting several small tower sections together. They had found them in a scrap metal yard and smuggled them out on small fishing boats.

No sooner had they made peace with the laws of physics, however, than they had to face lawless hijacking and sabotage by Caroline's opponents. Raiders took control of their vessel, smashed their equipment with sledgehammers and metal grinders, and silenced their transmitters. The British members of the crew refused to abandon their vessel.

Fourteen months later Radio Caroline came to life again using homemade transmitters.

In 2014 I could listen to Radio Caroline from my home 5,000 miles away in Houston, Texas. On the Internet, of course.[5]

Since 1991 the *Ross Revenge* has been cared for by enthusiastic supporters, who turned her into a floating museum.[6] Photo: eylard@eylard.nl.

VERONICA LOSES HER ANCHOR

Radio Veronica's transmitter ship MV *Norderney* pitches wildly as a storm drives her helplessly towards the shore. Earlier, a crew member had taken the microphone after the deejay had read the rest of the news, assuring wives and family on land that there was no cause for panic: they had stopped taking on water and rescue boats were alongside.[7] All made it home safely. It was the 2nd of April 1973.

Source: Endnote[8]

VERONICA STRANDED

A few days after the storm on the 2nd of April 1973, Veronica lay stranded beside the sand dunes on Holland's famous Scheveningen beach. I happened to be living nearby at the time and went down to see the pirate radio that had endeared itself so much to me. She looked peaceful there, though eventually she would have to be turned seawards to avoid being breasted by incoming swells. Luckily, Holland does not have a rocky shoreline, and they were able to refloat her.

Source: Endnote[9]

---

[1] Mike Kemble, "Radio Caroline – History," http://www.mikekemble.com/caroline/caroline4.html, created: 5th February 2003.
[2] "Before Caroline," *Offshore Echos Magazine*, http://www.offshoreechos.com/Caroline%2060/accueil.php?id=0, accessed 9th April 2014.
[3] "Bikini Atoll Nuclear Test Site," *Unesco*, World Heritage List, http://whc.unesco.org/en/list/1339.
[4] "Listen," *Radio Caroline*, http://www.radiocaroline.co.uk, broadcast 9th April 2014.
[5] Ibid.
[6] http://www.rossrevenge.co.uk/history.htm, accessed 19th January 2015.
[7] Henk Hendriks, "Radio Veronica 2 april 1973," *YouTube*, http://www.youtube.com/watch?v=9G5iilCiZlw, accessed 19th January 2015, Dutch language.
[8] Idem, video freeze frame.
[9] Harry KrisKras, "*Nu 41 jaar geleden* [right now, 41 years ago]," www.radiodagblad.nl, online report, 2nd April 2014 at 8: 54 pm, under "Harry KrisKras @ 20:54:00, Categoriën: PIRAAT berichten over (illegale) radio [Categories: PIRATE reports on (illegal) radio]," Dutch language, accessed ca. October 2014.

20

MY FIRST BIKE

It was Easter Sunday. I was catching last Mass. Sandymount Catholic Church was packed and the air was getting stale from so many exhaling lungs. Dead quiet descended over the bowed heads as the priest went through the most solemn part in the liturgy, the Consecration. This was my favorite part of the Mass—a still point where you could think deeply, on your own. But this time I needed to get out of the church quickly and was just hoping that the Mass would not last too long. I was glad it was not Father O'Hare who was saying Mass, because he was so slow you could count on an extra fifteen minutes when he did. (That's why we nicknamed him Father *O'Snail.*) I had not committed any mortal sins that week, so I joined the people shuffling up to the altar for Holy Communion. After receiving the spotless Eucharistic host I filed back to my pew and bowed my head in prayer. The Christian Brothers at school had taught me to do this. But this Sunday I was having trouble transcending the temporal world for the one where material things did not count.

Because all I could think of was my new bike.

The priest finished his silent reflection, gave us a final blessing, and dismissed us with a message of peace. I was excited in the extreme now because I had kept my pledge to give up some things for Lent and, besides, the solemn Latin Mass had made me feel good about myself and everything around me.

Nor was this just a spiritual thing: my new bike was waiting for me at home.

I had a bit of a nose cold, but that was incidental and would not slow me down one bit as soon as I got home and jumped on that bike.

It had a Latin name—*Vox Populi*, "Voice of the People." Latin was taught in secondary schools at that time and it would have been understood by a lot of people. Maybe they figured using a classic language would connote a bit of class. If so, it worked on me.

I had been campaigning a long time with my dad to have a racing bike. He relented and I was given a budget. I did not care at all about matching or beating the models that my friends had—I just wanted to have my *own* bike. A bike would give me unbelievable freedom: freedom to ride outside the bus routes of the city, and even in the hills of Dublin County and Wicklow.

Before getting the bike, my pals had told me to go to a special shop near Capel Street in downtown Dublin. This shop had a great collection of colorful sporty bikes. A somewhat aloof shopkeeper showed me the models that he judged would be in my price range. (He probably thought I was just looking and would never be able to buy any of the bikes.) They were hanging upside-down by their front wheels, like slaughtered steers in an abattoir. Mindful of my spending limit, and not letting the very expensive super-light racing bikes infect me in any way, I settled on the metallic-blue Phillips Vox Populi.

It was to be my Easter present, a few weeks before my sixteenth birthday, in 1958. As soon as my dad gave me the okay (and the money) I took a bus into O'Connell Street. It was the last bus I would take for a while, I hoped. Hurrying down Moore Street past the fruit stalls, I barely heard the racket made by the women shouting out their sales pitches in deep-grained Dublin accents:

My First Bike

"Apples and ord'n-ges only tuppens a piece! Get your apples and ord'n-ges here!"

I brought the shopkeeper over to my pre-selected bike and paid for it with the big one-pound notes my dad had given me. Then I wheeled it out of the store like a proud father rolling his firstborn out of the maternity hospital in a pram.

As soon as I got home from Mass on that Easter Sunday, I just *had* to show off the new bike to my pals. They lived just over a mile away, near Sandymount Green. I rode up and down the road, and cautiously let them take a spin on it. Unlike the staid bike models of the 50s, this bright-blue metallic wonder had a nifty set of gears and a shiny gear-change lever on the handlebar. There were two bottle holders on the handlebar, with lightweight aluminum flasks to carry drinking water when you went on long trips. The pedals had straps that fit tightly over your feet so you could pull up with one foot while pushing down with the other. Great for hills! And it had that essential distinguishing feature of the racing bike—dropped handlebars!

My pals all made the required Ohs! and Ahs! as I exhibited my bike with unrestrained joy, not tainted by any show-off stuff.

My nose cold persisted throughout the day, but that did not in any way dampen the exultation over my new status: I now had my very own bike.

The next day, Easter Monday, I went into the garage and took the bike to pieces completely. I dismantled anything that could be unscrewed, unlatched, or unpinned until the bike had revealed all its secrets to me. Soon I presided over an array of nuts, bolts, levers, ball bearings, cotter pins, sprockets, handlebars, a saddle, two pedals, and a metallic-blue tubular skeleton. I spread them all out on the floor until they looked like an exploded view of a car engine from a repair manual. My father came into the garage but quickly resigned himself to what I was doing. I think he understood only too well.

Then I put the bike back together. I noted carefully how the ball bearings were nested into a groove in the hub of the wheel, how the nut holding everything together needed just the right tension for things to work right—loose enough to allow the parts to move freely, but tight enough to stop the wheel from wobbling. I noticed how little teeth known in bike language as pawls would "bite" into a sprocket in the wheel hub to drive it when you pedaled, but would let go as soon as you stopped pedaling and started to freewheel. Very clever. And that was the clicking noise you heard when flying down a hill. Now I would be able to diagnose any problem instantly, and fix it.

But what was more important, it relieved my compulsive urge to know how the bike worked.

Over the next eight years I remained fused to my bike. It was part of me—like a silent brother who was always there for me. The very thought of going out the Wicklow Road on my own was exciting, because it triggered images of heathery wilds, evergreen forests, and mountains with mysterious rocky crags near their lofty tops. But in the 1950s the Wicklow Road was still a narrow route that twisted and turned to conform to the largely unaltered ground it was given, or to cross a river. Once you got past Bray, however, there was a fairly straight but very steep ride up to Kilmacanogue and Kilpeddar, then, up–up–up–up–and–up to Newtownmountkennedy. (This town's long name was sung to the tune of "La donna è mobile," when you got your breath back.)

What made this so exciting was that you were able to explore all the wild scenery with your own buddies, without having to wait until the grownups could take you. On the way back, the hills would return the energy you had put into them and let you glide down the smooth tarmacadam racetrack at incredible speed, your head almost touching the front wheel. At least until you came to the River Dargle: at that time there was no freeway, and the main road twisted over the dogleg bridge that today is an access road.

When the summer holidays were over I started to go to school on my bike, instead of taking the train as I had done for years. It was only about three miles to Westland Row. Once I arrived I would wheel the bike down a long corridor covered with well-worn linoleum, carry it over a few flights of steps, and place it in a big bike rack. There was not much fear of your bike being stolen in those days.

The release from school in the afternoon was always a happy time. Riding *home* from school was of course more fun than riding *to* school. On the way to school in the mornings, I usually had a foreboding of untempered discipline and of being force-fed subjects I didn't take to naturally. Now, of course, I wish I had taken to them. In any case, cycling home brought relief from the downer of school discipline. That was true even when we passed through the "wind tunnel": a section of Grand Canal Street where Boland's Flour Mills rose up suddenly like one wall of the Grand Canyon. The huge brick façade tunneled the wind and slammed it into your face as you headed home. All you could do to avoid being blown off course, or stalling in your tracks, was to bend low, squint forward, grip the handlebars tightly, and push hard.

Sometimes I rode home with a particular school pal who was very athletic. He would go all out in the wind tunnel to prove his strength. The first time we went through it together I tried to finesse my way out of this tacit challenge by not breaking the rhythm of my speech (thus not letting my distress show) while at the same time pedaling like mad. But, eventually, I had to plead for a break:

"Boy...(pant)...the...(gasp)...wind...(pant)...sure is...(gasp)...strong today!" I labored.

"Yeah—that's why they call it the "wind tunnel," he responded, without a hint of strain, as if we were relaxing on a lawn chair watching a game of badminton.

After you crossed the bridge over the River Dodder, you would be rewarded with a pleasant glide past the colorful shopfronts of Ballsbridge. But on Merrion Road you would have to keep a keen eye out for tramlines. For although the old trams had disappeared from the road a good ten years before I got my bike, their rails had not disappeared: they remained embedded in the surface of the road. If your wheel keyed into the groove that ran alongside the rail you would get a sickening, sinister feeling of having lost control over your steering (if not your life). All you could do at that point was brace yourself for the fall that was certain to come.

So, as you passed the professionally maintained lawns and shrubbery of the Royal Dublin Society on Merrion Road, you had to stay on the lookout for the iron relics of the Dublin tramways. But here—as in so many other areas of childhood—the "hot stove rule" applied: once you got caught in the rails and hit the road (once you touched the hot stove), the shock inoculated you from ever getting caught again.

It is worth digressing a moment here to the passing of the Dublin trams. I was seven years of age when they were taken off the road, in 1949. That was probably the best age to travel by tram, because one of my strongest childhood memories is the excitement of riding in the open top as the tram clattered along the rails.

By the time I got my own bike, the Dublin Tram had of course been replaced by the iconic British-style double-decker bus. Except that in the Emerald Isle our busses were green. At least in the fifties they were; the drive to have everything painted green wore off in later decades.

The fat rubber bus tires that replaced the iron wheels could drive back and forth over the old tram tracks as if they were not there. More to the point, diesel power set the busses free of having to stay on a tight line in order to suck electricity from fixed overhead wires: now they could weave all over the road as they pleased.

My First Bike

In fact, the fearless Dublin bus drivers got more out of the British busses than their designers had intended, so artful were they at darting in and out of traffic lanes. This is not to criticize the Dublin bus drivers. Not at all: a workable mutual understanding had evolved between cyclists, pedestrians, and bus drivers. This could have been because, when bus drivers were off duty, they probably rode a bike themselves (cars being still out of reach for many). Never did I feel threatened by a weaving bus; challenged, yes, but threatened, no.

Nor were ordinary cars a threat to us cyclists, at least not nearly as much as they are now. This was a time when nearly every Dubliner got on a bike at some time or other. It was natural. Those who drove cars would instinctively put themselves in the saddle of the cyclist. They knew that a cyclist about to overtake a parked car could swerve into their path quickly, without looking behind for approaching cars. The proportion of motorists to cyclists was of course much lower then, and I cannot recall being able to avail of a single dedicated bike lane.

But there are no guarantees, and life can be shockingly, unexpectedly, and inexplicably tragic: in Sandymount Village one youth did lose his life to a bus. I do not know the exact circumstances of the accident—what unfortunate error was made—only that the youth met a violent death under the wheel of the bus.

Fortunately my encounters with cars and road surfaces were relatively minor. One wet Saturday afternoon I was passing Trinity College, on Nassau Street, when a traffic Garda (policeman) suddenly signaled a stop. It was one of those drizzly Dublin days that made the city roads very slick. I braked hard, the front wheel locked, and in a split second I came crashing down, providing a nice spectacle for the motorists sitting cozy and dry in their four-wheelers. Concern turned to a "That'll larn ye" after they saw that I was able to get back on my bike unaided.

I had a closer call one night coming back from the suburban village of Rathfarnham. Approaching the T-junction at The Appian Way I aligned myself correctly left of the road centerline for a right turn (Ireland drives on the left). A car came skittling around the corner very fast, saw me at the last second, and swerved into a lamppost. The driver crunched his nose on the steering wheel. (Seatbelts were a long way off then.) The door of the crazy car swung open from the violence of the turn, knocked my bike from under me, and left me in the air. I came down. The driver had a broken nose. I had a broken wheel. I was lucky not to have a broken neck.

Going back to our cycling trips into my belovèd County Wicklow. At first we would not venture very far—perhaps only to The Scalp. This is a V-shaped gash in a ridge gouged out by an Ice Age glacier crunching its way across Wicklow. Luckily for thousands of Dublin daytrippers, the glacier left a neat little valley with just-climbable slopes exposing large jagged boulders. Those boulders that had not already broken free of the earth, and gone to the bottom of the valley, were poised for their turn to roll. On the narrow road at the bottom, graphic signs warned you to look out for fallen (or was it fall*ing*) rock.

There was still plenty of safe ground, however, and in the long Saturday evenings of the Irish summer we often had céilí— get-togethers with traditional dancing. These were held in a simple community hall near the entrance to the valley. Inside, well-worn floorboards provided that characteristic woody-musty smell of a country gathering place. Between dances, the girls would sit on a bench lining one wall, the boys on the wall opposite. The dancing was lively, with plenty of hops, skips, and swings to make the floor boards creak and the dancers laugh out loud. There was a lot of mixing and changing partners, or as Yeats described it, we were

> Weaving olden dances,
> Mingling hands and mingling glances
> —Yeats[1]

Further south, our big glacier friend had carved out another recreation area for us: the Glen of the Downs. This long scar was in line with the other one, The Scalp, showing the path the glacier must have taken. It was a little farther afield, but still well within the reach of an easy daytrip. We were not sensitive to any need for meeting or beating specific long-distance standards: we just wanted to have fun, and we had lots of it.

On the east side of the Glen of the Downs there was a stand of dense trees. In the autumn the glen had a colorful carpet of fallen leaves. We would rest our bikes against the wall by the old valley road and climb up the slope. Soon we would be enjoying the strange silence of the forest, where decaying leaves and deadwood twigs muted all sound. In a few weeks the trees would be completely denuded and the comfortable autumn air would be replaced by the chills of winter. On the crest of the valley were the ruins of a small gazebo—a little turret-like stone building with several windows that offered a privileged view of the valley below. It was said that a landowner had built the gazebo there for his daughter, who had tuberculosis, hoping the healthy Wicklow air would bring her some relief. We gulped down lung-fulls of that free air as a reward for scampering up the slope.

Around midsummer 1958 two friends and I set off for the southern city of Cork on our bikes. The round trip would be about 300 miles, far longer than anything we had tried up till then. We loaded our bikes with all the camping gear we thought we needed—and some more. I had bought pannier bags for the back of my bike to take small items such as cups, a frying pan, a primus stove, etc. I also had two simple brush handles tied to the crossbar with string; these were our tent poles. The tent itself was a heavy, army-surplus canvas job, waterproofed with thick linseed oil. We did not have titanium pans or Gore-Tex. But off we went anyway.

The first day—with muscle power fired by great enthusiasm—we rode a record 120 miles, even with all our impediments. (Enthusiasm is an even better motivator when mixed with naiveté.) We stayed that night in Mountain Lodge, a youth hostel run by An Óige, the Irish Youth Hostel Association. (You could translate *An Óige* loosely as "The Young Ones.") It was in the lovely Galtee Mountains, County Tipperary. The narrow dirt road leading in to the hostel was banked on one side by a tall, dense growth of flowering rhododendrons. A wall of color bathing you in peacefulness.

That night I was so tired I could not eat any solid food and had to settle for a bowl of soup.

On the way back from Cork we were freewheeling down a steep slope near Dungarvan, relaxing in gravity's reward after a long slow climb. Suddenly, we hit a patch of loose gravel. My whole bike began to rattle and shake, unraveling the string that tied the brush-handle tent poles to the crossbar. One of these slid forward into the spokes of my front wheel, undoing me without mercy. Over the handlebars I went, tent poles, arms, and legs flying. The forward momentum I had gained from gravity was now pushing my body along the surface of a road with sharp, angular stones, together with my bike and several loose pieces of gear. After a good half hour of de-shocking and wound-licking, I continued the journey. Your bones are much more supple at that age.

About a year later I had a fall of a different kind. I was riding my bike back to school after lunch. All was routine until I came to a bus stop at the Royal Dublin Society, in my Dublin suburb. A few schoolgirls around my own age were standing there waiting for a bus. My eyes fixed instantly on one of them: brown hair curling down on slender shoulders, girlish bangs in front, dark eyes peering out (that's all I saw). I didn't want to stop looking, but I had to, since I was flying past on a bike. Besides, I was bewildered why I wanted to look anyway.

Not long afterwards I saw the same girl again. This time, I was definitely not ready to whizz past—not ready to give up the chance of getting more of whatever it was I was getting. Propelled by instinct, I began to tail the bus on my bike to find out where this non-boy was getting off. Haddington Road. Over the next few weeks I fine-tuned the act to alternately pass the bus when it stopped, let it pass me when it moved off again, and always just happen to be right behind it as she stepped off. I did not even consider that my pretense might have been utterly transparent (no surprise there).

I had heard all the jokes and vulgarities about the girl-and-boy stuff. I usually just stayed silent then, half-pretending that I knew it all as well as they did, and had no need to join in, whereas in fact I knew next to nothing. But this was different, completely different; the guys had missed it completely. Then school ended. During summer I glimpsed her twice—or convinced myself that I did—while passing in my dad's car. Then I saw her at Mass, coming down from the altar after Communion. Great: in the middle of a packed church, during the most solemn part of the Mass. Even less convenient than flying past on a bike or passing in a car.

I never saw her again.

* * *

By 1964 I had gradually stopped riding my metallic blue bike, and in fact I do not know where it ended up. I had lost interest in cycling and turned to hiking instead. But the interest would come back.

That was the year I left Ireland to work in Germany, Holland, and Belgium. Somehow I never joined the biking clubs in Belgium or Holland when I worked there, despite how popular the biking culture was in those flattened countries. I didn't even catch on when visiting cycling clubs came to the *pension* where I lived in Ghent, Belgium, and I would find a jumbled heap of bikes parked on the tiny front lawn, as if some exotic species of rubber-and-steel bramble had grown there overnight. It would be many years before I corrected that omission and returned to the Lowlands with a good bike.

Around the mid-1990's, when I was living in Houston, I bought a really light, carbon fiber-frame bike from money saved working overtime on a survey boat. My criterion for a "really light" bike was that I should be able to lift it with my little finger without dislocating my finger joint or flinching too much.

Over the next fifteen years or so I cycled through the Houston environs, from the scenic, bike-perfect hills of Burton and Lake Somerville to the flat–flat–flat roads of Brazoria County. The rides were nearly all high-spirited charity fundraisers with volunteer riders and volunteer safety back-up along the road. In hot and steamy mid-June the volunteer firefighters in Danbury would set up their fire truck and crack the valve of their water hose just enough to send a fine spray of blessedly cool water into your path. As you rode into the hot Texas afternoon, the warmth bounced back at you off the baked surface of the blacktop as if you were looking into an oven. You grimaced at the foul smell of putrefying roadkill, were revolted by the signature smell of the skunk, and hoped to find a roadside tree where you could take a break in the shade. But then, all of a sudden, a hand would stretch out of a truck that had crept up behind you silently, and proffer you a wet paper towel straight from the icebox.

Yet, true to Texas tradition, the weather changes could be abrupt and extreme. One February weekend, in a burst of enthusiasm, I turned a deaf ear to the weather forecaster. (As did many others that day.) But about twenty miles into the ride the promised "blue norther" arrived. These notorious Texas cold fronts have a leading edge of ominous dark blue cloud that sweeps in low to dominate the northern horizon. When they hit, you can expect the temperature to drop very suddenly by twenty or even thirty degrees Fahrenheit. Caught in the cold rain squalls whipped up by the blue norther that day, I was shivering uncontrollably by the time I had whimpered back to my car. As I thawed out in the blast of hot air from the heater, I could well understand how blue northers have found their way into Texas lore: imagine being on a horse, in light shirt and chaps, far from shelter, when one of these hits.

The next day my fingertips developed mild chilblains— something I had not known since my boyhood days in Ireland.

But there really *are* no guarantees. I found this out one sunny Texas afternoon while freewheeling down a slope without a care in the world. Suddenly a pesky dog (who had probably been overfed and dozing) darted out from nowhere and started snapping at my feet. I tried to outride him (bad idea) but he spurted ahead and tried to cross in front of me (just as bad). The wheel locked sideways and sent me flying over the handlebars, snapping my collar bone like a matchstick. The dog was not much better off. My biking colleagues made little of this by stating that the collar bone is the most frequently broken bone in the human body. Another cycling friend suggested I get used to it, for *he* had done it three times.

After a few months I resumed cycling. I presume the dog switched to chasing cars.

The best-known bike ride in Texas is the MS 150, a two-day, 175-mile ride from Houston to Austin. The event helps victims of Multiple Sclerosis, a disease of the central nervous system that can lead to paralysis (and certainly can keep you off a bike). I did this ride many times and each time I got swept up in the excitement. Not much had changed in this respect since I left my own country more than a generation earlier. Except the size: whereas our weekend cycling trips in Ireland drew about fifteen boys and girls at most, the MS draws up to thirteen *thousand*. But not everything in Texas is big: apart from some really spiky (and dangerous) hills in Bastrop State Park, most of the route is either flat or has only fairly modest hills. (You participants from Colorado may not even have noticed the hills.) After two days and plenty of saddle cream, the route ends a few blocks away from the Texas State Capitol in downtown Austin.

* * *

In 1998 I took my carbon fiber-frame bike to Holland on a two-and-a-half year working assignment. Cycling now with my family—all in teens or above—we had some glorious days gliding through the lowland polders. We "discovered" dikes and windmills unknown to my Dutch friends who had whizzed by them many times on the freeways. We even got sun-reddened faces in February, when others had stayed at home not trusting the skies. We biked the narrow roads in the Delftland, between medieval Delft and gin-loving Schiedam; we dodged the human denseness in the towns by ducking through secret stiles and underpasses known only to cyclists with special cycling maps; then we continued through pastures dotted with idly gazing cows and their attendant cattle egrets. Often we had to tack into the North Sea wind by taking oblique paths to avoid coming to a complete stop, the roads often running for miles through two dead-straight lines of poplars. Most bike tracks were smooth, but some were cobbled, in which case you and your bike ran the risk of being rattled to pieces.

Or, on warm summer afternoons, we rested at popular roadside cafés and yielded freely to tempting signs offering coffee and cold drinks. We took our respite in mossy, cobblestoned yards corralled between orderly stands of poplars and decorated with big red splotches of geraniums. We watched sedate, Heineken-sipping Dutch couples who dressed sensibly and owned sensible bicycles. As pert, matter-of-fact waitresses brought us some Dutch apple pie.

* * *

Today, in 2015, I still have my prized Specialized Epic bike and still ride it around my neighborhood in Houston. I can't lift it with my littlest finger any longer, however, for fear of knocking that finger out of joint.

They say the strongest memories often go back the furthest. That seems to be especially true for highly-charged memories tagged to an incidental smell or sound. Sure enough, whenever I get a particular strain or type of cold virus—only that specific one—it shoots me back instantly to Dublin on that Easter Sunday of 1958.

You will not find me complaining about these flashbacks that so often let me relive the day I got my first bike.

MY VOX POPULI BIKE

This was probably a short camping trip. The tent on the back carrier was decidedly low tech, and very heavy: army surplus canvas soaked with linseed oil to make it waterproof. The panniers below the tent were handy for loose items such as a primus stove for cooking a hot lunch. The old-fashioned light (on the handlebars) was common in the 1950s; it was bulky, but sturdy and reliable.

Photo: County Wicklow, ca. 1959. Background: Sugarloaf Mountain.

---

[1] Yeats, "The Stolen Child."

21

HOW I GAVE UP SMOKING

My head was swirling almost out of control as if somebody had kept turning me upside down. I needed to be alone—to hide away before anybody saw me and noticed how strange I was acting. Where better to do this than in the privacy of the bathroom? I went inside, locked the door, checked that it was locked, put the seat cover down slowly, and sat down. I held my head firmly in both hands and rested my elbows on my knees. It needed only the smallest effort to remain in this position, and that's all I had left—the smallest effort. Then I closed my eyes. For at least half an hour I sat there, thankful for not having to move, and thankful that nobody knocked on the door in urgent need of using the toilet. My brain seemed to be swirling around in an unknown and frightening place. This was definitely new, and bad. Where was it going? Slowly, the pain and the swirling inside my head began to ease off to a level I could handle. I didn't need to be assailed by any more fearful thoughts while I tried to ease the soreness in my head. When I thought the worst was over I left the bathroom as quietly as I had entered and slipped into bed. With great relief I lay my dizzy head on the pillow and hoped the poisons would ebb before I woke up.

It was my first cigarette.

I had two very good pals when I was growing up in Dublin during the 1950s. We lived only a few houses apart and would meet up by mutual, spontaneous inspiration whenever we were free. We had been together for as long as I can remember, since that twilight of memory where real events become enmeshed with imagined events—and become indistinguishable from them. But now we were changing: we had climbed enough trees, busted enough chestnuts, scrambled over enough high walls to grab a few sweet apples or pears, stared down enough barking dogs, annoyed enough cranky grownups.

It was the time when a cigarette dangling from Humphrey Bogart's lip was as much a part of his essence as his dark, immobile eyes, his sloping hat, and the cool, measured words he dealt to those unfortunate crooks who crossed him. Or the way he brought those tall, slim ladies under his spell when he didn't appear to even want to do it. It would not be too many years before full-page magazine ads would project the Camel Man at us with his head in a cloud of blue smoke. That smoke deftly diverted most of our attention—but not all—from the beautiful background of verdant green foliage in some remote jungle clearing. The Camel Man held a cigarette prominently in one hand, while with the other he balanced a heavy airplane propeller on his shoulder. That shoulder did not look like it was used to handling such heavy loads—as, for example, one might expect of a roughneck on a drilling rig—yet the Camel Man with his cigarette seemed to carry the big propeller effortlessly. The scene implied that he would soon mount it back on the airplane's nose and continue his he-man adventure into the wild outdoors. The cigarette was insinuated by design into one's concept of toughness and manliness.

In case anybody missed that message, the Marlboro Man would surely clinch it for them. Sitting astride the rough-hewn wooden fence of a corral in the West, the Marlboro Man pauses from the dangerous job of breaking in wild horses. He is clad in a denim jacket, leather leg covers—chaps—and of course a cowboy hat. The fingers of both hands are cupped around a very visible, white cigarette sticking straight out of his masculine mouth. Swirls of fresh blue smoke curl upwards to show that the flame has taken hold on the tobacco. With a coil of rope balanced lazily on his knee, he exudes confidence as he surveys cowboys galloping after some runaway horses. The scene is capped by hazy blue mountains in the distance. It's pure satisfaction. You'd want to identify with that, for sure.

Even without the movies or magazine ads, it seemed that *everybody* smoked in the adult world back in the 1950s. One could not separate the smell of cigarette smoke from grownups. They just went together. On Sunday afternoons my dad would sink deep into his armchair as ribbons of blue-grey cigarette smoke spiraled upwards and spread out on the ceiling. When his cigarette was down to the butt—either through active smoking or sleepy neglect—he would fold the newspaper over his head like a tent and quietly slip into slumberland. Our sitting room—and that of many others—was almost always suffused with cigarette smoke. Occasionally a thin burn mark covered with a carcass of ash would betray a cigarette left to smolder itself out alone. Even one of the piano keys bore the dark brown signature of an unfinished smoke.

Cigarettes were part of our lives. They were called "fags." One of my duties was to rescue the smoker-out-of-fags by dashing to Sandymount village on my bike and fetching a shiny, cellophane-wrapped box of Twenty Players. Kids could buy cigarettes freely then, because it was understood they were for the fag-needy grownups at home. People really down on cash could even buy single cigarettes.

The movies were much more important to us then—before television. Every Sunday afternoon we looked forward to going to "The Shack," our local picture house. Inside, John Wayne and Bugs Bunny would act out their dramas on the big canvas wall as wisps of cigarette smoke rose from a hundred patrons slumped into the seats. The rising tendrils would flare up when they got caught in the shafts of light from the projector, until they rose above it to join the murky haze trapped under the ceiling. Occasionally some smart aleck would blow a few smoke rings into the spotlight. When the sensational Technicolor movies arrived in the early 1950s, and Dorothy skipped down the yellow-brick road, the smoke caught in the projector's light took on color, too, though we knew it was still just the same old dull smoke. The smell of stale cigarette smoke was everywhere—like a weak spice with a touch of mustiness. It was as much a part of going to the pictures as the seats we were sitting in.

And yet, not all of the smokers were adults…some were not much older than we were…

Smoking *had* to be a natural step in growing up. It had to be right, had to be okay. Had to be cool. And what better way to become part of the tantalizing grownup's world than to start smoking?

Yes; we were changing.

Getting hold of cigarettes was easy. For reasons I still do not understand, adults would sometimes only smoke half a cigarette and then discard the rest on the street. (Perhaps they were trying to give up the habit.) Some of these street finds were well over an inch long. Some had filters, some did not. Some had lipstick—ugh!—and we rejected them outright. After rain it was a lost cause: any potentially salvageable cigarette would have turned into useless mush. Eventually, though, we would be able to get a few good clean cigarette-halves or -quarters to work with. As for matches, these were always to be found. No boy of any worth would ever be lost for a box of matches. Having your own matches taught you to be responsible—another step on the way to becoming a grownup.

So where could we smoke our cigarettes without being seen and having to argue the point with grownups (who would never get it anyway)? In our den, of course. Our den was in the hollowed-out trunk of an old tree in somebody's front yard, on Sandymount Avenue. The once-majestic tree had been cut down, leaving only its fat trunk sticking out of the ground. Many damp Irish winters had rotted out the inside, but a crust of resistant bark remained to form the walls of our little den. The owners of the house didn't seem to know or care that we were occupying their relic tree. But then again we never used it in daytime, or in summer, when people would be around. It was the cold, dark winter nights that turned our thoughts to our cozy little den.

The hollowed-out stump was just big enough for all three of us to squeeze into. (We had not yet gone through the pre-adolescent growth spurt.) At least, in my memory, that's how big our den was. The rot had the extra benefit of creating a soft floor, even if it would get a bit mushy after it had rained. Climbing up into the den was easy because you could get a good leg-up by wedging your foot between the tree and an old granite wall beside it. And it was high enough to raise you above the eyelevel of passing adults.

On the night we had chosen to ascend into Adulthood, we nestled into our den with knees bent and legs folded double. Each of us put a piece of salvaged cigarette between our lips and gingerly touched the tobacco with the flame of a lighted match. At first I drew a small amount of air using my cheeks as a bellows—without expanding my lungs—so the nicotine-laced smoke would only fill my mouth. I didn't feel very much—just a slight weird sensation. I told myself that this was a grownup sensation, and that I was up to it. Slowly I began to test myself further by taking a small breath and drawing some smoke down my windpipe. That's when it hit me: my lungs rebelled, and I gagged. After that I continued much more cautiously, trying to get a feeling for how much smoke I could inhale without choking. Not much. My two pals seemed to be doing the same thing, but I was not paying too much attention to them. Each of us was too busy absorbing this new sensation to notice how the others were doing. I was trying to find the right balance between getting enough air for my basic body needs and drawing enough smoke into my lungs to really live this grownup experience. Surely I could breathe in a bit more smoke? Surely I would get used to it—get better at it. But now I was starting to become dizzy, and my head seemed to be swaying involuntarily from left to right. I dared not bow my head and rest it on my knees—not now, while my pals were watching. I felt somehow I just had to keep my posture and stick it out. Finally I tried to check how my two pals were doing. They were as quiet as mice and I could not divine whether they were finding it any easier than I was.

We probably spent not more than half an hour hunkered down inside the tree stump. Then, by some virtual nod, we reached a mutual agreement: we'd had enough. We climbed out of our mossy den and slowly walked home, a distance of about half a mile. My walking was not too steady. We said "see ya" to each other quickly as we peeled off to our own homes. Luckily, it was early in the evening by Dublin standards—around 9:30 pm, and *quiet:* neither my dad nor any of my three siblings noticed me slipping in through the front door.

That's when I had to hide in the bathroom to recover.

After that night I lost all interest in images of adults dangling cigarettes from their mouths, impressing others with the quick draw of a cigarette lighter, or lighting up while breaking in wild mustangs. My two pals continued smoking, though. At least they had not quit by the time I last saw them, when each of us left the street we had grown up in.

* * *

Well over a decade later I was working a summer job in Brussels, Belgium. In that wonderful city they seemed to specialize in displaying fat cigars in open boxes, stacked side-by-side the full breath and height of their shop windows. I had just completed my second year in engineering school, had emerged from two months of reclusive swatting, and was awaiting my results.

How I gave Up Smoking

Now it was "summer in the city," and my defenses were down. I deserved a break, right? It was a visual thing: the rich brown finish on those handmade cigars in their rustic wooden boxes. So in I went and sampled one. Next day, another. And so on for a few weeks, maybe. It was nothing, I told myself, because I did not inhale. But it was certainly not okay with those who shared my office, nor was it okay with me when I realized I was getting hooked, so I nipped the habit in the bud.

Since my clandestine cigarette smoke in that tree stump, the tide has turned against cigarette smokers. This became quite obvious towards the end of the 1900s. We all know the good reasons, but what would Bogart have used as a prop when putting on that mien of confidence in his victory over the bad guys? How would he have captivated the ladies without coming to their rescue with a fast draw of his cigarette lighter?

Nevertheless, the wave of change in the smoking culture did not—has not—swept the world uniformly. I got a stark reminder of this in the late 1980s when I flew from Houston to the pleasant town of Woking in Surrey, England. It was early winter and (since I had grown up in a similar climate) I knew from the "feel" of the air and the look of the skies that snow was in the offing (and was not disappointed). We were on a low budget, and at around ten pm we walked into a pub-guesthouse to ask for lodgings. The cold and damp outside seemed to propel us into that warmly lit inn. I saw vague images of people and faces nested together in the back of the pub, and heard the clinking of glasses and bottles above the sound of many lively but well controlled, simultaneous conversations. But when the receptionist appeared and addressed me I could not speak for a few seconds—gagged by the sudden change from clean, outside air to the thick, smoke-laden air inside.

Moving on a bit, back to Dublin, sometime in the 1990s, standing idly at a bus stop in Dún Laoghaire. There, I happened to notice a fourteen-ish girl drawing rapid pulls from a cigarette. What caught my attention was that she was dressed in a smart school uniform. She had paused with her back to an open wrought iron gate and was looking out onto the street with a vacant expression. Then she threw down the cigarette, stubbed it out with a few sharp pivots on her toe, and walked briskly through the gate. The name of her private school was displayed in ornate wrought iron letters on an arch overhead.

It must have been her only chance to take a furtive smoke between home and school. I wondered idly (while waiting for my bus) how kids at that time got initiated into the adult right of smoking. In a tree stump? Did they recycle half-smoked cigarette butts from the street? Probably not.

Around the same time—the late 1990's—my family and I went to live in Holland for one of my job assignments. We had got used to the smoke-free environment in the US—in the office and at home—but the change in smoking culture was still on its way across the Atlantic. Holland is the land of my inlaws, so I let my wife handle this one. The local hardware shop had just what she needed to keep our home smoke free: a big sign with a bold red circle and a red bar running through the words *"Verboden te Roken"*—"No Smoking." Anybody not taking the sign seriously had this house rule explained in very frank terms: Smoke outside, or don't visit us at all. It worked (after a short learning curve).

Yes, the tide was turning.

Then, in the early 2000s, Ireland took a bold initiative: it banned smoking in *pubs*. A courageous move, then, as anybody can imagine who has ever enjoyed the fun that can be generated by spontaneous combustion in the simplest of Irish pubs, how quickly it can loosen up a crowd, and how deeply this social culture is embedded.

But it worked.

After the holdouts had surrendered, little tables started to appear outside pubs, where smokers could grab their puffs. Clustered around these little tables (often resting on beer barrels), the smokers seemed oddly separated from the patrons inside. It was not the same: standing outside the pub like an outcast rather than sitting at the bar like some cool dude in a vintage movie. Culture had "turned the tables" on the smokers, I guess.

Even now, in 2014, whenever I travel outside the US the first thing I notice is the smell of cigarette smoke and the sight of people smoking (especially young people). That's not to say that this annoys me: on the contrary—and perhaps a bit perversely—I actually enjoy catching the whiff of a little cigarette smoke blown my way from a beer barrel outside a pub, somebody passing me on a street, or from the smokers' enclosure of a restaurant. That's because the smell triggers something and propels me back at lightning speed to Dublin in the 1950s, evoking pleasant feelings locked in memories of family and friends in smoke-filled living rooms, picture houses, and public places. And therein lies the paradox, for I strongly suspect that smoking eventually ruined my father's health.

So now I let others do it: I stopped smoking cigarettes that night in the tree stump. And I never bought any more of those seductive cigars.

BANISHED SMOKERS, 2013

A young woman envelopes herself in cigarette smoke on a street in Madrid, Spain, as she and her colleague take some hurried puffs. By 2013, the smoking culture had changed, and this was a common sight.

Photo: Calle Doctor Drumen, Madrid, January 2013.

22

BORN IN WORLD WAR II

At two o'clock in the early morning of the 31st of May 1941 the navigator of a German bombing raid looked down and saw a big city below. The city was easy to spot from the air, because it was not blacked out. The airplane opened the bomb bays. The first three bombs made craters in roads, caused other property damage, but did not hurt anybody. The last one, however, was deadly: its jagged steel fragments ripped indiscriminately through the bodies of civilians, and its force crushed others with shattered masonry. Twenty-eight people were killed and 300 houses were destroyed or damaged.

In that terrible year, German planes were bombing Great Britain. World War II was "only" two years into bringing out some of the worst extremes of human nature, and Britain was fighting with only its Commonwealth allies and the resistance forces of Poland and France at its side. It had been four years since Japan started World War II in the Pacific, by invading China. In that May of 1941, Pearl Harbor was still a safe place for American troops to be stationed, and the US was not in the war. The outcome for Britain was by no means certain.

But the city that had kept its lights on below the bomber planes was not part of Great Britain, nor was it part of the war with Germany: it was Dublin City, capital of the Irish Republic, a country that had chosen to be neutral in the war. The German Government eventually apologized, saying the Luftwaffe had made an error of navigation.[1]

A year later, in 1942, when the war was about halfway through, I was born in that same city. Two weeks later the Germans felt the Blitz on their *own* home soil for the first time in the war—saw bombs dropping out of their *own* skies for the first time, on the beautiful cathedral city of Cologne. This was the start of the relentless and determined *riposte* by the Allies that would eventually reduce urban Germany to rubble.[2] But not yet: It would still be another two years before American and British soldiers waded across the beaches of Normandy to face the piercing sprays of bullets from the bunkers on the cliffs above. The war continued a further fifteen months after that, before Japan was made to surrender five days after a second city in their homeland had been incinerated in the fireball of an atomic explosion.

Back in neutral Dublin my father, my mother, my siblings, and I were shielded from the direct effects of all the dreadful destruction. We were not spared the indirect effects, of course—the rationing of food and materials, the general disruption of our lives—but this pales to insignificance compared with the sufferings of the countries that were directly hit.

A year before the war ended my mother died during childbirth, leaving my dad with four children. I was the youngest, at two years of age. He never remarried, and went on to rear all four of us and keep the home together until he died nearly thirty years later. I only have very vague and unreliable memories of the last three years of the war—the first three years of my life. And I do not have any memories at all of the staggering shock it must have been for my dad to lose his one-and-only, with four young children looking on in innocent expectation. A then stranger who ran a public house near the maternity hospital recalled my dad coming in, sitting down, ordering a drink, and saying: "I just lost my wife."

One of my clearest and earliest memories is an event that must have occurred near the end of the war. I cannot fix the timing because only the subjective impressions remain from those toddler years, without clue as to when it might have happened. Like most young children, I was keen on exploring everything I could walk to or climb onto. I became very interested in a car sitting up on blocks in the garage of our suburban semi-detached house. It was an Austin Seven, the British answer to Henry Ford's Model T. The British working man's car. My dad had bought it in England and brought it to Dublin after he returned to settle there, around the mid-1930s. When the war came, of course, there was no petrol for private cars, and he had to put it on blocks.

But that was a windfall for me: the Austin Seven had a box cabin, and the windows and doors had been left open—the perfect place to make a den. But there was a problem: the family cat, with characteristic disregard for all other sentient beings, had already claimed it as *her* home. Sharing the cabin of the Austin Seven with the cat was not an option: she had poor toilet training, and as soon as you came near the car you would be repelled by the disgusting stench of stale cat pee. Then she suddenly produced a bunch of little kittens and started nurturing them on the foul-smelling jute sacks that covered the back seat.

The human brain seems to be extraordinarily capable at permanently linking highly emotional experiences with the specific smells (and other sensations) that accompany them first time around. This is true even if the association is purely coincidental. Thus, even today, if I come across that revolting smell it will bring me back instantly to that cat's stinking bed on the back seat of our old Austin Seven.

The next memory I have comes from a time not all that long after the war. No healthy kid can or should resist exploring an attic. The musty smell, the undisturbed layers of dust, and the lack of any signs of adults having been there for a while—all these beckon the young explorer. Getting to the attic (when my dad was at work) just meant wedging my bare feet between the jambs of the door just below the opening and jacking my body upwards (like a rock climber wedging himself up a "chimney"). Once I got within grasping reach of the attic opening, I could push the cover off, grab the wooden rim and swing up into it like a little monkey.

There were all sorts of interesting things up there. My dad's old fiddle—complete with rosin and bow, and a wind-up gramophone with a cornet horn like the one in the logo for "His Master's Voice." A dusty little compartment inside the case yielded a stash of bright stainless steel gramophone needles for playing the old 78s. These big disks were made of brittle Bakelite then, since vinyl had not yet arrived. The needles were so sturdy and sharp that they appeared to be plowing the grooves into the Bakelite rather than coaxing tiny vibrations from them. It was not long before I got curious how the winding mechanism worked, but my probing finger got caught in the cogwheels and I was left with a big blue bruise covered with grease and blood.

Later I used the "cornet" as a bullhorn to address our whole block from my upstairs window (when my dad was at work). If I was in a more sensitive mood I would put the inlet of the horn to my ear instead of my mouth and listen to the greatly amplified tweet–tweets of the birds. Sometimes—by accident—I would pick up conversations between people walking down the street several houses away—people who thought they were out of earshot.

There was also a box of *gas masks* in that attic.

My dad told me the masks had been distributed to all families during the War in case there was a poison gas attack. After all, poison gases had been used in World War I. There had also been about six "conventional" bombings in Ireland during WWII, apart from the deadly one in 1941 that killed the twenty-eight people. Furthermore, the motives of those bombings were still subject to speculation. Why, for example, did the Luftwaffe pilots not realize that the city below them was in a neutral country, since it was not blacked out like those in Britain, or Belfast, in Northern Ireland? Was this Hitler's idea of a "subtle" warning to the Irish Republic to stay out of the war, and not to come to the aid of Britain secretly? After the horrible stories from World War I of soldiers being blinded by tear gas, slowly suffocating in agony from chlorine gas, and being disfigured by painful blisters from mustard gas, who would want to take a chance?

But by the time we kids discovered the gas masks in our attic, the war was over, and they had become toys. They had a transparent visor, a rubber mask to cover your face, and a big canister in front of your mouth. Like most gas masks, they did nothing to improve your appearance: you looked like a mutant wild pig, your head narrowing to a bluff-shaped "nose" formed by the big black canister.

One of the first things we did was to take the top off the canister with the kitchen can opener to see what was inside. We found what looked to us like coarse grains of black sand (these must have been charcoal—to adsorb and neutralize the toxic gas).

One summer I got an idea. I had been fascinated by movies of divers looking for pearls or sponges in the lucent aquamarine waters of the tropics. The movies had taken hold of my imagination completely: swarming shoals of brightly colored tropical fish, natural sponges waving with the subtle movements of the water. Seasoned, bronze-skinned sailors would have to hand-crank an air pump on deck to keep the life breath flowing down to the diver. The scenes were charged with drama as animosities festered among the hardened sailors and sinister motives were hidden. As if the natural dangers of the underwater world were not enough.

In one movie the diver was stranded on the bottom without air because the sailor on top had stopped turning the handle of the air pump for some dark reason. When any of these dangers arose, the diver would have to make a desperate dash for the surface, and the movie director knew exactly how to stop *your* breath and put you on the edge of your seat. This was the type of screen magic that transported us to other worlds in what we called "The Shack," our local picture house.

So I got to thinking: Why not use one of the old gas masks to make a diving helmet? If we could just find a way to supply it with air while we were under water...

I persuaded one of my pals to go along with the idea. To get air down to the mask, I replaced the filter canister with a tin can fitted with a long rubber tube coming out the bottom. Then we waded into the sea off Sandymount Strand until we were about waist deep in the water. My pal was supposed to keep the open end of the air tube above water while I went below. I was excited about this project and did not even think of failure: I would glide above the sandy bottom, taking my time to study the shining quartz grains, the cockle shells, and the pulsating patterns of sunlight projected on the seabed. It would be just like the divers gathering oysters in the exotic tropical seas (though we knew from experience that very few fish ever ventured that near to shore).

But my grasp of physics was not as solid as my enthusiasm for tropical diving. The water pressure quickly squeezed the rubber mask, molding it to my face as tight as a surgeon's glove. It pressed against my eyes with such unexpected force that I had to shut them immediately— shut my eyes to the wonders of the tropical waters at Sandymount Public Baths!

It would be years before I got real swimming goggles, let alone a snorkel.

One day a large parcel arrived in the mail. My dad opened it up and soon we were all passing around an assortment of shirts, pants, and other clothes, examining them carefully. I would have been around six at the time, and what sticks in my memory is the concern (possibly implanted by my dad or my siblings) that one would need to have a certain amount of "guts" to wear these clothes on the street, so colorful and bright were they. (At that time charcoal grey was very much in fashion.) The risqué shirts and pants had come from America, a sort of "care package" to help us recover from the war years. I remember them as being used, but spotlessly clean, and neatly ironed and folded. They were completely free of any rips, tears, or frays that might have raised the suspicion of their having been of no further use to whoever donated them. And then I thought: What a strange place that must be, America, where people go around wearing such bright colorful clothes!

The next memory I have of my dad's Austin Seven was sometime after the war, when he had it running again. The war ended when I was three years of age, and he must have told the cat to find a new home, thrown out the smelly old sacks, and fumigated the back seat of his prized Austin Seven.

Although my dad had to raise us four kids on his own, he seemed to find plenty of time to play tricks on us. One that I remember vividly was when he showed us the hidden force of electricity. He had parked the Austin Seven in front of our garage with its bonnet open (called the "hood" in the US). He started the car (possibly with the hand crank) and let the engine idle at a nice rhythm. Then he had five or six of us kids hold hands and stand in a wide semicircle around the open engine compartment. He took the hand of the kid closest to him and asked the one at the other end of the chain to put his free hand on the metal chassis of the car. Then, suddenly, he put one finger of his own free hand on the high-tension terminal of the ignition coil—the thing that puts the spark into a spark plug. This sent an electric shock through the whole chain of kids. It was not a strong shock—just enough to give you a little tingle and a funny sensation of vibration. Not enough to make you break your handclasp with a yelp! I was in the middle of the chain, and was delighted by this game.

That was electricity. I got to know it—and to *feel* it —at a very early age. My dad explained how an electric circuit must be closed before any current can flow through it. That was part of the act: we did not feel anything when we took each other's hands—only when he closed the circuit by slyly touching the ignition terminal. My dad seemed to be tickled by our startled "Ohs." I'm not sure how (or whether) he satisfied himself that the amount of electricity flowing through our young arms and chests would be harmless. But I can definitely confirm that it was much less than the sting you get when you straddle a fence that you didn't know was electrified.

My dad must have kept the Austin Seven for several years after the war, because I have clear memories of riding in it as a very young passenger. He often took us up the winding white-gravel tracks where the Dublin and Wicklow Mountains merge. Up there, a six-foot blanket of turf covers the granite bedrock below. This turf could be cut, dried, and brought home as fuel to heat the house and provide hot water. It burned very well (though not as hot as coal), and it only cost the labor that you yourself put into its harvesting.

I must have been too young to work the bog, because, apart from the thrill of driving up a mountain, I only remember eating mushy tomato sandwiches, drinking hot tea, and playing in that white gravel.

On the way home we often drove with the windows of the Austin Seven rolled down. When we reached a certain cruising speed, the pulsating "br–br–br–br" of the engine got locked in step with the vibrations in the cabin caused by the wind buffeting the open windows. It was like the resonance set up in a wind instrument—an enormous bassoon, say—but completely void of any sonorous timbre. In a peculiar effect, the rhythm seemed to lock on to the pitch of my dad's voice, distorting it and making him sound like some sort of a robot or space alien. Once again, a specific sensory stimulus had tagged an early childhood experience, to be revived with incredible fidelity whenever I heard that same resonant sound again. We all share this experience, yet I still find it very "useful" for reviving anecdotes from the distant past. (One rarely hears this resonance now—only where vehicles with simple engines and open cabins are still used.)

One day, while driving under the low railway bridge at Ranelagh Road, my dad told us of a tragic accident that happened there. A man was sitting on the top of a lorry, looking backwards, as it passed under the bridge. He probably never knew what happened as his head hit the low crown of the bridge.

The old railway line was abandoned in the late 1950s—and the rails taken up—but it was rebuilt in splendid style during the early 2000s. Sometimes, when I go over the bridge in the new Luas train, or drive under it in a rental car, I think of the role that chance plays in our lives—how it can undo years of intelligent planning with one wicked wildcard.

With time my dad had to part with his Austin Seven. He had to be on the road most of his working hours, so it must have been a tough choice when he gave up the protection of the old Austin Seven's cabin for a motorcycle exposed to the wind and rain. My lasting recollection is hearing him say, some years later, that he would have to "get a roof over his head soon": the raw Dublin winter must have been catching up with him.

The 40s and 50s were no time for what is now called "discretionary spending" by the marketing folks (spending the money left over after paying all the bills that cannot wait). Discretion was of little use when making one-choice decisions on how to feed your family.

We were minimalists when minimalism did not come with the luxury of choice.

When my hair got too long, my dad sat me down on a chair in the middle of the kitchen, tucked a towel into my collar, and snipped away at my mop with comb and scissors. Soon the linoleum floor would be covered with little tufts, curls, and separate hairs strewn around like grass from a lawn mower. No matter that he favored the bowl cut, and that I may have looked a bit like Moe of the Three Stooges when it was done: it would be a long time before the 50s brought the crewcut craze, a long time before my hair meant anything to me at all.

And when all my running and playing wore holes in my shoes, my dad put on his apron and sat on a stool in front of his cobbler's last. He traced out my small footprint on a sheet of leather and cut it to shape with a little knife. He had sharpened the knife so often that the grinding stone had worn a big arc out of the blade. Every time he made a delicate cut, he pointed to an old scar dangerously close to his main wrist artery.

"That was a chisel," he would say.

"Lad, *never* put your hand *in front* of a blade; always cut *away* from you. If no part of your body is in front of the blade, the knife can't possibly cut you, now can it?"

I remembered that sound logic most of my life, and, although I had some near misses with power saws, some of the fingers I am now using to write this story I probably owe to my dad's advice.

Having cut out the new leather sole, he attached it to the upper of my shoe either by nailing it down on the last—the easiest way—or stitching it with a hand awl and waxed thread. To give the job a professional touch, he blackened the sides and the stitch lines with melted pitch.

The home shoe repair worked well. Occasionally a nail that had not been fully flattened down on the last would announce itself with a sharp prick to your big toe. But that was much better than not being able to walk through puddles without getting your feet wet.

There's nothing more miserable than getting your feet wet.

The profound truth is that I was actually a very rich child in those postwar years: I had *enough;* more than I expected, more than I could even imagine. Among the many "sweeteners" added to our young lives was my dad's ritual of bringing home a bag of assorted chocolates *every* Friday night.

* * *

Coming back to my failed career as a diver and harvester of exotic sponges, perhaps the dangers of diving are not overdramatized at all by the movies. When I grew up my work often required me to spend many weeks at sea on marine construction jobs. We worked very closely with divers: they were our eyes and our hands under the water. On my very first job, in the tropical waters off Kharg Island in the Persian Gulf, I worked with some divers from Louisiana. Four of us shared a tiny cabin for over six weeks. (These guys were true Cajuns, a species I have learned to seek out as companions because of their ready and unassuming friendliness and the rub-off you get from their unique culture.) One of the divers was about my own age, and we were especially good buddies. When I was leaving the barge he offered to buy my white designer T-shirt so he would have something stylish to change into for the few leisure hours one had in the common room of a compact work barge. These luxury items were highly valued because they were hard or impossible to get once you left port. (I just gave it to him of course.) But not long afterwards he died in a freak accident inside the diving chamber, died in a cruel and unspeakable manner.

That's only one example of the many tragedies that can quickly sober divers to the dangers of their profession.

A few months after becoming an American citizen in 2006, I attended a conference on Oceanography in Caen, France. Not far from that beautiful city, the Allies had waded in from the beaches through those sprays of piercing lead from the German machine guns. That was, of course, the 6th of June 1944.

A few years earlier, I had taken my family to some of those landing beaches. Anybody who has visited them will surely have been moved deeply by the silent testimony of the battered concrete bunkers and the graphic exhibits in the war memorials. (When we visited, our children played in the surf as I tried to visualize myself jumping out of a landing craft and heading inshore towards one of those bunkers. There were some well-dressed young French students prancing across the forecourt of one of the museums, absorbed in excited conversation. Given their ages—mid teens—I casually wondered whether they were more excited about getting to hang out with their friends on an outing, or about learning what price had been paid for their freedom.)

On this latest trip—to nearby Caen—I had a work colleague who was a natural-born American citizen and had never seen the Normandy landing beaches. We had one free day after presenting our work at the conference, and he asked me to drive him to one of the sites.

I picked Omaha Beach.

It was fairly late when we arrived, but we still had enough time to take in the affecting experience of walking solemnly along the now peaceful beaches. We stared in silence at the now quiet pillbox bunkers where one morning just after dawn the peace was shattered by the rat-tat-tat of machine guns spewing death—until silenced by a grenade or a flame thrower.

It was dusk by the time we finished our short visit. We stopped by a simple restaurant in the town of Vierville sur Mer, eager for some coffee and sandwiches before the long drive to Charles de Gaulle airport.

We also needed some time to reflect.

There was a restaurant that seemed to have been built especially for people in our state of mind, and body, so we went in and took one of several vacant tables in the large dining room. While we were talking among ourselves in subdued voices, I casually noticed a couple sitting a few tables away. They seemed about ten or so years older than I was at the time, putting them at around 75 years of age. When we left the restaurant they were lingering outside on the parking lot, looking towards us. The man came over to us:

"Are you Americans?" He asked.

Since I had just become an American citizen, I answered for both of us, with a bit of a smile:

"Yes, we are."

"Thank you for what you did in 1944," said the stranger.

My American colleague was stunned.

I wondered what that man and woman had been doing when, in 1944, I was two years of age, in the neutral city of Dublin, trying to make myself a den in the back of my father's Austin Seven? They would have been about, say, twelve or thirteen years of age. I don't think their main worry would have been some smelly old jute sacks.

They probably took gas masks much more seriously, too.

FORTUNE UNTOLD

My mother with an ad hoc fortune teller, around mid-1930s. She died young—on her own 30th birthday.

Source: Family print of uncertain origin.

Born in World War II

WORLD WAR II: WALKING OUT IN DUBLIN

My farther is proud of my two brothers and my sister, all dressed up for a walk through Dublin's city center. In March 1945—the date written on this print—US troops had just crossed the Rhine at Remagen Bridge; six weeks later the Soviets launch their final offensive, encircling Berlin; two weeks after that Hitler commits suicide in his bunker; seven weeks later Japan surrenders the island of Okinawa to US troops. The Irish Republic was neutral in the war, though it was bombed a few times "by mistake."

Our mother had died eight months before the date on this print. Dad never remarried. He gave all four of us a very happy childhood through the lean years that followed, and went on to grandfather my sister's and my brother's kids. He died in 1974, five months short of eighty.

My three siblings are, from left: Louis, Marie, and Tom (died 2012).

Source: Probably O'Connell Street; probably by a street photographer. My dad wrote "March 1945" on the print, but we don't know for sure when the photo was taken.

A DAY'S OUTING—IN THE BOG

Although Ireland was neutral in World War II, the threat of invasion was always there. Shortages and rationing could not be avoided, leading to a period of tense restrictions and sacrifices. This was known as "The Emergency"; it lasted from 1939 until 1945. Like many Dubliners, my dad used to cut his own turf to keep the kitchen fire alive. The narrow gravel road in this photo leads up to a bog straddling the line between the counties of Dublin and Wicklow.

Before the hungry turf cutters arrived, and over a period of three or four thousand years, peat had formed where once there had been mountain woodland.[3] The blankets of peat lying undisturbed on the ancient bed of granite had made themselves a quilt decorated with fluffy white tufts: bog cotton. And from this arose a name familiar to any Dubliner who ever ventured beyond awing the city lights with the mot from the car park at Killakee: the Featherbeds. When my dad had petrol for his Austin Seven, he would fearlessly drive it up this gravel road, or one near it, and all four of us kids would enjoy the heck out of it.

The image above is the best I can do to reproduce the scene, but it does use some license: The family photos are from unconnected occasions (from the 1940s, some possibly earlier). The Austin Seven is a stock photo (but the same model as my dad's). And I took the background photo over sixty years later.

The white quartz gravel was still there.

Source: Cut-and-paste from late 1930s (?) to 2000s; inside Austin Seven, from left—my dad, my brother Louis, sister Marie, and I (separate photos, ca. 1940s); background—Glendoo Mountain, just north of Military Road and just inside Wicklow county border (2012).

---

[1] Dublin City Council, "Records of the North Strand Bombing May 1941," http://www.dublincity.ie/main-menu-services-recreation-culture-dublin-city-public-libraries-and-archive-heritage-and-histo-17, accessed ca. 12th April 2013.
[2] United States Holocaust Memorial Museum: Holocaust Encyclopedia, "World War II: Timeline," http://www.ushmm.org/wlc/en/article.php?ModuleId=10007306, accessed 10th April 2013.
[3] Michael Fewer, *The Wicklow Military Road: History and Topography* (Dublin: Ashfield Press, 2007), ISBN 13:978 1 901658 66 8.

23

LEARNING SCHOOL

I was five years of age. My sister led me through an enormous gateway into a wide courtyard and handed me over to the nuns. I was about to feel the cool hand of impartial discipline.

It was my first day in school.

Events that arouse strong emotions can engrave deep memories—much deeper than those that only stimulate the rational mind or cause physical sensations. We can easily forget how to solve those algebra equations, and, although we can well remember how our finger hurt when we touched the hot stove, we can't actually *feel* that pain simply by recalling the event (unless we touch the stove again). But when something stirs up the emotions we *can* feel it again. It can come back instantly and clearly—with all the original flavors of emotion—when the little memory capsule is opened by some trigger. Happily all the memories I have from my first experiences of school are pleasant.

Except for one, perhaps.

Lakelands Convent was a Catholic school run by nuns. It was also an orphanage for children who somehow ended up without any parents to care for them. I had already lost one parent, but it never occurred to me that this might have brought me halfway to becoming an orphan myself. At that age, you never ask yourself why you have the things you have, nor waste precious child time worrying about their being taken away. They're just *yours*, like your soft-boiled egg for breakfast, your bread and jam for tea, your warm bedclothes at night. The days are sunny and long in summer; in winter there is Christmas and there might be snow. It will always be like that.

My sister Marie, three years older than I, was already attending the same school, and she simply took me along with her when it was time for me to start. The school was close by, and we only had to walk about five minutes along suburban roads lined with middle-class, semi-detached houses, like our own. The trees planted on the sidewalks were young—probably around the same age in tree-years as I was in human years. But the ground on which the new roads were laid was also "young," and was still shrinking from the heavy loads. When the inevitable cracks opened up in the white concrete paving, they filled them in with the inevitable black tar. Thus I would forever associate this image of "giant crazy pavement" with a vague feeling of uneasiness and fear of the unknown as my sister led me to the gates of the school. So, I was very glad that she was so carefree and cheerful that morning, because it gave me a sort of protective umbrella to ward off my first-day jitters. My sister was the only female in our family of five, so she got very early lessons in being a mother. Besides, my dad had left me in her care, and if he was not concerned, and she was not concerned, then why should I be concerned? Losing one parent is not nearly like being an orphan, any more than losing one eye is like being blind.

The school and the orphanage were run by the Sisters of Charity, an order of Catholic nuns well known for their sanctity and selfless service to others. It would not be long before I noticed that ritual prayer was central to their lives, and that they intended to make it central to ours, too.

The whole convent was surrounded by a sturdy wall. This seemed to be for keeping the orphans in as well as keeping the public out. Its granite stones were blotched with moss, and weathered to that brownish color typical of old property boundaries all over south Dublin. Inside, there were mature trees and nice playing fields.

The first memory I have after my sister dropped me off at the big gate is being corralled with lots of other kids and made to file into long hardwood benches. The room was very large, somewhat dark and gloomy, with a high ceiling. Several nuns were standing in front looking at us (either to make sure we understood that they were in charge, or to size up the incoming class). Their faces were framed in spotless white cloth wrapped tightly from chin to forehead. The "wrappers" seemed to be fixed with what looked like one of those stiff collars my dad sometimes wore on his shirt. All this resplendent brightness was sharply contrasted by black veils flowing over the shoulders and merging in with formless shapes below.

They looked untouchably clean.

One of the nuns was trying to assert herself over a clatter of children's voices that had not yet felt the jolt of classroom discipline. As far as I could tell, the black-and-white figure down in front of me kept repeating something about a "ten shilling note." Her voice had an urgent tone, but was nevertheless well controlled, so I did not feel threatened. I could not understand what she meant, however. I knew from listening to the adults at home that a ten shilling note was a piece of paper with bright colors, and that it was the same as money—like silver coins—only somehow more important than coins. The grownups kept them to themselves and never let us kids play with them. There appeared to be so much money in them—and they were so far out of my reach—that I never even bothered to think what they could have bought me in an ice cream shop or a sweet shop. I might have been able to buy the whole shop with one, for all I knew. So I just wrote off the message that the nun was trying to get through, knowing that if it was really important she or somebody else would eventually bring its meaning home to me.

It was some time afterwards before I realized that I had come across a new word, and that in fact the nun was shouting "Pay attention! Pay attention!" (possibly in a country accent).

The only sound I had stored in my memory lobes up till then that matched her "a-ten-shin" was "a-ten-shilling."

One of the staples in a Catholic school is a rigorous discipline of prayer, of course. (Or at least in the late 1940s it was.) So the next memory I have is of reciting prayers with all the other kids, led by the nuns. It was not long before my vocabulary let me down again, as the nuns in the starched coifs and black veils constantly repeated new words that mystified me. One prayer that was repeated often had the words "chase room" in it. I knew what "chase" meant, since we were always playing chasing games on the street. We would hide behind bushes, walls, or even behind lampposts, if trapped by our pursuer. (Our bodies were slimmer than the base of a lamppost then.) So what exactly was the nun on about? A room where we could play chase? No: She was having us recite a prayer in honor of the Virgin Mary that included the words "…in the *chaste womb* of the Virgin Mary…" Whereas I was used to being chased, the word "chaste" had no meaning for me whatsoever. And since I knew that babies were delivered in bunting knotted to the stork's beak, I had no need for the word "womb," and nobody saw the need to explain it to me either.

But, as long as we repeated the prayers, the nuns were very pleased. Besides, there was a certain soothing effect when all our voices recited the words in unison; a sense of togetherness that gave you a feeling of security.

I was a carefree boy and I regarded the whole world as one big playground full of new things for me to try out, even in school. I have pleasant memories of colored sticks of chalk lying in their own dust on trays below the blackboards, and how they "melted" into colored lines on the blackboard when you rubbed them across it. It was fun breaking a stick of chalk, too; it didn't bend first like a twig from a tree: it made a satisfying "snap" and a faintly ringing "dink." You only had to watch out that the nun was not looking when you played with the chalk. But, most of all, it was the perception of color itself that excited me. Colors seemed to have their own, very distinct "personalities"—they seemed to evoke different feelings. Yellow was warm and made me happy; blue was quiet and tame; green was friendly; and red was lively. All were stimulating. All left lasting impressions.

During class breaks the students played together, so we got to mix socially with the orphan boys and girls. I became aware in my young mind that the orphans' world was very different from mine. They told me they did not go home after school every day, like I did. I wondered how that must have felt. And of course they did not spend their weekends at home, either. On Saturdays and Sundays they stayed within the convent grounds—within those big stone walls—and slept in communal wards. No doubt they had to pay lots of a-ten-shin, and talked a lot about chase rooms.

It did not help that the orphans would ask you as a matter of routine whether you were from the outside or the inside. It did not help either that you could read the thoughts behind their expressionless faces when you told them you would be going home after school. I could *feel* the difference between us. One day a boy suggested that I take him home to play with me in my house. But that was not on, of course.

That impression has stayed with me, too.

I must have been a rather average student. I have concluded this because I don't recall either having been praised as an exemplary learner, or being made an example of for the opposite reason. But I did become the center of attention in class one day. The distinction I got does not fit neatly into any normal level of learning, such as being the dunce or the genius. On that morning the class must have been dragging a bit, or else I was starting my lifelong habit of daydreaming. In any case, I found that if I wetted my finger with spit and rubbed it on the cover of my school book, the glossy paper would get soggy and turn into pulp. You could then rub this pulp into little rolls and flick it off. Once you got below the glossy part, you could bore through the soft brown cardboard underneath with very little extra effort. This became more interesting to me than whatever the teacher was talking about at the front of the class. So I kept at it until I had a nice hole in the cover of my book, through which I stuck my big finger.

The next thing I remember was looking up from my handiwork and seeing the teacher right in front of my desk, her eyes boring down on me like a drill bit. I have no memory of her exact words, but I am very clear about their meaning. It sounded like this:

"WHAT do you think you are DOING! Stand up here in front of the class! We'll get your sister down here and let her see what you have done!"

Within minutes my older sister came into the classroom, a bit sheepishly, not knowing exactly how much trouble I was in. The rest of the class awaited the outcome eagerly. Until then I had not really *felt* the force of school discipline, and this was a bit like walking unexpectedly into a glass door. My bewildered sister was made to stand with me in front of the whole class and witness my being severely rebuked for this thoughtless act of destruction. I was exhibited to the whole class as a warning to others who might not yet have understood the purpose of school.

Most parents will probably agree that their children enter a truly magical age when they reach seven. There is a marked uptick in maturity, a sort of quantum step. They suddenly astound you with statements that show acute observation, deep comprehension, and penetrating insight. Their powers of deduction alarm you, and you resolve to watch what you say much more carefully. (That blossoming of intellect is delightful, unlike the eruption of independent thought that will come at age thirteen.) Thus, in the Catholic belief (and many others, no doubt), seven is the "age of reason." You are now ready to confirm the commitment to the church that you made at baptism (when you were a tiny helpless baby held over a marble fount full of holy water). This implies that you also confirm your agreement with all the things you have been taught in Catholic School between baptism and the age of seven. (I never knew anybody who declined to confirm.)

The Confirmation ceremony itself is a festive day for seven-year-olds. Boys appear in new two-piece suits, with short trousers, and a big medallion in the lapel. Girls look like they are going to their own weddings, with pretty white dresses and colorful bows. All join in a procession to the church, where a high-ranking priest asks God to give the girls and boys spiritual qualities such as wisdom and understanding. (Gifts we certainly could use in the seven or eight decades to come.)

After my own Confirmation ceremony, I must admit that my main understanding was that it all would be sweetened by an envelope with a silver shilling inside—an upfront payment for passing that critical milestone on the way to heaven.

Although my short-trousered suit was neat, I always felt better in clothes that I could horse around in without fear of staining them. One Sunday I was in my Confirmation suit playing outside on the street. It must have been a hot day because the tar that was used to fill those big cracks in the road had been softened by the sun. I found that if you got a sharp piece of stick you could dig into the tar and use it as a pen to write on the road. That was great fun until I went inside and discovered big tar stains on my new Confirmation suit. My dad was very distressed, but somehow seemed to understand. That was one of the things that made for a good relationship between us—he seemed to be easy on me when my intentions were clean, even though the results of my actions were not.

After that I must have behaved reasonably well during my earliest school years, for I have no further memories of them, good or bad. In fact the only spot on my record was that hole I made in my schoolbook, and that too was sort of unintentional.

I guess I should have been paying more a-ten-shin.

* * *

In the early 2000s I got a very lucky break: I was sent to work for a few months in the charming city of Madrid, Spain. As soon as the February rains had eased off, the evenings had got brighter, and the trees on the sidewalks had begun to sprout some leaves, I started to walk home from work. This was far better than squeezing into a rush-hour bus and being jolted around, hanging on to the bar with white knuckles for fear of being flung against some mute, expressionless passenger (and, in certain cases, wondering whether they harbored the suspicion that it was not entirely unavoidable). But far more important, it's difficult to unfold the character of a new city for yourself when you are in a bus that swerves through narrow concrete underpasses and your view out the window is blocked by power hairdo's and tall men.

To get the most out of this opportunity, I took a different route each evening for my stroll to Mar de Cristal metro station. Often, a seemingly unimportant detail offers valuable insight into the culture of the people you are living with. It's as if you get to peek through a little window into their lives, but without having to snoop. Soon I noticed that the little suburban photo shops had filled their display windows with prints of girls and boys dressed up in elegant children's clothes—white dresses and bright bows for the girls, smart suits with shirt and tie for the boys. The kids were undoubtedly dressed for their Confirmation, and those photos would live long lives on proud parents' walls. The images flashed me back to my own Confirmation at Lakelands Convent in the late 1940s: the feel and smell of a brand-new suit, neatly pressed and creased; a medallion hanging from a ribbon in my collar; a colorful procession with lots of other kids; solemn prayers with strange words.

And a bright silver shilling.

Best of all, I believed I could actually feel the emotions of the seven-year-olds in that Madrid suburb, bringing me a little closer to people whose city I was sharing.

Let the little children come to me...

—Jesus Christ

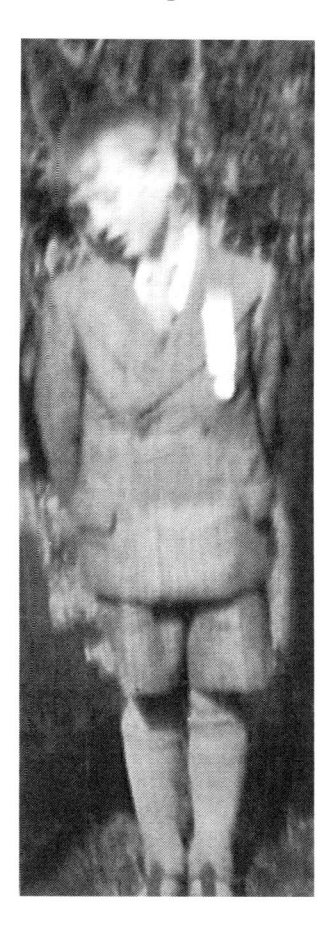

1940s CONFIRMATION SUIT

You were expected to be able to reason things out for yourself when you reached the age of seven. Your Confirmation ceremony bestowed spiritual gifts such as wisdom and understanding, but you also got a nice suit, a bright medal, and at least one bright shilling.

This is my brother Tom, in May 1947.

—Source: Family photo.

24

CLIMBING TREES

Somewhere in the brain of most boys there appears to remain a primeval instinct that compels them to climb trees. I can clearly recall clinging tightly to the slender branches of treetops that swayed back and forth as I moved. Often the trees spread their limbs over hardtop roads, so any slip would have led to broken bones, at best.

Strolling idly with my pals, the sight of a "good" tree might suddenly unleash an irresistible urge to climb. The urge seemed to hit all of us spontaneously, resulting in a sudden dash for the tree. It was as if a tree gave us a friendly challenge: "I bet you can't climb me!"

Why are kids driven to climb trees, with so many other things to do like playing soccer or cricket in the street? We were not trying to peer over any high walls to spy into secluded backyards, or to get at any ripe fruit. Nor was tree-climbing ever recognized as an official sport, such as school football. And only rarely did we climb a tree to hide from a pursuer. One could speculate a lot as to why this might be, given what has been revealed about the evolution of humans, because nearly always we seemed to be just following an instinct that did not need to be explained.

You or your pal would start climbing up the trunk. This could be difficult on old trees because the bark was often too smooth to get a hold, and our arms were too short to reach the lowest branch. Here, you had to get finger- and toeholds on healed-over wounds in the bark, where branches had long since rotted away or been cut off. Sometimes two of us would start climbing together, but take opposite limbs once we got above the trunk. A basic instinct compelled you to always keep at least one hand and one foot securely fixed on the tree. These were your anchors points. You could sense some muscles tightening involuntarily when something outside your control started to affect your balance—a branch flexed too much or a support began to give way. Once you were sure of your holds, you could safely reach up to a higher branch with your free hand. You might have had to test the branch first by carefully moving some weight onto it before abandoning a secure anchor: New growth could be springy and weak. Sometimes, an apparently healthy branch would turn out to be rotten inside and snap off as soon as you grabbed it, sending a little cloud of dust and debris into the air. As a test, you could carefully bounce up and down on it a little—in effect asking it to carry more weight than it would have to when you put your whole trust in it.

With practice you got a feel for how much the branch could take, and how safe you were up there on that tree. You never tried to move up or down by over-extending your reach and springing to what you *hoped* would be your next hold. And you never raced anybody: there was no time limit for finding a good hold when you were on a tree twenty feet above a concrete road.

As you climbed into the topmost branches, the limb that you were climbing on would start to bend under your weight. The higher you went, the more you swayed from side to side (and the less palatable the idea of falling to the ground was). Sometimes a grownup would walk past on the street below, and you could startle them with a sudden cry from your perch on the tree. Eventually, the sway of the branches would start to rule the game, and you had to decide whether your urge to climb higher was worth the risk of falling—an unthinkable event. No matter how high any of my pals climbed up a tree, I would always climb higher (at least, as far as I can remember...).

How high up you got depended on how well you thought you could judge the strength of the branches and the firmness of your holds. By this time you would have had a well-grounded feel for what it meant to be "out on a limb," even though you might not yet have come across that phrase used as a metaphor for some less obvious danger in life.

The fear of falling is indeed a powerful instinct. Possibly because of that, in spite of all the raw elements in our playful climbing and the spontaneity of our impulses, none of us ever fell. Nor can I recall any of us ever having lost sight of the risks or acted recklessly. But then you could argue that since we never knew exactly where the limits were—when a branch might break or a hold might give way—we never knew either how close we might have been to going over some limit, and falling.

Sadly, that argument seems to be valid, for not all the boys in our suburb survived the urge to climb trees: one day we were shocked to hear that a boy had died after falling from a tree in Sandymount Green. That was less than a mile from my home. We did not know the boy personally, nor did we hear how he lost his grip—only that, by callous chance, he landed on a spiked railing.

These and other memories of my boyhood prompt me to wonder how any of us ever reached the age of twenty-one without meeting with a serious accident or worse.

25

CHESTNUT BROWN

The description "chestnut brown" may evoke different images and different thoughts for all of us, but it is never dull. It may mean the rich brown luster of human hair, endowed free to some, eagerly sought by others with the willing help of the cosmetics industry. I definitely value that occurrence of chestnut brown, but here I want to talk about real chestnuts just out of their spiky jackets.

As boys growing up in Dublin, we got to know the lustrous brown of chestnuts long before we began to seek out that color for beauty sake alone. That's because we were continually gathering chestnuts to play conkers. It's true that the rich brown appearance added to the value of our conkers, but only as a side benefit. And let's not forget the *fragrance* of fresh chestnuts—a very distinctive mix of aromas that was quite pleasant, at least to us. The spiky husks covering the chestnuts had a stronger smell—bordering on pungent—and they left a dark brown stain on your fingers. Nevertheless, the stain from a chestnut husk was not nearly as good as that from a walnut, whose near-indelible, penetrating dye could survive one or two days' hand-washing (by a boy). The walnut stains were apparently accepted by adults and teachers without any need for explanation.

In the game of conkers, the chestnuts became the "conkers." (The derivation might have something to do with "hitting on the head.") Each boy had a chestnut with a string threaded through it and knotted firmly at the bottom. The defending boy held his string by the top, letting the conker hang down freely by about eighteen inches. The opponent positioned his conker in strike mode with one hand, holding the top of the string in the other. With a fast downward sling, he tried to whack the defending conker and knock it off its string. This could be done either by shattering the chestnut or forcing the knot at the bottom to ream through the hole in the chestnut from the shock of the strike. In either case, a well-aimed, fast shot was required. If the aim was off, the attacking chestnut could miss the other one, entangle the strings, and leave you smarting from the sudden jerk of the string biting into your finger.

The contestant whose chestnut suffered enough damage to be knocked off the string lost that round. The winner would then notch up one more victory for the chestnut, hoping that it or another one of his would survive the season. It was not unusual for a chestnut to boast about five or even ten shattered opponents.

Conkers that survived one season, or were spared the dangers of battle to serve as hardened soldiers the following year, were called seasoners. By the time they became seasoners, though, the lustrous brown would have turned to a dull matte. We hardly counted that as a loss, however, because we had not yet been struck by the beauty in the original color as something to be valued for its own sake. In fact, the duller they got and the more wrinkles they had, the better we liked them: that was a sign that they had dried out nicely and had become hard enough to face battle.

The gradually changing seasons in Ireland's soft climate left us with plenty of variety for outdoor play. By the time the autumn equinox returned in late September, the long summer evenings would have slipped away from us. Suddenly, we would become aware that the shortening of daylight hours was becoming more acute with each passing day. Never mind; this

Chestnut Brown

would not dampen our sprits—even if the sense of loss was compounded by our having to go back to school. And how better to forget the desertion of the sun than to switch to autumn things—like gathering chestnuts? So in the mornings, on our way to school, we would keep an eye on the chestnut trees. This helped to mellow the back-to-school blues, at least enough to make them bearable.

We started to get excited when the chestnuts on the trees matured into spiky green balls. At a certain time the palm-shaped leaves would turn yellow, causing the chestnuts nestled among them to stand out. When they were ripe enough, some natural tree-signal would snap their stems and send them to the ground. We learned that after a night of blustery wind we could expect a nice harvest of chestnuts to be strewn on the grass below the trees. The most mature among them would treat you to the sight of that hallowed lustrous brown peeping out through a split in the husk.

We had our favorite spots to look for these windfalls—usually houses with large front gardens. One particular house, near the railroad crossing on Sandymount Avenue, had several huge chestnut trees that spread their leafy umbrellas over a spacious lawn. There was an unwritten rule that nobody would mind you trespassing on their property to gather chestnuts. Or at least we hoped so. We selected the chestnuts for size, mainly—some of the biggest being easily an inch-and-a-quarter across.

We usually brought home about ten of the best specimens. Next, we bored a small hole through the chestnut with my dad's gimlet. We started the hole at the strongest part—a woody welt where the stem had been attached. As we bored through, curls of soft chestnut fruit would fall from the spiral groove of the little wood auger and gather in curls at our feet. This inner "filling" was very soft and looked like you could eat it. On your first try, however, you found that it had an uninviting, bitter taste as well as an off-putting smell. This was the *horse chestnut*, and now

I read that it is in fact mildly toxic. It would be many years before I would wander the streets of Continental Europe in winter and savor the taste of the roasted *sweet chestnut*. And briefly join some strangers standing in the warm glow of a brazier.

We played conkers wherever we had enough space. We brought them to school and kept them ready for any schoolyard challenge that might arise. Whenever you met any of your pals, on the street or at school, someone would be sure to ask, "Like to play conkers?"

Eventually, though, some change in mood or season would trigger the end of the chestnut-bashing season. It would be time to start thinking about making candle lanterns out of fruit tins and blackening our faces with burnt cork for Halloween night. Surviving conkers—if there were any—would be archived in a shoebox along with the untested ones. Those would do battle as seasoners the following year.

That is, if by the following year we had not grown out of this boyhood phase altogether. But I never outgrew my fascination with nature's gift of chestnut brown.

The color that still evokes the fun of finding a fresh chestnut peeping out at me from its jacket.

* * *

I went back to the chestnut trees on Sandymount Avenue in 2013. It was close to the middle of September. The leaves were still green, but nestled among them was what looked like a fairly good crop of chestnuts. I reckoned they lacked about two weeks before they would mature, and begin to fall.

But I would be gone by then.

Not that it mattered much, because a large apartment block had been built on the old spacious lawn. And you needed a digital code to open the gate.

CHESTNUT BROWN

We loved to see a bright chestnut peeping out at us from its spiky jacket. These horse chestnuts have a nice range of color from rich brown to almost pure red.

>Source: Stock photo from Dreamstime, modified to show split coat.

26

DÚN LAOGHAIRE PIER

Nature gives many gifts to youngsters born in Dublin (perhaps to compensate for the weather). One of these is the coastline around Dublin Bay: steep cliffs, sandy beaches, miles and miles of tidal flats, and big rocks sticking up out of the ground. We could dive straight into the water off these rocks at Seapoint. Holding our breath as long as we dared, we would marvel at beaded ribbons of seaweed floating lazily among the boulders. Back-lighted by the sun, the curling seaweed looked like long-haired girl swimmers with no bathing caps. The bottom was covered with pure, clean sand—no muddy silt to cloud the water. We kept to safe depths—about four to six feet. Ripples on the surface of the water twisted the sun's rays like crude lenses, projecting light shows onto the seabed: sinewy bands of light billowing into bloated circles and wiggly squares, before collapsing into ropy braids. Grains of mica shone back at us from the sand like sequins. There were limpets to be prized off the rocks near Seapoint's Martello Tower, and games to be played with the crabs hiding in the seaweed under the rocks. We wanted to capture the crabs and hold them by the carapace so their pincers would open and close in vain, but we forever feared they would suddenly dart out sideways from under the seaweed and nip us in the fleshy part of the toe. That was probably an ungrounded fear, driven by the sight of those formidable claws. When we were tired of swimming and playing in the water, we lay on the granite slabs between the seawall and the railway listening to the trains rattling past—a mere twenty feet away—and just soaking up the sun.

Indeed, the rocky coast at Seapoint was a perfect place for children to spend their free summer months. But a hundred and fifty years earlier, in 1807, those same rocks must have brought unimaginable terror to twenty-nine children huddled below deck in a boat. After enduring freezing rain and heavy snow, a vicious wind drove them helplessly towards the coast and dashed their boat to pieces on those same heartless rocks. That was just the children: a total of 265 perished on that troopship—the *Rochdale*—and 120 more went down at Blackrock with the *Prince of Wales*[1] (though the captain saved himself). The victims' baggage was strewn around the shore and troops had to be posted to prevent looting. That same night, a coal ship was lost with all hands in the inner part of Dublin Bay, and another vessel was seen bottom-up at Bray.[2]

Beneath the ground in much of South County Dublin there is massive bed of granite. With time on its side, and the relentless pounding of the sea to help, nature ate away much of the softer ground and handcrafted the exciting landscape that we now have in Dublin Bay. That explains the rocky holdouts that spike the coastline, and the jagged rocks that stick out of the sand—rocks that appear and disappear as the tides come in and go out.

In fact, that old granite gave us much more than natural diving boards and quartz sequins on the seabed: it baked the overlying rocks into beautifully different forms. For example, the silvery mica that flashes the sunlight back at you on the hiking trails (when the sun is out); the stubborn spike of quartzite known as the Great Sugarloaf that dominates the approaches to Enniskerry and the aspirations of every first-time climber from the city.

Add to this the shifting sandbanks and it's easy to see why Dublin Bay had always been a treacherous place for boats. The devastating storm on the 18th of November 1807 probably strengthened the resolve to build a safe harbor, protected by the Dún Laoghaire piers.

The piers were built between 1817 and 1860, about a hundred years before I discovered them. They are shaped like the open claws of a big crab. Boats pass in and out through the open gap between the "crab's pincers." At the ends of both piers there are massive, rotunda-like bastions of granite. Any ship that hit one of those walls of rock would surely come out the loser.

The two piers actually have very different personalities. Both are about the right length for a casual walk—about a mile—but the East Pier was just made for promenading. It starts at the center of life in Dún Laoghaire town, and otherwise has more to divert the attention of the carefree walker. A gentle curve ensures that your perspective changes continually as you stroll out. As small children we used to look back every so often and congratulate ourselves on how far we had walked, clearly proven by how much the pier had curved around behind us, and how small the church spires in Dún Laoghaire had become.

Sometimes there would be a brass band playing in a small stand near the shore end of the East Pier. One weekend there was a group of traditional Irish dancers performing there, and I asked my dad why the boy dancers were wearing skirts like girls. He pointed out that they were kilts, not skirts, though they looked the same to me.

Wherever there are crowds of relaxed people and sunshine, there is sure to be ice cream. My dad never failed to buy us a nice big cornet—a custom I have tried to preserve even if it is not the HB brand. In winter, though, the atmosphere was very different. For one thing there were far fewer people, and no ice cream at all. The wind always seemed to find a way down the front of your neck and draw off whatever body heat remained in your chest. A heavy twill coat with high collars was your best bet. The pace and style of walking were different, too: you would have to walk briskly, head down, hands gloved or stuffed into pockets, shoulders hunched up. As you passed other people, their faces would be contorted and their eyes scrunched up too, just like yours. When you got to the end of the pier you would turn around instinctively and head back. If you relished the strong wind—and I always did—you could walk back on top of the windbreak wall and let the wind try to blow you off.

Within the two piers there was a marina that sheltered at least a hundred small boats. On breezy weekends you would see little yachts passing through the crab's pincers—where the harbor piers gave access to the open sea. It was a welcome diversion to watch yellow-clad figures dart to one side of a little boat and lean far out, almost touching the water, to counter the roll caused by a sudden gust of wind. In some seldom-trodden hinterground of my mind, I wondered vaguely how the people who were decked out in those fancy sailing clothes, and who owned their own pleasure yachts, may have been different from us.

A passenger ferry known to everybody as the Mail Boat served the route between Dún Laoghaire and Great Britain, across the Irish Sea. Standing at the lighthouse on the end of the East Pier, you could watch the Mail Boat sail by in all her quiet majesty. She passed so close you could read expressions off passengers' faces.

The MV *Hibernia* served as a Mail Boat then. It had a berth inside the piers where passengers could embark from trains with connections to Dublin and key cities throughout Ireland. At that time the Mail Boat was probably the best known icon of Irish emigration. There was hardly anybody in Dublin for whom it did not evoke powerful emotions. If somebody was said to be "for the boat" it meant they were going to leave their home and family to work in Great Britain. The move was mostly driven by necessity, because Ireland did not have enough jobs to go around, but in some cases it was just plain wanderlust that led people to go. There were other drivers, too: It was said that girls who suddenly found themselves expecting the unexpected—a taboo in 1950s Catholic Ireland—would sometimes "choose the boat."

Years later, when I was living in Germany, I was stunned to find that a German writer, Heinrich Böll,[3] had distilled into magically simple prose the unforgettable experience of sailing on the Mail Boat. For most of us that meant sailing in steerage—the least expensive section. It was difficult to believe that Böll had not been born and raised in Ireland, that he had not lived through the years of Irish emigration in the 1950s as I had. His description of traveling through Ireland had made such an impression on the folks in postwar Germany that every time I identified myself there as an Irishman (to anybody who read books) I was immediately told that I just *had* to read Böll's *Irish Journal.* So I bought a copy out of the small reserve I had kept for luxuries such as hardcover books.

Böll describes the human scene he found crossing to Ireland on the Mail Boat: climbing over boxes, suitcases, and the outstretched legs of the passengers who owned them. He was looking for a place to sleep—or at least to rest—during the crossing. I know only too well where he was: on the open deck. You were clear of the crowded lounges, but poorly protected from the cold night wind. In the 1950s, most Irish emigrants in Great Britain came home at least once a year to keep in touch with fathers, mothers, brothers and sisters, and sometimes grandmothers and grandfathers. The country was fiercely Catholic. If a young girl or boy went to England and "lost the faith"—stopped practicing the Catholic religion—they could be faced with a painful dilemma on returning home: how to break this shocking news to their parents without breaking their parents' hearts as well. If they only stayed for about a week (that is, spent only one *Sunday* at home), the least harmful all round would have been to just go to Mass and hope that there were no awkward questions.

Among the passengers on the Mail Boat, priests and nuns were very common, and of course very recognizable. (At least in steerage, where I traveled.) One of these priests found a place for Böll to sit down, and the writer began to overhear a conversation between the obliging priest and a young girl. After a bit of to-and-fro about religion, which the priest deftly prevented from escalating into rudeness, the touchy question eventually came up: given what she had just said about the church, why did she go to Mass when she went home? But she had the trump card: How could she be so cruel to her parents as to *not* go?

Böll concludes the episode: The young girl politely excused herself and wrapped her blanket tightly around her slender shoulders to get some rest. The priest sighed and turned up his collar to do the same.

At the time Böll wrote about this encounter on the Mail Boat, I would have been around fifteen years of age, in high school. Within seven years I, too, would be making myself comfy and trying to catch some sleep on the open deck of the Mail Boat. But I was going the other way—to Germany. A few years after that I, too, would return home and face the same dilemma as that girl.

Böll was also quick to pick up one other revealing symbol of how we lived in the 1950s, when we could only afford the bare necessities: behind his upturned collar the priest had a little stash of safety pins. My dad told me never to forget to leave a few safety pins fastened behind my collar when going anywhere important. Keeping a piece of string in your pocket was another wise contingency. At that time, you wore your clothes as long as possible, to get your full money's worth out of them and to put off the cost of buying new ones. When your clothes approached the end of their lives (something to be denied as long as possible) they could rip unexpectedly at some critical seam, at the wrong moment, in the wrong company. So, indeed, that safety pin behind your collar might suddenly become pure gold.

(Years later—but too late for me—I found out that when Heinrich Böll was traveling in Ireland gathering material for this book, he had been a frequent customer in a pub owned by my sister-in-law's family in Achill, on the west coast of Ireland.)

Back to Dún Laoghaire Pier. The Mail Boat described by Böll was an overnight service that left Great Britain from the port of Holyhead in Wales. It arrived in Dún Laoghaire early in the morning, just as Dublin City was awakening. That way, passengers returning to Ireland had the whole day in front of them, though they would not have had a good night's sleep behind them. On the outward trip—from Ireland to the Great Britain—a boat left Dún Laoghaire in the evening and arrived at the then dreary Holyhead port in the raw, early hours of the morning. Most of Wales was fast asleep as the wan-faced passengers were shunted from the Mail Boat to trains waiting to take them to Euston station in London, or to major railway junctions along the way, such as Crewe.

Although the Holyhead boat terminal could indeed be dreary when you arrived there from Dún Laoghaire—just as you were enjoying the best part of your sleep—I do have one very good memory of the terminal. I had gone with a hiking buddy to Wales, a country with great mountain scenery and the type of simple hiking trails that allow you to get intimate with the environment. When planning a trip on a minimal budget one has to carefully parse it into its discrete stages and reality-check it against available time and money. The plan was necessarily tight: hitchhike as much as possible; avoid train fares; stay in youth hostels or sleep in the open; and, of course, never even *think* of taking a plane any more than you would think of making a side trip to the casino in Monte Carlo.

This particular hike had gone very well: we had conquered a new land, we could prove it by showing off colorful stamps in our youth hostel membership cards, and we had climbed a ridge that led us to Mount Snowdon's mist-ridden cairn at 1085 meters.

When we arrived back in the Holyhead boat terminal, we had exactly the planned amount of money left for our last meal before boarding the Mail Boat back to Dún Laoghaire. We studied the menu in the cafeteria very carefully and chose what we thought would give us the best value. Then we took a table and ate our rations with artificially prolonged relish. Staring at the soon-empty plates, my buddy lapsed into an unrestrained fantasy about what he *could* have eaten had we not been left with only our bus fares from Dún Laoghaire boat terminal to our doorsteps in Dublin. A moment later a guy with a British accent came over from the next table and told us quietly that he would treat us to the meal described by my friend in his reverie.

Kindness endures: I never forgot that spontaneous act from a lone stranger.

Nor were the delights of Dún Laoghaire's East Pier limited to genteel promenading, listening to brass bands, or eating ice cream. At least not for boys around the age of ten, who naturally assume that the human body is indestructible. Why think otherwise, if no painful accident has yet left its mark on your pliable body? At that age, any obstacle in your journey of discovery is just one more experience to be exploited to the fullest.

The East Pier is flanked by big granite boulders on its seaward side. These "armor stones" protect the pier from being slowly undone by the storm waves that broadside it from the Irish Sea. They are perfect for that purpose: large and heavy, irregular in form. Their bluff shape absorbs the force of the slamming waves very well, while the voids provide a ready path for the seawater to retreat when its fury has been spent.

They were also perfect for a bunch of boys testing their skill at boulder-hopping. This required springing at least several feet from boulder-top to boulder-top. We did not walk: we ran. Ran at what seems to me now to be a frightening pace. It required radar-like, continuous scanning of landing conditions—the distance, shape, slope of the rock face, whether slippery or not. You just had to be sure-footed; one error or lapse of attention could send you down between the rocks in a heap of bruised limbs and injured pride.

But none of us ever slipped.

The West Pier was far less interesting. There were no brass bands—summer or winter—practically no lazy promenaders, and far fewer walkers. It was mainly for fishing.

At the end of the West Pier there is a granite rotunda matching the one on its twin to the east. The side exposed to the open sea has a high wall that drops almost straight down to the water. It seemed to me—at that age—that it dropped about thirty-five or forty feet (at least at low tide). But for sure if you had fallen into the sea, there would have been no handholds to grab onto when you came up for air. *If* you came up for air. You would simply have been knocked about in the water until you made it to one of the boat landing steps inside the pier, or to the thick bands of seaweed waving in the surf outside the pier. Or until somebody threw you a lifebelt. Yet in all my time fishing off that high pier, I did not see anybody fall, or even hear of anybody falling.

It was mainly men and boys who fished, with the occasional mother, spouse, or sister (presumably) pressed into service for company or for support. The fisher-people would sit or stand passively beside a small pile of belongings marking their territory on the stone parapet: a box or a crude tin for fishing tackle, an old mat to sit on, a bucket of bait, and—most important of all—a lunch box. The experienced and organized also brought hot tea in a big "flask"—our name for a thermos bottle.

We were a somber bunch, we fisher-folk, our pensiveness broken only by some mild gesture or utterance to acknowledge a trophy taken from the indifferent sea. Seagulls circled endlessly overhead. Their constant squealing blended with the sound of the waves slapping against the bottom of the wall and the muted sounds of civilization drifting out from Dún Laoghaire town.

It was a perfect way to rest the senses.

Much later I often thought that fishing off the pier induced a stilling of the mind, as when one meditates. Was there some inner pull that led us to the serenity of the pier, or did the pier induce the calmness of mind once we got there, with no direct or indirect intention on our side? Which really came first?

We did not have fancy fishing rods or indeed any other gear beyond the basic tackle needed for hooking and landing fish. Some grownups did have nice varnished rods with high-end mechanisms for unreeling the fishing line at great speed. You would see them whipping these rods over their heads with the cool confidence of experts. Those advanced reeling mechanisms also protected their lucky owners from that worst of all problems—the tangled fishing line.

We assembled our fishing gear from materials we had lying around the house. Except of course for the hooks. And the line itself, which was usually made of catgut. Four barbed hooks dangled from little wire hangers like trinkets on an ornament, held taut by a lead weight (the sinker) at the end. We made the hangers out of wire recycled from orange boxes, twisted together with my dad's pliers. With minimal skill we could melt lead in a bean can over the gas stove in the kitchen and manufacture a sinker as good as the fancy ones they sold in fishing stores.

Where did we get the lead? Don't ask that.

When the chain of hooks and hangers was held carefully in the hand about shoulder high to a boy, the weight of the sinker would keep it straight. If you let it droop onto the top of the wall, the hooks could easily snag the line and turn the whole thing into an ugly mess. Standing on top of the wall—three stories above the water—you would swing this complex hook-and-sinker several times over your head (having made sure nobody was behind you) before letting it fly into the air. You had to stand with feet apart to brace yourself for the reaction of the throw, so one foot would be very close to the seaward edge of that high wall.

When you let go of the weighted tackle—and if all went well—the fishing line would uncoil like a seasoned whaler's harpoon line. If not, you had at least a half-hour's worth of untangling to do. Not to mention the gratuitous displays of sympathy from strangers sharing the wall with you. ("Poor lad!") On a good throw, you measured your success by the distance to splashdown.

This was bottom-fishing: the line was designed to sink to the bottom and stay there. There were no brightly colored floats to bob up and down to alert you that a fish had taken the bait. Once the line was firmly on the seabed you would take up the slack so that any pull on the hooks would send a slight twitch back up the line. With practice, you learned to delicately balance the line tension against the muscles of your index finger so you could tell when a fish was nibbling, biting, or had been hooked (you hoped). If a tiny jerk turned into a definite pull, you knew you had a catch. Often this would happen very soon after the line was cast, possibly because the fish had seen the bait dropping through the water in a trail of bubbles. Then the careful haul-in would begin. On the way up you could build your expectations by trying to gauge the size of your catch from the resistance in the line. Sometimes the line would suddenly go limp and you would just have to haul it in and try again, without complaining. Fishing makes one stoic.

A nice speckled plaice was the prize to be hoped for. Sometimes we would have to take the consolation of small dabs—not exciting to look at. Not exciting to eat, either.

At evening time the harbor would reverberate with the Mail Boat's deep bass notes, warning the little yachts that the big ship was about to make its nightly lunge for the gap between the ends of the piers. Soon she would be passing ever so close, her powerful engines propelling her with unexpected swiftness. Once again we would read expressions off passengers' faces—adults looking pensively over the rail, excited children straining to take in everything, now that the boat had finally pulled away from the wharf and was giving them a tour of Dún Laoghaire harbor.

For a moment I would gaze at the figures on the boat and idly contemplate the difference between us—how different their motivations were from ours. For although our paths had approached to within a few hundred feet, it was a very critical few hundred feet: they were on a boat that was taking them swiftly out to sea, to a different life in a different culture, while we were standing passively on the stone wall, tethered to the seabed by our slender fishing lines.

After one of those Sunday afternoon fishing trips to the West Pier, I begged my dad to let me go on my own so I could spend a whole day fishing, not just a few hours. I was on my summer holidays and had plenty of time. To my delight he agreed: agreed to let me stand on the high wall swinging that awkward hook-and-sinker, when at best there would only be a few grownups on the wall near me. My dad was like that—he would boost your self-confidence by showing his own confidence in you.

The following Thursday I took the bus alone to Dún Laoghaire with my bag of fishing gear, my bait, and my lunch box. The bus stopped near the Purty Kitchen, a much-loved restaurant in the old town of Dún Laoghaire, and from there I walked the one mile to the end of the West Pier. I had finally got my wish to spend a whole day on the high wall, unconcerned with the passing of time. There were only one or two others throwing fishing lines off the wall that day, and nobody walking the pier for exercise.

The result was a bit unexpected for me: I must have had "too much of a good thing." The long bus trip; the walk to the end of the pier and back; the lonely hours on the wall baiting and coiling my fishing line, slinging it into the sea. I had nobody to talk to, nobody to share my enthusiasm with. I believe on that day I lost that *kick,* that wonderment one gets from each new youthful experience.

The fish themselves seemed to have been in on the conspiracy to give me this lesson in life: all I got were a few nibbles.

* * *

In October 1964 I made one of those pivotal decisions that radically change the course of one's life: I gave up my badly sputtering career in cost accountancy, left my family and friends, and went to live in Germany. I was compelled to do this by chronic, overpowering wanderlust. My plan was to go for one year, which is what I estimated it would take for a full cure.

Actually, it is taking much longer.

I had chosen the Mail Boat—what else?—to start my journey through Great Britain and thence to Austria and Germany. I planned my trip just like that hiking trip to Wales, except that I allowed myself a train ride to Vienna to get a "quick launch" deep into Continental Europe. Since I would not be coming back for a year, and had no job lined up on the Continent, I had to avoid the uncertainty of a long hitchhike where one is dependent on passing strangers for a ride.

I carefully packed selected essentials into one big rucksack. The badge of a seasoned hiker-camper at the time was the Icelandic Wall-Quilted Sleeping Bag, made by Blacks of Greenock, in Scotland. I had become a proud member of the club when I bought one of these on a hiking trip through

Glasgow. Compact, cozy, and light, this essential piece of gear gave you spiritual as well as physical comfort in a life where you might unexpectedly have to sleep outdoors. (The "wall quilting" was the key feature: it kept the down thick and fluffy within walled pockets. Otherwise it would be squeezed to nothing at the stitch lines, and you would wake up around three o'clock in the morning mentally noting the parts of your body that had been chilled to numbness.)

Having said all my goodbyes and long since come to terms with my decision to leave Ireland, I found a bench on the upper deck of the Mail Boat. This would be my bed for that short night: as soon as the boat was clear of land I would unfold my comfy Icelandic Sleeping Bag and snuggle into it. At least I could rely on a few good hours of sleep to bolster me for the rude early-morning shuffle in the Holyhead boat terminal.

We were heading away from the sun, which I knew was soon to disappear abruptly, since the sky was clear. But for the time being the sun was still backlighting the Dublin Mountains, reducing them to dark, featureless profiles. I looked back emotionally at the city I was leaving—Dublin City. The city that had mothered me. I thought of the family and friends I was leaving behind. I had so many friends there that I could hardly walk down O'Connell Street without at least passing a nod to a casual acquaintance, or stopping for a chat with a friend. On the following day, most of my friends would continue their lives just as before, whereas I was abandoning all claims to the routine and the predictable.

The Mail Boat had picked up speed quickly and was now passing the ends of the piers that marked the exit from Dún Laoghaire harbor—and from Ireland. It was great weather; lots of people were walking on the East Pier—parents with children, young couples with their arms cross-wrapped around each other's waists, pensioners, loners. I'm sure all the children had been provided with ice cream cones. Some walkers had stood to watch our big boat pass. On the West Pier opposite, a few late fishermen stood on the high wall holding fishing lines that sloped into the sea. They were so close they appeared to be looking me in the eye, reading my thoughts.

We had changed places: I had taken the boat.

JUST ANOTHER FERRY?

The Mail Boat M.V. *Hibernia* leaving Dún Laoghaire harbor. To the Irish emigrants who huddled on her windy decks, or shared stories of home and exile in her crowded lounges, the Mail Boat must surely have become part of their very souls.

On one of these crossings to Ireland the German author Heinrich Böll sat down beside a priest and a young country girl returning home for a family visit. From this brief encounter Böll gives a stunningly accurate and touching picture of an Irish emigrant in the 1950s.

The Hibernia sailed the Mail Boat route from 1949 until 1976. In 1980 she made her final voyage—to a scrapyard in India. That was a far better ending than the RMS *Leinster*, torpedoed by a German submarine in 1918, a month before the end of World War One. 501 people lost their lives.[4]

Source: ©http://www.flickr.com /photos/ jimlightfoto/

SKIES DARKEN OVER DÚN LAOGHAIRE PIERS

Left: Walkers stroll back from the end of the West Pier as the last rays of a November sun make their final splash on the massive granite walls. Right: rotunda at the end of the East Pier.

Photo: 2012

Dún Laoghaire Pier

FISHING OFF THE HIGH WALL

We used to stand on top of this high wall for hours, slinging our fishing tackle over our heads into the sea, and waiting. Others had fancy fishing rods like the ones in this photo. We learned to be realistic about the risk of falling off the wall, and took sensible precautions.

The Mail Boat passed very close to us as it slipped between the piers on its way to Wales. When I re-visited my old fishing spot in 2012, many of the fishermen were speaking a language I could not understand. No, it was not Irish. It sounded like Polish.

Photo: November 2012

JAMES JOYCE TOWER

The Martello Tower dominating Sandycove Point houses the James Joyce Museum. The gunrest on top of the tower used to have a cannon that could be swung around to blast any Napoleonic ship that might have come visiting. None did, but in 1904 Buck Mulligan used the gunrest as the "altar of God" for his irreverent parody of the Catholic Mass.[5] Later his plump body plunged into the sea at the Fortyfoot swimming area (above, left of Joyce's tower), where to this day hardy men swim bottomless all year round, regardless.

Photo: 2012; telephoto shot from East Pier.

THE HITCHHIKER'S BEST FRIEND, 1960s

My Icelandic sleeping bag, bought with great pride in Black's of Greenock, Scotland. This piece of gear distinguished the serious hiker from the daytripper in the 1950s. It was compact, cozy, and light—a true friend to the backpacker with absolutely *no* contingency for fancy lodgings.

Much later, I used mine for sleeping under the stars in Texas. For fun, of course.

Photo: 2012 (Houston).

---

[1] Edward J Bourke, "The sinking of the Rochdale and the Prince of Wales," National Maritime Museum of Ireland, http://www.mariner.ie/history/articles/ships/rochdale, downloaded 11th October 2012.
[2] Ibid.
[3] Heinrich Böll, *Irish Journal* (McGraw-Hill, 1967). Originally published in German under the title *Irisches Tagebuch* (Köln-Berlin: Kiepenheuer & Witsch, 1957).
[4] References differ on number of casualties; the 501 comes from the Official Site of the *R.M.S. Leinster*, http://www.rmsleinster.com/sinking/sinking.htm, downloaded 20th October 2013.
[5] James Joyce, *Ulysses*, Telemachus (first few sentences of novel).

ACKNOWLEDGEMENTS

This book would not have been written without the initial prompt by my daughter Tara, and the enthusiastic follow-up by my two other children Amanda and Mark. If you have read this far (without skipping too much), I would like to let you know that you might not still be reading had Tara and Mark not focused their professional eyes on my narratives and enriched them with incisive and sometimes excisive comments.

I am indebted to my brother Louis, my sister Marie, and to Lucy, my brother Tom's widow, for agreeing to let me publish some family photos.

To Bernard Agard, for tutoring in computer graphics.

To Don and Mai Palmer, for hosting me so often in Dublin, and for guiding me back to some people and places that were part of my growing up there.

To the volunteers in Sweny's Chemist, Dublin, for keeping the flame alive, for dispensing their indispensable medicines, and for the photos in Chapter 17.

To CreateSpace.org, for keeping me afloat when I jumped into writing and publishing with no formal training.

To Terra Earth Images, for their wonderful satellite photos.

I have taken pains to provide sources for material that is completely outside my own direct experience (though most of it is relevant in some way). Any images presented without sources, and all the cartoons, are my own doing.

Finally, to my wife Yvonne, who stood by me during the endless writing and rewriting.

ABOUT THE AUTHOR

John E. "Gene" Mullee was born in Dublin and grew up there through childhood and adolescence. He is now a retired civil engineer living near Houston, Texas.

On completing his secondary education at Westland Row Christian Brothers School, he worked in Dublin for four years in a fruitless attempt to latch on to a career in cost accounting. At age twenty-two he left Ireland (and accounting) to work in Germany, and, later, in Holland and Belgium. He did various jobs there, ranging from boiling precision-timed eggs for breakfast guests in a Munich hotel, to carrying a survey staff over the beautiful hills of the Bavarian countryside. After four years at that he returned to Ireland to follow his original inclinations towards physics and engineering. In 1972 he graduated from University College Dublin with a bachelor's degree in civil engineering.

Since then he has lived and worked in many countries, some with highly contrasting cultures and landforms, following projects in design engineering and marine geophysics. In 1982 he bought a home in Houston, Texas, which became his permanent base, and in 2006 he became a US citizen.

Gene has been married to Yvonne for thirty-nine years. They have three children and two grandchildren.

He began writing a year after retiring from his day job in engineering. He was sixty-nine years of age, and there was no point in waiting any longer.

The author at age seven, when some of the events in this book were taking place, and at around seventy, when he started to write them down.

Printed in Great Britain
by Amazon